LATIN

A HISTORICAL AND
LINGUISTIC HANDBOOK

LATIN

A HISTORICAL AND LINGUISTIC HANDBOOK

MASON HAMMOND

HARVARD UNIVERSITY PRESS
CAMBRIDGE, MASSACHUSETTS
LONDON, ENGLAND
1976

Copyright © 1976 by the President and Fellows of Harvard College
All rights reserved
Printed in the United States of America

Library of Congress Cataloging in Publication Data

Hammond, Mason, 1903–
  Latin, a historical and linguistic handbook.

  Bibliography: p.
  Includes index.
  1. Latin language—History. 2. Latin language—
Grammar, Historical. I. Title.
PA2057.H3   470′.9   75–33359
ISBN 0–674–51290–1

PREFACE

This handbook is intended to present a historical and linguistic introduction to Latin. It does not claim to offer original research into Latin linguistics, but does suggest the current state of historical and linguistic work on the language. The book was undertaken in the hope that it might provide a background for study of the language in a form more easily comprehensible than is that in the usual scholarly and technical discussion. It will achieve its purpose if it persuades the reader that the study of Latin grammar and syntax is not an exercise in the memorization of seemingly arbitrary paradigms or rules, but is rather an approach toward understanding how Latin developed its complex and often apparently inconsistent structure, as well as how this development illustrates the nature of linguistics.

The book was begun during the academic year 1965–66 as an exercise for three students in the program at Harvard University leading to the Master of Arts in teaching Latin. Chapters drafted by the students were wholly revised and then mimeographed by the Department of Classics of Harvard. The resulting book was circulated in the winter of 1967 to a number of school teachers of Latin and others. Their comments were collated and integrated into the text by Gregory Nagy, currently Professor of Greek and Latin in Harvard University. Another revision was prepared during my two half-years as Acting Director of the Harvard Center for Renaissance Studies at the Villa I Tatti outside Florence, Italy. The resulting text was further corrected by Prof. Nagy. It also incorporates revisions by an anonymous reader for the Harvard University Press. Various stages of the text have been typed under the auspices of the Department of Classics of Harvard University, by Gloria Ramakus, secretary at Villa I Tatti, Sirena Tabet, secretary in the Department of Comparative Literature of the University of Wisconsin, Janet Beane of Cambridge, Mass., and Marie Allen of Roxbury, Mass. Virginia LaPlante, an editor at the Harvard University Press, has, with firmness veiled under charm, greatly improved the style and clarity of presentation.

The author is most grateful for all this advice and assistance. He is particularly indebted to Prof. Nagy, who from the beginning encouraged the preparation of the book and contributed greatly to it from his thorough familiarity with linguistics.

A difficult typographic decision concerned the use of quotation marks around English words cited as examples or for meaning. After Latin words, the equal sign ($=$) is used to signify "means" or "meaning," in which case quotation marks are omitted around the English definition. Otherwise quotation marks are used. Every effort has been made to give the English equivalents for Latin words and phrases on each occurrence, on the assumption that after an interval of text beginning students may not recall the meaning. In most cases the derivation from Latin or Greek, with English equivalent, is given for the grammatical, syntactical, metrical, or stylistic terms used.

Latin long vowels are marked with a suprascript long mark ($^-$) except in the chapter on versification, where such marks belong to syllables, not simply to vowels therein. Explanation or interpretation relevant at different points in the book is often repeated, as an aid to reinforce memory and understanding.

Indications of errors and suggestions for improvement will be most welcome.

CONTENTS

CONTENTS

CONTENTS

TABLES

LATIN

A HISTORICAL AND
LINGUISTIC HANDBOOK

I

LANGUAGE AND LINGUISTICS

Language has been the most important factor in the advance of human civilization, more so even than the development of the hand or the mastery of fire. Animals produce sounds that surely convey such instinctual emotions as hunger or fear. But scholars are not yet agreed whether these sounds, perhaps in more advanced species of animals, reach the level of protolanguage. Upon such agreement would depend the determination of whether mankind's great advance of attaching to sounds meanings capable of communicating complex desires and ideas was a slow improvement of the system of sounds uttered by his simian ancestors, or whether it represented a major breakthrough in the progress from animal to human status.

At all events, while it seems probable that for any given species of animals the connection between sounds and conveyed meaning is fairly uniform, among humans the meanings of sounds have become highly complex and infinitely varied. Different groups within the human species have developed their own particular agreed systems of sounds and of connections between sound and meaning. A given group may have either sounds or meanings (concepts) not used by other groups. This wide variation fosters communication within that group but inhibits it with members of outside groups. Hence among humans there have come into being from three to four thousand mutually unintelligible systems of meaningful

1

sounds, or languages. Each language may have variations within itself, or dialects, which do not differ enough from each other to be mutually unintelligible.

Whatever was the process by which human speech arose out of simian sounds, the evolution of languages must have been gradual and long drawn out. By careful analysis and correlation of known languages, scholars have been able to group them into related families and to reconstruct hypothetical original tongues from which evolved the varied patterns of divergence that now differentiate the members of each family. However, no generally accepted explanation has yet been advanced to account for the very dissimilar ways in which the major families alter or combine words to constitute units of meaning, or sentences, by expressing relationships between the component words. The biblical story of the Tower of Babel offers what is called an aetiological myth, an attempt by early men to account for the diversity of tongues by representing them as the confounding of an originally single language. It remains uncertain whether the correct explanation for the divergence of the major families is that of the Tower of Babel myth, a remote breakup of a basic human language, or whether several groups of primitive humans, widely separated in space from one another, and perhaps at very different times, each independently made the critical advance from animal sounds to intelligent and meaningful language.

The study of language is today called "linguistics" because the older term "philology" is used, especially in classics, for the study of both language and literature. "Philology" comes from the feminine noun *philologia,* which was borrowed into Latin from Greek. In Greek it is compounded from the adjective *philos* = loving and the masculine noun *logos* = word, or reason. Thus *philologia* means "love of reasoning, or of argument," and then "love of learning, or of literature."

"Linguistics" is based on the Latin feminine noun *lingua* = tongue, or language. To this was added in English as early as the sixteenth century a noun suffix *-ist,* which comes from the Greek *-istēs* and indicates an agent or practitioner. Hence a "linguist" is "one concerned with, or a student of, language." The suffix *-ist,* though Greek in origin, is added in English to words of both Greek and Latin derivation, such as "dramatist" (Greek) or "horticulturist" (Latin). In the nineteenth century there was added to "linguist" a second, adjectival suffix *-ic,* which comes from the Greek *-ikos* (Latin *-icus*) and means "pertaining to." Thus "linguistic" means "pertaining to the study, or science, of language." The plural of this adjective, "linguistics," came to be used as a noun meaning "the study, or science, of language." Generally the suffix *-ic* appears in English on words of Greek origin, which are basically adjectives but which may also serve as nouns in either the singular or the plural, such as "music," "rhetoric," "physics," "politics," or "ethics."

Linguistics, like anthropology, sociology, psychology, and other disciplines concerned with human behavior and thought, can to some extent be called a science, since the phenomena that it studies, though they result from the behavior of different individual humans, are capable of almost as rigorous analysis as are the phenomena of the physical sciences. From such analysis may be constituted patterns or laws that serve both as general statements of observed processes of change and as predictive guides for the classification of future observations. Nevertheless the development of languages adheres less strictly to its laws and produces more numerous eccentric results than do operations within the physical sciences. Linguistics is therefore far from an exact science.

Linguistics approaches the study of languages in at least four different ways. Descriptive linguistics analyzes a given language in terms of its vocabulary, grammar, sounds, and style. Comparative linguistics compares languages that have been studied as separate entities to see whether they show common features which might prove a relationship between them. Historical linguistics traces the development of one or more languages, often focusing on their separation from a common origin suggested by comparative linguistics. Theoretical linguistics seeks to derive from the results of descriptive, comparative, and historical studies of many languages general principles for the nature and function of language as such.

DESCRIPTIVE LINGUISTICS

Descriptive linguistics regards a given language as basically a system of utterances that involve both form, or the actual sound, and meaning, or the significance of the sound as accepted by both speaker and hearer. The relationship of the sound to the accepted meaning in any given language is probably a matter of convention, but to achieve communication, the convention must be familiar to all speakers of the language.

A meaningful sound or combination of sounds is called a "word." Words in turn are combined in speech to form a sequence which expresses a complete idea, and such a sequence is called a "sentence." A sentence may express either a simple or a complex thought. The meaning of the sentence is given by the relationship between the component words. This relationship may be one of order, or of the form of the words themselves, or of their connection to one another by certain of the words that serve to signify given relationships. When the relationship of one word to the others in a sentence is indicated by its form, this may be achieved in several ways. There may be an internal sound change, a change in the stem, as in English in the change from "sing" to "sang" which places the verb in past time. Prefixed or suffixed sounds, single or multiple, may be annexed. Such prefixes or suffixes may be originally independent words, like the prepositions joined to the beginning of a simple verb or noun, or they may be sound groups that have meaning but do not occur as independent words. The addition of a preposition is illustrated by the English word "income" to denote "what comes in." A two-syllable prefix not occurring independently in English is the Latin preposition *ante*, as in "antedate," meaning "to date before." The English suffix *-ly* makes an adverb out of an adjective, as in "happily" from "happy."

Descriptive linguistics therefore studies and systematizes a language with respect to its sounds and their changes, its word forms, and the ways in which it joins words together to express ideas.

The linguistic description of a language is called its "grammar," a word derived from the Greek verb *graphō* = I write. Grammar deals with three main aspects of language. The study of sounds and their development is called "phonology," from the Greek *phōnē* =

4

sound plus *logos* = word, here in the sense of rationale or science. The study of forms and their development is called "morphology," from the Greek *morphē* = form plus *logos*. And the study of constructions, or the way in which the appropriate forms of words are put together in correlated sequences to express larger units of thought, is called "syntax," from the Greek *suntaxis* = a putting together.

Phonology establishes patterns among sounds—namely among vowels, consonants, and syllables—and rules for their changes when combined with other sounds, or when used to express different relationships between words, or when alterations occur in the passage of time. It thus becomes useful for the study of the historical evolution of forms in a given language and the relations between cognate languages. Phonology may require a hypothetical reconstruction of the probable original sounds from which developed the various sounds actually found in the different existing languages or in the developed form of a given language, and the use of signs or invented letters to represent these sounds by linguistic convention. While phonology helps to understand the historical development of a language, it is not so important for an appreciation of the final result, the formalized structure or grammar of the language. In this book, therefore, attention is paid only incidentally to the role of phonology, whether in the linguistic antecedents and connections of Latin or in Latin grammar itself. Nor is use made of the signs and invented letters employed in phonological study. Emphasis is placed on the system of forms, or morphology, and on the system of constructions, or syntax, of Latin.

HISTORICAL LINGUISTICS

The present book seeks not merely to describe Latin as it was spoken and written in the first centuries B.C. and A.D., that is, the classical Latin of the Ciceronian and Augustan periods, but to show how its forms, sounds, and constructions—namely its morphology, phonology, and syntax—developed from older stages of the language and ultimately from a linguistic ancestor which gave issue to a wide range of cognate languages, including Latin. To this linguistic ancestor is applied the general term "Indo-European."

Modern linguistics uses the term "synchronic" with respect to the phenomena of a language studied descriptively at a given point in time, such as those of classical Latin. This term derives from the Greek prepositional prefix *sun-* = with and the noun *chronos* = time. It is equivalent to the English word "contemporary," which derives from the Latin translation of the Greek, namely the prepositional prefix *con-* (*cum*) = with and the noun *tempus* = time. The historical study of a language over a period of time is called "diachronic," from the Greek prepositional prefix *dia-* = through and *chronos*. Latin and English offer no equivalent translation for this word. Since the terms "synchronic" and "diachronic," however useful in advanced linguistic studies, do not at the level of this book differ materially from "descriptive" and "historical," they are not ordinarily employed here.

COMPARATIVE LINGUISTICS

Comparative linguistics compares not only the actual sound-symbols, or words, of different languages but the ways in which words are put together to express complex ideas or are changed in form to show their relationships to other words. That is, it compares the structures of various languages, which individually are the concern of descriptive linguistics.

Translation from English even into a language such as French, which has a relatively similar structure, involves far more than the simple substitution of the French equivalents for English words. In the first place, two languages seldom have words with exactly equivalent meanings; their connotations extend out in different directions. Thus a dictionary usually provides for a given word in one language several alternatives in another, among which the translator must choose that which most closely approximates the meaning of the original word in its given context. Second, no two languages integrate words into sentences in exactly parallel fashion; each language has an individual structure. Whereas the comparative study of English and French, for instance, might show more similarities than differences of meaning and structure, the comparative study of English and a language from some totally different group, like Chinese, would be concerned largely with differences. The close relation between language and thought means that individuals using languages whose sound-symbols and structures are alien to one another will find difficulty in understanding each other's ideas and processes of thought. People not only speak according to their patterns of thought but think according to the structures of their speech. Hence language exercises a profound influence on outlook, understanding, and philosophy.

Comparative linguistics formerly classified most languages structurally into three categories: isolating, agglutinating, and inflecting. Although no language falls completely into one of these categories and although various sub- or cross-classifications are now made, to the extent that some linguists reject entirely the validity of this classification, nevertheless the tripartite scheme may still suffice to indicate important differences in the structure of languages.

Chinese is an example of a language that is primarily isolating. Its words, for the most part monosyllabic, show no changes in form when placed in combination with other words to make a unit of meaning or sentence, but are simply strung along one after the other. Changes of meaning, as in the time of action, the person who acts, or the like, are usually indicated by the addition of separate words, without changing the original word. This occasionally occurs in English, as in "one moose" and "several moose," where the English termination to denote more than one, -s, is not added to "moose," or in "I hold" and "I will hold," where futurity is indicated by adding "will," without changing "hold." In Chinese, generally only the position of a word conveys its relation to other words in the sentence. Whereas in English the order "him do I see" expresses without ambiguity the same thought as "I do see him," in Chinese, since there is no change of form between the subject and the object, an inversion in word order ordinarily results in an inversion of meaning. Indeed, this is generally true in English too, as in "the man sees the dog" as against "the dog sees the man."

Inflecting languages use changes in stems or the addition of endings to show the relationship of individual words to the meaning. In such languages, as in Latin, word form rather than word order is the major key to understanding the sense of a sentence. Agglutinating languages, such as Turkish, put together long clusters of significant sound groups so that both insertions within the cluster and additions at the end serve to give meaning. Sentences in an agglutinating language consist of series of such clusters, which may only loosely be regarded as words.

Although Latin and English are for the most part inflecting languages, they also have characteristics both of isolating and of agglutinating languages. Meaning may be affected by the addition of words, as when the neuter Latin past participle *factum* = done becomes part of a perfect passive verb by adding the auxiliary verb *est* = is, so that "it is something which has been done" = "it has been done." Or, as in the English instance of "the man sees the dog," the meaning may be changed by altering the word order. Thus in Latin, *robur non habet cor* = an oak does not have a heart, as against *cor non habet robur* = the heart has no strength. Or there may be an internal shift of sound, as in Latin *făcit* = he makes, as against *fēcit* = he made.

However, the inflecting languages place chief importance on changes in the ending of words, namely on the addition to a basic stem of suffixes indicating the varying relationships in which a word may stand to other words or to the whole idea. Where Chinese would simply add to the word for "love" other words indicating "I" and past time to convey "I have loved," and Turkish would compose a word cluster of various significant sound groups, Latin either makes changes within the stem of a single word or adds suffixes and occasionally prefixes, or sometimes does both.

For example, to the stem *am*($\bar{a}$)- = love (as a verbal concept) Latin adds a simple long -$\bar{o}$ to yield the concepts both of present time (now) and of the speaker as the subject of the action expressed by the verb, producing a form known as the first person singular active present indicative, *amō* = I (now) love. When Latin wishes to express the same person as having acted in past time, it inserts a consonantal -*u*- between the stem *amā*- and the special ending for the first person active indicative in past time, long -$\bar{i}$, producing the first person singular of the perfect active indicative, *amāuī* = I loved, or I have loved.

In the verbal form *cecinī* = I sang, or I have sung, three ways of showing past time are used: the repetition or reduplication of the initial consonant *c-* with the insertion between the two *c*'s of an accessory (sometimes called a "glide") vowel, short *-e-*; the weakening of the short *-a-* of the present stem *can-* = sing to short *-i-*; and the use, as in *amāuī*, of the ending long *-ī* to indicate the first person singular active indicative in the perfect (past) tense.

No two languages, however closely related, have such similar structures that one grammatical scheme will serve to describe both. Even dialects—and the line between a dialect and a language is often one of degree rather than of kind—show structural variations as well as differences of vocabulary and pronunciation. Latin borrowed its grammatical terminology and organization from Greek, not always with complete descriptive accuracy. And the application of Latin grammatical formulations to English is often even less successful.

For instance, Latin expresses a simple unqualified verbal idea by a verbal form which, though it has a special ending, does not change to show its relation to other words in the sentence. Since this form serves simply to name the action expressed by the verb, it is called a "verbal noun," or an "infinitive," and, since it does not change its form like ordinary nouns, it is said to be "indeclinable." In English, the verbal concept may be named either by a prepositional phrase or by a verbal noun that resembles in form the English present participle. For example, the Latin infinitive *īre*, unchanging in form, may be expressed in English either by "to go" or by "(a) going."

Latin has a far wider range of forms of nouns and verbs to show different relationships. For instance, the subjunctive has almost vanished from current English. In contrast, English makes a much wider use of compound verb forms to express shades of meaning or emphasis. Thus the Latin *eō* may be rendered, according to the context, by English "I go," "I am going," or "I do go." Latin classifies nouns in three genders, namely masculine, feminine, and neuter, which have little basic relation to sex. English nouns are masculine or feminine only when actually or metaphorically they refer to males or females.

THEORETICAL LINGUISTICS

During the past century or more, scholars of linguistics in various countries have sought to develop from the findings of descriptive, historical, and comparative linguistics general principles concerning the nature and function of language. They have devised a variety of linguistic theories, and often their theorizing has become far removed from the actualities of any specific language. Indeed, many express their concepts of the structure of language in nonverbal formulas almost algebraic in character. Not only have theoretical linguists reached into mathematics, but they have also ventured into such fields as sociology, aesthetics, physiology, and psychology in their search to interpret the nature of language. As illustrations of modern linguistic theory, two widely used approaches and one special field are here briefly described: structuralism, transformational linguistics, and semantics.

Structuralism, or structural linguistics, seeks to establish the underlying patterns both of sound (phonological) and of word structure (morphological) that serve to organize a variety of languages. These patterns begin with minimal units or "building blocks." In phonology, the units may be the individual sounds that distinguish otherwise similarly sounded words. For example, in English, the different initial sounds of *p* and *b* distinguish such otherwise similarly sounded words as "pit" and "bit" or "pan" and "ban." In morphology, the units have fixed functions to distinguish meaning. Thus, again in English, the suffix *-ed* shows that "talked" is past in time in contrast to the simple present "talk." In syntax, the units are the smallest meaningful combinations of words, as in English "of a man," which combines three words to show that a man possesses something. Structural linguistics therefore tries to determine in any given language the structure of relationships between its basic units of sound, form, or syntax. The structural linguist may then go further and generalize structures or systems into a sort of algebraic formula which can serve to organize any language.

Transformational linguistics derives rules and procedures by which longer utterances can either be broken down into smaller units or expressed in alternate fashions to define their meanings

10

more sharply. The transformational linguist holds that beneath the specific utterance, or what is termed the surface structure of speech, lie deeper relationships between meanings, called the underlying structure. These underlying structures, when discovered, may even be generalized for all, or at least for several, languages. A commonly used example is the sentence "flying planes can be dangerous." As it stands, this sentence is ambiguous, so to determine which meaning is intended, it must be rephrased, or transformed, into either "to fly planes can be dangerous" or "planes that fly can be dangerous." A transformational linguist would also maintain that the active sentence "John reads a book" can be transformed without change of meaning into the passive "a book is read by John."

The transformational linguist further tries to establish a limited set of formulas or rules for any language from which a great variety of sentences can be constructed, that is, which are "generative" of all permissible grammatical constructions in the given language and which predict what combinations of words will be poorly or ungrammatically put together. For example, a rule that a sentence, to be a meaningful and complete utterance, should have at least a subject and a verb permits "John reads" as a sentence but precludes "John book." Naturally both subject and predicate may be much expanded beyond the single noun and verb used in this example.

Finally theoretical linguists have elevated to almost independent status the study of meaning, called "semantics," from the Greek verb *sēmainein* = to signify. A given sound-symbol, or word, is usually joined in speech with others to form a meaningful utterance or sentence which expresses either a simple or a complex thought. In a given sentence, the denotation that a word would have when standing alone may be widened or altered by the general context of thought, by the speaker's tone of voice, by the subject of discussion, or by the social environment of the speaker and his hearer.

For instance, in the sentence "he gets sick" the English verb "gets" has a different meaning from that in "he gets a book." Likewise, the meaning of words has changed historically, or diachronically. In the seventeenth century, in the phrase "faith, hope, and charity" in the King James version of the Bible, "charity" has the general meaning of "love," not its restricted modern meaning of "generous giving to the poor." Thus the full connotation of a word is not merely its denotation or denotations, its meanings as defined in a dictionary, but the implications which it conveys in a given sentence.

Furthermore the accepted meaning of a word may have overtones that vary according to the personal experiences of the speaker. Among peoples who believe in an afterlife of rewards and punishments, dwellers in hot climates, for whom the word "heat" has unpleasant connotations, conceive of Hell as a place of eternal fire. But northerners for whom warmth is a boon and cold a bane regard Hell as a place of eternal ice. In the same way, the conditions of life may affect the development of vocabulary. Eskimos have several distinct words to express differing conditions of what in English is simply called "snow." Latin used the single adjective *altus* to express a concept differentiated in English into "deep" and "high." Semantics therefore involves the consideration of the temporal, social, or cultural environment of the speaker and the psychological or philosophical background underlying the utterance.

The semanticist also asks whether the relationship of meaning to sound is arbitrary or has some rationale. He thus revives the old Greek debate between analogy and anomaly. Analogy, from the Greek prepositional prefix *ana-* = according to and the noun *logos* = reason, as well as word, means that sound and meaning have a rational or logical connection. Anomaly, from the Greek negative prefix *a-* = not and the noun *nomos* = law, or rule, means that the relationship is without rule, or arbitrary. There are in most languages words that reproduce sounds, like the English "buzz" or "cuckoo." The formation of such words is called "onomatopoeia," from the Greek noun *onoma* = name, or noun, and the verb *poiein* = to make. However, even onomatopoeic, or sound-reproducing, words are not necessarily the same in different languages. In English the sound made by a dog is reproduced as "bow-wow" but in German as "wauwau."

The use of totally diverse sounds in different languages to convey the same meanings generally makes it difficult to maintain that the relationship between sound and meaning is anything but arbitrary at the level of language. Of course, within a given language

12

communication is possible only if the speakers are agreed on the meaning or meanings to be attached to any given sound.

In conclusion, theoretical linguistics, including semantics, has undoubtedly helped to understand the nature and function of language, despite the wide diversity of individual theories. In due course the insights of the theorists may be applied to improve expression, communication, and in particular methods of teaching languages. However, this book is intended to clarify for beginning students of Latin the traditional grammatical formulations in which the subject is still presented to them. It does not, therefore, attempt to reformulate the structure of Latin grammar along lines propounded by modern theoretical linguists.

This book also eschews as far as possible the technical terms which have been devised by linguists for aspects or elements of their study but which are not essential for an initial comprehension of the history and character of Latin as traditionally presented. Some phonological and morphological terms, however, are briefly mentioned, in case students may happen to run across them elsewhere in their reading. For instance, linguists in the United States tend to call phonology "phonemics." "Phonetics" is used for the study of the movements of the vocal organs in uttering the sounds of speech. Two other common terms are "phoneme" and "morpheme." A phoneme, from the Greek word *phōnē* = sound, is a single unit of sound, not only a consonant or a vowel but any vocalization which, not itself fully sounded, conditions a consonant or vowel, as does aspiration. A morpheme, from the Greek word *morphē* = shape, or form, is a meaningful unit of sound. It may be a word like the English verb "see" or a single letter or syllable, like -*s*, which added to "see" yields "sees," the present active indicative third person singular form of the verb.

In short, the linguistic approach of this book is descriptive, historical, and comparative, but not theoretical. Its general presentation of Latin grammar is the traditional description and history of its morphology and syntax, with occasional attention to its phonology.

II

THE INDO-EUROPEAN FAMILY
OF LANGUAGES

Comparative linguistics, formerly called "comparative philology," is the study of the relationships and differences among languages. It was developed during the early nineteenth century. Sir William Jones, an English scholar in India, observed as early as 1786 resemblances of Sanskrit, the old sacred language of the Hindus, to Greek, Latin, and German. He proposed that all three had derived from a common original tongue. A century later, another scholar, Max Müller, who felt that Sanskrit had been brought into India by conquerors, applied the term "Aryan," from the Sanskrit *arya* = noble, to the speakers of the presumed original tongue.

Since community of language is no proof for community of race, because language may readily be imposed by conquest, borrowed by contact, or diffused by intermingling, scholars now prefer to call the original tongue "Indo-European," a term first used in 1813 as a purely geographical designation of the wide area over which this group of related languages is found. Inasmuch as the original tongue is no longer spoken by any of the various peoples using its derivatives, it can only be reconstructed hypothetically through analysis of the resemblances among these derivatives and by assuming common original sounds from which the later languages developed their particular forms according to their individual linguistic laws of sound change.

ORIGIN AND DISPERSION OF INDO-EUROPEAN

The approximate point or period in the development of human civilization at which the hypothetical Indo-European language first began to be spoken and the geographic area where this occurred are much disputed. Obviously a language is not invented at one moment of time. It must have taken a long time for the animal sounds uttered by the simian ancestors of man to become words. Nor can it be determined whether this development took place in one group of primitive humans located at some point perhaps remote from the centers of the later major linguistic families so that those families were gradually spread and differentiated by the migrations of subgroups branching off from the original speakers, or whether groups of humans in separate localities independently made the transition from animal sounds to the originals of the various linguistic families.

Thus, even if the area in which the hypothetical Indo-European was spoken could be fixed, this would not prove whether it had come into being there or had been brought there by some nomadic group of primitive humans. There is, indeed, no reason to suppose that the hypothetical original Indo-European was ever in fact a single language; it may from the beginning have been differentiated into dialects basically similar but differing from group to group or from place to place. This would perhaps account best for the differences between the derivative languages carried to widely separate areas by the disperson of its speakers.

The original homeland of the first speakers of Indo-European has been variously located somewhere in the general region extending from eastern Germany through western Russia and from the Baltic to the Black Sea. It is not important for the study of Latin to try to define the location more precisely or to review the evidence used. Collaboration between archaeologists and historical linguists now casts doubt on the traditional chronology for the differentiation of the original Indo-European tongue into separate Indo-European languages and on the hitherto accepted correlation between changes of culture in various areas, as indicated by archaeological finds, and the possible movement of new peoples into these areas, who were presumed to have brought with them Indo-European languages. Some scholars now hold that the transition from the neolithic ("new stone") cultures to those of the Bronze Age did not represent a drastic change of culture, or anything more than a regular local progress, and that the cultural change more likely to have been the consequence of the intrusion of new peoples was that from the Palaeolithic ("old stone") Age to the Neolithic.

This transition, from the use of crudely made tools of stone and bone to the use of more finely shaped ones, was accompanied by another major advance, from the procuring of food by hunting, picking berries, and other forms of gathering natural produce to the deliberate cultivation of cereals and the domestication of animals. The English anthropologist Vere Gordon Childe called this cultural advance "the neolithic revolution," though it was no sudden alteration of life-style but a slow progress over centuries, at different times and at varying speeds in different areas.

It is still generally held that cultivation of crops and domestication of animals were diffused outward from their beginnings in Anatolia (Asia Minor) and the northern Middle East, southerly to Mesopotamia, Palestine, and Egypt, and northerly to the Balkans, the Danube Valley, and western Europe. Nevertheless evidence is accumulating which suggests that these new techniques for food production instead of food gathering may have originated independently in different areas and that only at later dates did intercommunication between these areas occur. Thus the recent hypothesis that the neolithic revolution was diffused by speakers of Indo-European is itself being subjected to reexamination.

Though the neolithic revolution permitted the establishment of more fixed places of residence than had been possible for the palaeolithic hunters and food-gatherers, nomadism remained common, to find either new soil for crops or new pasturage for animals. How far simple nomadism, or instead some such development as climatic change or growth of population, occasioned the dispersion of the speakers of Indo-European, whenever it began, cannot be determined. Probably the dispersion should not be thought of as massive migrations, such as those of the Germanic tribes that overwhelmed the Roman Empire in the west from about 400 to about 600 A.D. The Indo-Europeans movements were more likely of small groups seeking better land and slowly infiltrating new territories.

Nor would the diffusion of the Indo-European languages necessarily have required displacement of earlier populations. History affords many instances in which either a relatively small number of immigrants have imposed their language on natives by conquest or natives have adopted the language of immigrants as a superior vehicle of communication to their own, as witness the spread of Latin first through Italy and then over western Europe and North Africa. In this case conquest was the primary reason for the adoption of Latin by the natives, but the fact that Greek resisted Latin in the east shows that it, unlike the languages of Italy and western Europe, was felt to be a superior vehicle of communication even by the conquering Romans.

Whatever the date and method of the original dispersion of the speakers of Indo-European from their presumed original homeland, by the end of the third millennium B.C. peoples using Indo-European languages were impinging on a wide arc of lands extending from central Asia and northwestern India (Pakistan) through the Middle East, Anatolia, the Balkans, and in due course further west into Italy and Gaul.

At the same time, a significant cultural advance was occurring, the spread of techniques for smelting and casting or hammering copper to make weapons, tools, and other utensils. In fact, the Neolithic Age was giving way to the Bronze Age. These techniques seem to have been discovered at the beginning of the fourth millennium B.C., perhaps even earlier, in Asia Minor and somewhat later in Egypt. At first copper was used pure; then it was found that an alloy of copper and tin called bronze was more satisfactory. It used to be held that migrating speakers of Indo-European learned these techniques and spread them to Greece, the Balkans, and western Europe, but archaeologists now question whether the introduction of the Bronze Age into Greece and Anatolia was necessarily the work of invading speakers of Indo-European. However, in Italy the arrival of speakers of Indo-European does seem to have coincided with the beginning of the Bronze Age. In fact, bronze came to Italy not only from the north, but also from the south, imported by traders from the Aegean area during the second millennium B.C. The introduction of copper and bronze by no means displaced stone, bone, or pottery, which remained common materials for making tools, weapons, and containers throughout antiquity.

Speakers of Indo-European who migrated later, in the course of the second millennium B.C., seem to have brought with them the horse and the war chariot, although wheeled vehicles drawn by animals had been known since early in the second millennium at least in southern Mesopotamia, in ancient Sumer. Some of these later migrants had also learned to smelt iron, perhaps from peoples of eastern Armenia who had invented the necessary techniques. Thus their arrival in any given area signaled the beginning of the Iron Age. However, because iron requires high temperatures for smelting and working, it remained throughout antiquity a less commonly used metal than was the more easily handled bronze.

INDO-EUROPEAN SOCIETY

Study of the vocabulary common to the various Indo-European languages and of the social and political organization of the different Indo-European speaking peoples when they emerge into historical light shows common elements that must go back to the society of the original speakers. This society was based on the family, and the head of the family was the father, not, as in some societies, the mother. Such a society, ruled by a father, is known as "patriarchal." Larger groups of families were assumed to have descended from a common ancestor, actual or invented. With the passage of time this presumed original ancestor might sometimes come to be regarded as having been superhuman, a deified hero or a god. In such groups of households, presumably related by kinship, leadership was exercised by some forceful head of a family, whose position as chief was not necessarily hereditary, though it often tended to become so. The chief was assisted, and controlled, by a council of heads of families or households, often known as elders.

The chief also had ultimately to command respect and support from an assembly of the men old enough to fight; women and children had no political rights, nor did such outsiders as resident strangers or slaves.

So primitive a society had no elaborate political forms or documents. Oral tradition played a large part in establishing custom, the predecessor of law, and in preserving oral folk memories, probably expressed in verse, which became the ancestor of history. Slavery undoubtedly existed. Property belonged rather to the family or whole tribe than to the individual. Worship was of a skygod of the daylight or sun, and probably also of lesser natural powers and phenomena, which may not have been personified but were simply regarded as friendly or hostile forces (Latin *numina*) to be honored or placated. The dead seem to have been thought to continue a vague existence and to require offerings and placation so that they would not harm the living.

Since from the earliest period the speakers of Indo-European were presumably already separating into nomadic tribes, it may be questioned whether the original forms (sounds) assumed as the source of similar words in the various Indo-European languages were ever actually spoken at the same time as a homogeneous tongue. The development of distinct tongues was presumably caused not by the breakup of an originally unified speech, as was described in the myth of the Tower of Babel, so much as by the increasing divergence of always somewhat variant dialects. It should not be assumed that all the dialects followed a common course of development. Those that were more isolated from contact with other languages and cultures preserved a more archaic character. Those whose speakers moved into highly developed civilizations were much changed in vocabulary, syntax, and pronunciation by the influence of and borrowing from the languages of such civilizations. As the migrant groups spread away from one another, their dialects followed individual patterns of growth until they became distinct languages, usually mutually unintelligible, despite the elements of a common origin that they preserved in vocabulary or structure. The same process was repeated in the later development of the Romance languages from Latin or of the Germanic tongues from a proto-German.

19

GROUPING OF INDO-EUROPEAN LANGUAGES

The surviving languages of the Indo-European family, and also some no longer spoken which are attested by written record, can be classified not only into such closely related groups as the Germanic, the Romance, the Slavic, or the Indic, but also into broader relationships, which presumably represent a more primitive stage of divergence. The establishment of such broader relationships is often not precise because different criteria may assign a given language partly into one relationship and partly into another.

A major distinction often made within the Indo-European family of languages is that between languages which preserve an original hard *c* or *k* sound and those in which this has been softened to a soft *c* or *s* sound. This division is exemplified by the contrast between the initial consonants of the Latin *centum* and the old Persian (Avestan) *satem*, both meaning "hundred"; thus the two groups of languages are called the *centum* and the *satem*. Later changes may have obscured the original treatment of this sound in some members of either group. For example, in the Germanic languages, from the *centum* group, the original hard *c* has become *h*, as in English "hundred." It used to be held that the *centum* languages were western and the *satem* eastern. But this distinction is by no means absolute. For instance, two Indo-European languages of the east, namely Hittite in Anatolia and Tokharian in central Asia, are *centum*. Other criteria also cut across the *centum/satem* distinction, which makes difficult the establishment of major classifications of the Indo-European families of languages.

Among the languages that are either still spoken or well attested by written materials, lesser groups can be established more readily. The accompanying table of the Indo-European languages assumes, for simplicity of presentation, the validity of the *centum/satem* or east/west division. Moreover it presents the recognizable families of Indo-European languages in a roughly chronological order, based on datings that today would be regarded by some scholars as probably too late. These dates are not those of the earliest attested evidence for the various languages but the approximate times at which archaeological and other researches suggest that their speakers first occupied the areas in which the languages themselves are later found. Centuries, not to say millennia, may separate the original arrival of the speakers in a given area from the period when evidence for the language is first available. Despite these uncertainties, the table indicates the variety and spread of the Indo-European languages both in time and in space.

The table in no way purports to offer a "family tree" of the Indo-European languages. The groupings are based on similarities of vocabulary, morphology, syntax, or phonology; and in more recent, well-attested cases, chronological sequence or geographical distribution may show descent, as of the Romance languages from Latin. But the major division into *centum/satem* or western/eastern, given the number of other crosscutting criteria, cannot be regarded as representing two major "lines of descent."

Nor for the earlier groupings does the chronological order of appearance in their final homelands establish any sure order of dispersion from the original Indo-European. The most that can be said is that languages on the geographical fringes of the dispersion tend to be more archaic in character, such as Tokharian in Central Asia or Latin among the Italic languages. But such archaism may be evidence not for early separation but merely for isolation from other languages, whether Indo-European or not, which meant that such fringe tongues were not stimulated to develop by outside contacts, whether linguistic, cultural, or intellectual.

In the table, no clear distinction is made between significant dialects and languages, for it would be difficult to determine precisely when a dialect became so unintelligible to a speaker of a related dialect that it could justly be regarded as a distinct language. Moreover, still spoken languages are not distinguished from those known today only from written records.

Of languages preserved only in writing, perhaps the least familiar is Tokharian (Tocharian, or Tocharish). This language appears in certain Buddhist and business manuscripts which were found in Chinese Turkestan, north of the Himalayas, between 1890 and 1909. The manuscripts, dating from c. 500–700 A.D., are written in a Hindu script, but the language itself is a form of Indo-European no longer spoken in the area and not closely related to other nearby Indo-European tongues, such as Sanskrit or Old Persian (Iranian). Tokharian, as well as Hittite, a language spoken

The Indo-European Languages

Possible earliest date of use in areas where attested	Western or *centum*		Eastern or *satem*	
3500 B.C.			*Anatolian* Luwian Hittite (*centum*) Lydian Lycian	
2500 B.C.			*Armenian*	
2200 B.C.	*Hellenic* Linear B (Mycenaean) Greek Homeric Greek Classical Greek Doric Aeolic Ionian Attic Others Hellenistic Greek (Koinē) Byzantine Greek Modern Greek and its dialects		*Iranian* and Old Persian (Avestan) Pahlavi Persian Pasto Tajik Others	*Indic* Sanskrit (Vedic) Prakrit (Pali) Modern Indic Bengali Hindi Urdu Punjabi Gujerati Sinhalsi Sindhi Marathi Others
1800 B.C.	*Italic* and Latin Oscan Umbrian	*Celtic* Irish Gaelic Welsh Cornish Breton	*Tokharian* (*centum*)	
800 B.C.	*West German* and *North & East German* Anglo-Frisian Scandinavian English Norwegian Frisian Icelandic Continental Swedish Dutch Danish Flemish Gothic German Swiss Yiddish			

The Indo-European Languages (*continued*)

Possible earliest date of use in areas where attested	Western or *centum*	Eastern or *satem*
1 A.D.	*Baltic* and Lithuanian Latvian Old Prussian	*Slavic* Russian Polish Ukrainian Czech Serbo-Croatian
600–800 A.D.	*Romance Languages (from Latin)* Rumanian Dalmatian Raeto-Rumanian French Provençal Catalan Spanish Portuguese	

in Asia Minor (Anatolia) during the second millennium B.C., even have some characteristics of the western or *centum* branch. Precisely who were the people who spoke Tokharian is not certain, and therefore the date given for their settlement in Chinese Turkestan is not a sure one. Tokharian, however, marks the most easterly known migration of speakers of Indo-European. And it serves to illustrate the problem of determining the interrelationship of the various Indo-European languages and the times at which the various groups of speakers migrated to their eventual homelands.

In the table, the Italic languages are closely grouped with the Celtic. Although the closeness of their relationship is much disputed, the Italic languages are in many respects more similar to the Celtic than they are to Greek, with which Latin is so commonly associated in the modern mind. It is possible that speakers of the two linguistic groups appeared on the central Danube about 1800 B.C. Thence speakers of the Italic group moved southward into the

Balkans and then around, or across, the Adriatic into Italy. The speakers of Celtic moved westward into Gaul (France), whence they eventually spread into Spain, northern Italy (the Po Valley), and the British Isles. The movement into the Po Valley seems to have begun only in the fifth century B.C., and offshoots of it are represented by the Gauls who sacked Rome in the early fourth century and those who moved through Greece into Anatolia during the third century. Since the Italic and Celtic groups were probably at best parallel developments from Indo-European, a comparison of the elements common to them is not here made.

III

INDO-EUROPEAN AND LATIN

The grammar and syntax of Latin, as compared to Greek, are in some respects more archaic; they reflect more closely the original Indo-European. Indo-European in general produced a heritage of inflectional languages. Such languages indicate the relations among words in sentences by adding endings to a stem that communicates the basic idea of a given word. Latin also indicates relationship by stem changes of various sorts, or by adding prefixes at the beginning of the stem. Though it is possible, but by no means certain, that the endings were originally in Indo-European separate words, as in Chinese, in all the derivative languages the endings are grammatical units which have no independent existence and appear only joined to stems. It is therefore safer to assume that in Indo-European they were similarly added to stems to afford the same determinative character.

The morphology of an inflected language establishes patterns or paradigms (Greek *paradeigma* = a pattern, or an example) of the possible forms that any given type of stem may assume by the addition of endings or prefixes and by stem changes, classified according to the relationships which these forms indicate. Nouns, pronouns, and adjectives add endings to indicate the relationships of gender, number, and case. Verbs do so to indicate relationships of voice, mood, tense, number, and person, and also to make noun or adjectival forms. That is, nouns, pronouns, adjectives, and verbs are inflected. The other parts of speech, namely adverbs, prepositions, conjunctions, and interjections, do not change their forms since their respective functions, or relationships, are expressed either by the stem itself or by the stem with a fixed ending, as in the case of adverbs. Adverbs, like adjectives, may also add different endings to express their degree of intensity, their comparison, in relation to some other word or thought.

These eight parts of speech presumably existed in Indo-European, though probably with less sharply defined functions. Their classification was the work of Greek and Latin grammarians, eager to reduce language to systematic regularity. But even in Latin certain words may function as two distinct parts of speech without change.

The addition of prefixes and endings to stems, as well as changes of sounds within stems, to indicate the relation of a word to other words or to the whole thought being expressed is called "inflection." Inflection is subdivided into the declension of nouns, pronouns, and adjectives, and the conjugation of verbs. The four parts of speech that do not change are said to be uninflected.

NOUNS: DECLENSION, GENDER, NUMBER, AND CASE

The declension of nouns, pronouns, and adjectives indicates two types of relationship: the number of persons or things involved, and the function that the word performs in the total development of thought, or its case. To denote these relationships, Indo-European developed different systems of endings for different classes of nouns or for nouns of different genders. Latin reduced the classes of nouns that it inherited from Indo-European to four and produced a fifth of its own. The first four of these systems, also called "declensions," derived from Indo-European but altered considerably the original forms of their endings both by interaction and borrowing among declensions and by phonological change and assimilation of sounds.

Indo-European differentiated nouns not only according to their declensional endings but also into three classes, which the Latin grammarians called "genders" because in some instances a difference of gender indicated a difference of sex. The three classes were defined as masculine, feminine, and neuter. In Indo-European, pronouns apparently had gender according to the sex of the person or thing to which they referred, that is, of their antecedent. But evidence from all the languages derived from Indo-European shows that by and large the gender of nouns did not depend on any general concept of sex. The significance of the three genders has not yet been convincingly explained. Even among the modern languages derived from Indo-European, English is the chief one that has made the gender of its nouns and pronouns correspond consistently with sex. French, for instance, has eliminated the neuter, so that inanimate objects are grammatically masculine or feminine just as are animate beings. In German, words connoting females may be neuter in gender, as is *Mädchen* = maiden, and inanimate objects may be of any one of the three genders.

In Latin, gender may be shown by the type of ending or even by the declensional class. But many nouns do not show their gender by their endings. Gender is important because most adjectives, including the verbal adjectives called "participles" and "gerunds," have different sets of endings for agreement with nouns of different genders. Only a few adjectives are invariable and do not change their endings to show agreement in gender, or even in number and case.

Indo-European distinguished not only between one person or object and many by its inflectional endings in both declensions and conjugations, but also between one, two, and many. These three numbers are called "singular," "dual," and "plural." Dual forms survived in Greek declensions and conjugations; in Latin the only dual ending is the final -$\breve{o}$ in the nominative masculine and neuter plural forms *du$\breve{o}$* = two and *amb$\bar{o}$* = both.

Indo-European used at least eight different endings in the various declensions to indicate the relationships in which a noun or pronoun, with modifying adjectives, might stand to other words or to the whole idea being expressed. These relationships are called in Latin *cas$\bar{u}$s* = cases. *Casus*, literally "a falling," derives from the verb *cad$\bar{o}$* = I fall. The noun was used in grammar to translate the

Greek word *ptōsis*, which has the same significance in Greek grammatical writers, that of denoting a mode or modification of a word, particularly of a noun.

Latin normally has only five cases for nouns, and in the various declensions there are similar endings for some of these cases. Latin uses the same ending for the nominative, or case of the subject of speech, and the vocative, or case of direct address, except in the singular of the second or short *-o-* declension, where these cases show different endings. Latin retains the Indo-European genitive, dative, and accusative. However, the Latin ablative absorbed the functions of three cases that Indo-European distinguished: a case denoting separation, called "ablative"; one denoting means or instrument, called "instrumental"; and one denoting place, called "locative." Some Latin words show distinct terminations for the locative in the first, second, and occasionally the third declensions. Locative endings are also preserved in some adverbs, particularly those of time or place.

PRONOUNS AND ADJECTIVES

Pronouns and adjectives show only the five regular cases in Latin.

Adjectives may add not only case endings in agreement with the gender, number, and case of the noun or pronoun that they modify but also endings, in their turn declined, to indicate degree of intensity. There are three such degrees: the simple or positive form, which has no special ending to denote intensity, and two degrees of higher intensity with special endings, the more intense or comparative form and the most intense or superlative form. The three terms indicating these degrees are adjectives formed from the perfect passive participles of three verbs: *positus* of *pōnō* = I place, *comparātus* of *comparō* = I compare, and *superlātus* of *superferō* = I carry, or put, beyond. Thus a positive adjective simply places on the noun that it modifies the limiting qualification given by its meaning. A comparative adjective signifies that with respect to its meaning, its noun is more so than something or somebody else. A superlative adjective shows that with respect to its meaning its noun is qualified beyond everything or everybody else, or is "tops" in terms of the adjectival qualification.

The phenomenon of comparison by adding inflected endings was inherited in Latin from Indo-European, as was the original form of the comparative ending: *-ior* (masculine and feminine) and *-ius* (neuter). Latin, however, developed special superlative endings of its own.

VERBS: CONJUGATION, VOICE, TRANSITIVE AND INTRANSITIVE, MOOD

The basic forms, called "stems," of Latin verbs in part went back to Indo-European and in part were developed in the preliterary period of the language. In Indo-European, the stems of verbs had been of two main types: those which added endings directly to the final consonant or vowel of the stem, and those which introduced a transitional sound between stem and ending. This sound was later shown in writing as either short *-e-* or short *-o-*, and these transitional vowels are called "thematic" from the Greek *thema* in its meaning of "stem (of a word)," because they became part of the stem to which the endings were added. Hence verbs that introduce a thematic vowel are themselves called thematic, while verbs that add the ending directly to the stem are designated as "athematic," a term in which the initial *a-* is a Greek prefix with negative force. Greek kept distinct its thematic and athematic declensions. Latin merely retained some athematic forms in a few primarily thematic verbs.

Ancient grammarians classified the almost wholly thematic Latin verbs into four conjugations. The conjugations are distinguished by the vowels which are added to the root to form the stem. The order in which these are arranged is arbitrary and not one of priority either in antiquity or in significance. First conjugation verbs add long *-ā*, as in *amā-*, the stem meaning "love." Those of the second conjugation add long *-ē*, as in *monē-*, the stem meaning "advise." Those of the third conjugation add short *-e*, as in *rege-*, the stem meaning "rule," or short *-i*, as in *capi-*, the stem meaning "take." Those of the fourth conjugation add long *-ī*, as in *audī-*, the stem meaning "hear." A few irregular verbs in general follow the third conjugation.

The action denoted by the verb may stand in at least three relationships to the person or thing acting, namely its subject. The endings used to express these relationships, which usually differ, are classified under general headings called "voices." If the action proceeds from the subject, the verb is said to be in the "active" or "acting" voice. The "passive" or "suffering" voice shows that the subject is acted upon; the source of the action, the agent or instrument by which the action is initiated, may or may not be expressed. Finally the subject may act upon him-, her-, or itself, in which case the voice is called "middle," namely between active and passive.

In Indo-European it seems that the middle and passive significances were not distinguished by different endings because the relationships so closely overlapped. In Greek, middle endings are used to express both middle and passive meanings except in two tenses, passive future and passive aorist (a simple past tense), which have distinct endings. Latin has no special endings for a middle voice; it shows simply active and passive forms. Normally action of the subject upon him-, her-, or itself is shown by the use of a reflexive pronoun, that is, a pronoun as object referring back to the subject of the verb as its antecedent. When the Latin passive has a middle meaning, chiefly in poetry and from the Augustan age, there is dispute whether this is a survival from a preliterary usage or represents an imitation of the Greek similarity of the middle and passive forms.

Within the active voice, the action may proceed from the subject to an object (a person or thing), in which case the verb is said to be "transitive," that is, one in which the action passes over from subject to object. If the action proceeding from the subject does not affect an object, the verb is said to be "intransitive." Verbs that express merely existence, or "being," are also called "intransitive." Both transitive and intransitive meanings are ordinarily expressed by the same active endings.

Indo-European distinguished by verbal endings the attitude, or mood, of the speaker toward the action expressed by the verb, that is, the modality of the action. At a preliterary stage, Latin had four such moods. The indicative mood indicated a simple statement of fact or a question; the subjunctive, or subordinating, mood, uncertainty or probability; the optative mood, wish or desire; and the imperative mood, injunction or command. Although the optative survived as a distinct mood in Greek, Latin incorporated its functions and some of its forms, such as subjunctive endings with the vowel -i-, into the subjunctive. In Latin, in addition to the three real moods (indicative, subjunctive, and imperative), the infinitive, an indeclinable verbal noun denoting the mere (unqualified) action, is usually also classed as a mood, since it shows different endings to indicate voice and tense, and it may have a subject, object, and adverbial modifiers, unlike an ordinary noun.

VERBS: TENSE

In primitive Indo-European, verbs apparently changed their stems not so much to indicate the time of the action in relation to the moment of speech as to show the character or type of the action itself, what is called its "aspect." The action might be thought of as in progress or at least as vividly contemporary with the utterance. Or the action might be regarded as a single or unitary occurrence, whether at the moment of speech or previous to it. Third, the action might be conceived of as already completed in the past and usually, therefore, as having resulted in a permanent condition or state. To draw an inadequate comparison, aspect in English would mean that "I do" also signifies "I am doing"; "I did" would refer to a single act whether past or present; and "it is done" would show that the work is finished, as God said to the author of the Book of Revelation 21:6 in the Latin Vulgate: *factum est.*

Later Indo-European languages came to assign temporal significance to the forms originally used for these three aspects by employing them to show the time of the action in relation to the moment of speech. Progressive action was looked upon as contemporary or present. In Greek, single or unitary action, called *aoristos* = undefined, was regarded as simple past action, as distinct from completed action. Latin combined the aorist and the completed past action under one tense, which was called the "perfect,"

31

from the Latin perfect passive participle *perfectus* = completed. Thus in Latin *agō* = I do, or I am doing, and *ēgī* = I did (a single past act), or I have done, that is, my past doing has resulted in a present completed state.

In the indicative mood, Latin developed three tenses each in the present and perfect systems. The present indicative tense denotes action contemporary in time with the speaking. The imperfect indicative shows action past in relation to the time of speaking but not having occurred at a single or undefined point of time. As the term "imperfect" suggests, the action may have begun in the past and still be continuing in the present, or it may have been continuous, repeated, or habitual in the past. The future indicative denotes action that has not yet occurred at the time of speaking but which will, rather than might, occur later.

The future was developed in preliterary Latin differently from its development in other Indo-European languages. In the first, second, and occasionally in the fourth conjugations it shows a -*b*- inserted between the stem vowel and the personal endings. This -*b*- may come from the imperfect ending of all declensions. In the third and usually in the fourth conjugations the future uses forms of the subjunctive. The latter usage suggests that preliterary Latin, like Indo-European, did not distinguish between futurity and possibility, between "will/shall" and "may/might."

In the perfect indicative system, the tenses are parallel to those in the present system. The simple perfect indicative combines the connotations of action completed in past time and simple past action at a single or undefined point of past time. The pluperfect, or more than the perfect, indicative is used for an action which had occurred before some other action in past time. The future perfect indicative indicates action that will be (or will have been) completed before some other action takes place, or took place.

In the Latin subjunctive system, only four tenses are used: present and imperfect, and perfect and pluperfect. These retain, more than do the tenses of the indicative, the original connotation of the modality of the action. Thus their temporal relation to the time of speaking is not necessarily absolute but may be conditioned in main verbs by the speaker's mood and in subordinate uses also by the time of a main verb on which the subjunctive depends.

In Latin, imperatives have active and passive voices, a present and a so-called future tense, and singular and plural numbers.

Among the verbal nouns, infinitives occur in the active and passive voices, which have present, perfect and, as compound forms, future tenses in both voices. The two other verbal nouns, the gerund and the supine, act purely as nouns in their incomplete inflections. Of the two verbal adjectives, there are present and future active and perfect passive participles, while the gerundive is only active.

VERBS: NUMBER AND PERSON

Indo-European indicated by differences in the verbal endings the number and person of the subject from whom or from which the action proceeded. In Latin, only in certain compound forms of the verb is gender also indicated by agreement of the endings of the adjectival part (participle or gerundive) of the compound with the gender of the subject. Since Latin did not preserve, as did Greek, special endings to denote two persons or things as subject (the dual), number in Latin is either one or several, singular or plural. As respects person, the subject may be the speaker or speakers, that is, first person singular or plural. It may be the person(s) or object(s) addressed, that is, second person singular or plural. Or it may be the person(s) or object(s) about whom the speaker speaks, that is, the third person singular or plural. Thus six personal endings (three singular and three plural) in both active and passive voices are necessary for a full expression of the number and person of the subject of a verb in tense systems that are complete. A simple pronoun need not be expressed as the subject of a Latin verb.

Though Latin inherited its sequences of personal endings from Indo-European, it changed considerably the specific endings in its own preliterary development. The personal endings in Latin are normally connected by a thematic vowel to the stem in uncompounded forms of the verb, namely throughout the active present and perfect tenses, and thus in six of the indicative, four of the subjunctive, and two of the imperative. In the passive, only the tenses of the present system, namely three in the indicative, two in the subjunctive, and two in the imperative, are uncompounded and add the endings directly. The past or perfect passive tenses, namely three in the indicative and two in the subjunctive, are compounded. In them the passive perfect participle is combined with the appropriate inflected forms of the auxiliary verb *sum* = I am. As a predicate verbal adjective, the passive perfect participle is in the nominative case and agrees with the subject of the verb in number and gender. Since the imperative has only present and future tenses, it shows no compound passive forms. In the compound forms of the passive perfect system the inflected forms are those of *sum*. In consequence, in the passive, personal endings occur only on the uncompounded forms of verbs, namely in the present, imperfect, and future.

The personal endings differ according to the person of the subject (first, second, or third), its number (singular or plural), and its voice (active or passive). The active perfect indicative (but not the other tenses of the active perfect system) has personal endings different from those of the active present system. The personal endings also differ for the moods, to a slight extent as between indicative and subjunctive, and considerably for the imperative. The active and passive imperative have only two tenses, present and so-called future. In the present they show only the second person singular and plural. In the so-called future, they show both a second and a third person singular and plural. All of these forms have special personal endings, except that the second person plural passive future is identical in ending with the second person plural passive indicative and often is not given in paradigms. The non-finite forms of the verb, namely infinitives, participles, gerunds, and gerundives, do not have personal endings, though many may show endings to distinguish voice, tense, gender, or number.

Any standard Latin grammar covers the various sequences of personal endings and the forms on which they occur. It also shows how to distinguish, by the stem changes that usually differentiate the perfect from the present system, between those forms in each system and in each tense thereof which have similar personal endings.

In conclusion, what is presented in the usual Latin grammar or textbook as the declensions of nouns, pronouns, and adjectives, as the conjugations of verbs, and as syntax represents the end result of a long process of development and systematization. The pre-literary forms, derived ultimately from Indo-European, were altered by centuries of usage and were adapted or broadened to cope with fresh and more elaborate thoughts. The writing down of the spoken language tended to inhibit change, particularly after a widely accepted standard of language was established by the outstanding authors of the late Republic and the early Empire.

This formation of a literary and consciously stylistic language also tended to introduce conformity and suppress variation, particularly through the work of grammarians and teachers who attempted to present the language systematically for learning by children or foreigners. In consequence, the forms and even the syntax both of preliterary Latin and of its ancestral Indo-European must be reconstructed by careful analysis of what survives, by comparison with developments in other Indo-European languages, and by hypothesis as to how changes may have occurred. Moreover, what is preserved in writing is only an approximation of the subtle variations in spoken sounds and may obscure differences of pronunciation by representing them with the same letters or combinations thereof. A spoken language is altered primarily by changes in sound (phonological), in forms (morphological), and in constructions (syntactical). Changes in the spelling and forms of written words or in the syntax of written texts only slowly come to reflect the alterations in speech.

An elaborate analysis of the development of Latin forms from Indo-European would be confusing here and only slightly helpful in understanding the grammar of classical Latin. It should suffice to know the nature of the problems involved, the results as well as the uncertainties of linguistic investigations, and the complex developments that intervened between the possibly more regular but also probably more varied inflections of Indo-European and those of classical Latin.

In this book the Latin that was developed primarily as a spoken language during the centuries from the arrival of Latin speakers in Italy to the beginning of Latin literature, about 240 B.C., is called "preliterary Latin," and the Latin spoken and written from 240 B.C. to about 150 A.D. is called "classical Latin." Classical Latin more specifically means the Latin used in the latter half of the first century B.C. and the first half of the first century A.D., in the so-called Ciceronian and Augustan periods. Literary Latin includes not only classical Latin but also the Latin of the middle and late Empire, of the Middle Ages, and of modern times. In all these periods works of literature continued to be written in Latin.

IV

LATIN AND THE OTHER LANGUAGES OF ANCIENT ITALY

Latin is an Italic language, one spoken in Italy. For convenience, however, it may be set apart from the other cognate Indo-European tongues spoken in ancient Italy, and those may be called collectively "Italic" in contradistinction to Latin. Besides the Italic tongues cognate with Latin, Italy became the home of at least three imported languages: Etruscan, Celtic, and Greek, while on the fringes of its western waters, in Sicily, Sardinia, and Corsica, Punic was introduced by the Carthaginians. Yet Latin was influenced only slightly by its contacts both with the cognate Italic languages and the imported or neighboring ones.

Older scholars assumed, because of the close connections between Latin and Celtic and also on the basis of certain archaeological evidence, that the speakers of the various Indo-European languages called Italic, including Latin, migrated into Italy from the northwest, over the western Alps, as the forefront of a general movement into western Europe of Indo-European speaking tribes, a movement which later brought the Celts into Gaul (France). Recent studies indicate, however, that Latin is not so closely cognate to Celtic as was once thought and that the speakers of the Italic languages moved from the central Balkans into Italy either across the Adriatic or around its northern end. Such a movement should not be conceived of as a series of mass migrations like the later Germanic in-

37

vasions of the Roman Empire but rather as the gradual infiltration of small nomadic groups or tribes into an area as yet sparsely settled by pre-Italic inhabitants still at a neolithic (new stone) level of culture. The newcomers, better equipped with bronze utensils and weapons and more advanced in herding and agriculture, either absorbed the previous inhabitants or isolated them in the wilder, more mountainous parts, such as the Ligurian Alps above Genoa, whose historical inhabitants, to judge from the little that is preserved of their speech, were probably neolithic survivors. So far as can be determined, Latin adopted little or no vocabulary, morphology, or syntax from the neolithic linguistic substratum, whatever may have been the physical or racial changes introduced by mixture with the neolithic peoples themselves.

The Indo-European speaking newcomers seem to have entered Italy during the second millennium B.C. in three waves. First came the speakers of proto-Latin, who were gradually pushed westward by later arrivals. Their speech survived only in the lower Tiber Valley as Latin, as the closely related Faliscan dialect spoken somewhat further up the valley around Falerii, and also, so far as scanty survivals suggest, as the dialects of other tribes scattered down the west coast of Italy and of certain tribes of Sicily, called "Siculi." The relative isolation into which the speakers of proto-Latin were forced probably accounts for the many archaic features in Latin, since linguistic archaism results from a language's lack of contact with other tongues or from the absence of new experiences requiring new modes of expression.

The next wave of Indo-European speaking intruders into Italy, who were perhaps more numerous than the speakers of primitive Latin, occupied the whole of the central mountains of Italy, the Apennines, from its ranges south of the Po Valley down into south Italy, and even pushed across the straits of Messina into Sicily. The material remains of these intruders attest a common culture which archaeologists call "Apennine." Literary citations and inscriptions from the period of the Roman Republic show that in historical times the many tribes throughout this area spoke dialects often so different as to constitute separate languages. Nevertheless, they have enough common features so that they may be classified under one general linguistic group with two main subdivisions. In north central Italy, the principal region is the extensive plain of Umbria. The subdivision spoken in this whole region is therefore called "Umbrian." In south central Italy the Greeks who settled around the Bay of Naples found resident there a tribe named the Osci. Their name came to be applied to the subdivision spoken throughout this whole region, called "Oscan." The Romans, however, called the various tribes of south central Italy collectively "Samnites." The principal Samnite tribe in the neighborhood of Rome was the Sabines or, in early and poetic Latin, the Sabelli. Hence modern philologists use the term "Sabellan" to cover the Samnite dialects. However, the compound term "Osco-Umbrian" is regularly employed for the grouping together of all the dialects spoken in historical times by the second wave of intruders, though their material culture is known as "Apennine."

Finally, just before what may be regarded as the beginning of the historical period in Italy, sometime between 1000 and 700 B.C., the east or Adriatic coast of Italy was occupied by a third wave of newcomers whose various languages, from Messapic in the south to perhaps Venetic in the north, were closely akin to the languages spoken on the opposite shore, the coast of Illyricum or the western Balkans. Recent studies suggest, however, that the language of the people around the north end of the Adriatic, the Veneti, may not be a latecomer among the Italic tongues but a survival from the first wave, since its scanty remains appear to show some kinship with Latin.

OSCO-UMBRIAN

One of the surprises of history is that Latin, the language of so small and isolated a tribe, should eventually have displaced the Osco-Umbrian tongues as the principal speech of Italy and then should have dominated the western Mediterranean. The triumph of Latin was the result of Rome's success in first overcoming her neighbors in Italy and later expanding her empire throughout the Mediterranean basin. Certainly classical Latin was influenced by its contacts with the other languages of Italy, both Italic and imported. But what seems remarkable about Latin is that in the course of expansion, despite such contact and the need for meeting new situations, it did not lose more of its archaic character. In their language the Romans displayed the conservatism so characteristic of them generally.

The close linguistic relation between the Osco-Umbrian tongues and Latin, reinforced by the geographical proximity of the respective speakers, made borrowing from the former into the latter easy. For instance, both Sabellan (Oscan) and Umbrian show a *p* where Latin has *qu*. The traditional second king of Rome was said to be a Sabine with the name Numa Pompilius. While Numa may be Etruscan, Pompilius is derived from the Sabellan *pompe* = five, equivalent to the Latin *quinque*. Similarly *popina* is a popular Latin word, undoubtedly borrowed from Osco-Umbrian, for the regular *coquina* = kitchen. Sabellan shows an *f* between vowels where Latin has *b*. Thus Latin *rufus* = redhead is a borrowing which corresponds to the regular Latin *ruber* = red. More complicated is the relation of the rare *bufo* = toad to the more common *bubo* = owl. *Bufo* is probably a Sabellan word whose derivation may have been different from that of Latin *bubo*, a term which is called "onomatopoeic," or "name-making," because it derives from the sound uttered by the owl. However, since Latin *bubo* shows a dialectical variant *bufo* or *bufus*, the Oscan and Latin words, if not similar in origin, must early have become identified.

ETRUSCAN, CELTIC, PUNIC, AND GREEK

The area north of the Tiber along the west coast of Italy was occupied during historic times by a people called the Etruscans. The question of their origins is much debated. Their language, written in Greek letters, can be made out and meanings assigned to many words from context or from occasional Latin translations. But not enough of it survives to give any sure foundation for assigning it to a linguistic group, that is, for determining whether it is Indo-European, a non-Indo-European language subject to Indo-European influence, or wholly non-Indo-European, perhaps native neolithic or possibly from Asia Minor.

Despite the long and close contact between the Latins and Etruscans, and the Etruscan domination of Rome during the sixth century B.C., the Latin language made relatively few borrowings from Etruscan and was little influenced in its own structure. Roman nomenclature imitated the Etruscan, however. Instead of a single name, the Etruscans, like the historic Romans, used a personal *praenomen*, a gentile *nomen*, and a family *cognomen*. Many actual Roman names appear to have derived from Etruscan, such as those ending in *-ō* (*-u* in Etruscan) like *Catō*, *Cicerō*, *Pisō*, or *Varrō*, and perhaps those ending in *-a* like *Catilīna* or *Murēna*. The names *Rōma* (of which *Rōmulus* is a derivative) and *Remus* themselves seem to be variants of the same Etruscan name. Some very common Latin words are Etruscan, like *amor* = love, *persōna* = mask, *ātrium* = hall, *īdūs* = ides (a fixed day in each month), and *balteum* = belt.

As the Celts expanded in Gaul, some tribes pushed over the Alps into the Po Valley in northern Italy. Though the Roman historian Livy dated this movement around 700 B.C., archaeological evidence indicates a date shortly after 500 B.C. A raiding party of these Gauls pushed south to sack Rome, traditionally in the year 390 (or 387) B.C. Another group moved through the Balkans, raided Greece in 279 B.C., and by the middle of the third century B.C. settled finally in central Asia Minor, in the region named after them, Galatia. From Celtic, Latin took a number of technical words, such as *carpentum* = carriage, *gaesum* = javelin, or *bracae* = breeches (originally a Germanic term), and also some more general words. Of the latter, *bāsium* = kiss is probably one, since it was first used by Cicero's contemporary, the poet Catullus from Cisalpine Gaul, and not thereafter in Latin, although in all the Romance languages it displaced the Latin *osculum* = kiss.

Punic, spoken only on the western fringe of the Italian area, had little influence on Latin. It was not only tangential but part of a totally different linguistic family, the Semitic. Moreover Carthage, more even than the Etruscans and Celts, was the enemy par excellence in Rome's middle republican period. Thus there was slight occasion for the type of contacts that might have led to borrowing.

The people of the Aegean area had been in touch with southern Italy and Sicily since the second millennium B.C., when the Minoans of Crete extended their trade into the western Mediterranean. Following on their traces, the Greeks began by the middle of the eighth century B.C. to settle both in southern Italy and Sicily, and also toward the head of the Adriatic at sites known as Spina and Adria. The latter achieved sufficient importance as a trading post to give its name to the sea. The colonies in south Italy and Sicily became flourishing and wealthy centers of Greek culture, so much so that the Romans called the area *Magna Graecia* = Great Greece.

Rome must early have come into contact with this culture, either directly or more probably at first through her Etruscan neighbors, who had close commercial relations with both Magna Graecia and Greece proper, as well as with the eastern Mediterranean. Roman legend traced her contacts with Magna Graecia and even with Greece back to her later kings, the Etruscan Tarquins who ruled during the sixth century B.C. By about 500 B.C. the Romans had adopted a Greek alphabet used by the Greeks at Cumae, just north of the Bay of Naples. Though they may have borrowed this directly, more probably they got it from the Etruscans, who had earlier adopted it. The common use in early literary Latin of such Greek words as *amphora* = a large wine jar, or *talentum* = a weight, usually of silver, or a sum of money represented by that weight, suggests contacts directly with the Greek cities around the Bay of Naples after Rome began military expansion into this area, known as Campania, during the second half of the fourth century B.C. From its beginnings in the middle of the third century B.C., Roman literature attests a familiarity with and the strong influence of the literature of Greece. Linguistically, Latin shows not only frequent borrowings of Greek words but also occasional imitations of Greek syntax.

In general, the contribution of the Italic languages to Latin was not great; at most it comprised elements of vocabulary. Nor did Latin accept much except an occasional word from Etruscan or Celtic, and even less from Punic. Despite the profound influence of Greece on Roman culture and the very considerable borrowings of vocabulary, Latin was little affected by Greek in its fundamental grammar and syntax even during the later Republic, when Rome ruled Greece and when any educated Roman was bilingual. To look further ahead in history, the same may be said about Rome's expansion into other parts of the Mediterranean basin. She imposed her tongue on her subjects but took almost nothing linguistically from them. Only as her power shrank under the later Empire and ceased in the west during the early Middle Ages did Latin begin to separate into different Romance languages, each of which was possibly influenced by the native speech of its area.

V

THE ALPHABET

Up to this point languages, including Latin, have been treated as far as possible in terms of spoken sounds as they existed before the introduction of writing. The representation of sounds by conventional drawn or written signs occurred at the beginning of history; indeed it might be held that the invention of writing marked the transition from the oral transmission of thought, primarily in myth, legend, or religious and legal formulations, to history.

Undoubtedly the earliest form of writing consisted of purely representational pictures, such as were used by some American Indian tribes until they came into contact with European writing. These representations of objects, called "pictographs" or written pictures, gradually came to be used for the sounds applied to the objects even when those sounds occurred in some other context with a different meaning. At this stage the signs are known as "ideographs," pictures of concepts. In the process of becoming ideographs, the signs became conventionalized so that it is often hard to recognize their original pictographic value, what they had first represented. Egyptian hieroglyphs, or signs used for sacred writing, and the cuneiform, or wedge-shaped, signs developed by the Sumerians in southern Mesopotamia had reached a stage in which some still had pictorial value but most had come to stand for syllables, combinations of consonant and vowel sounds. In an early form of writing found in the Aegean area and dating from the second millenium B.C., called "Linear B," ideographs representing syllables are combined with explanatory pictographs. For instance, a statement in ideographs that three jars were paid to a palace is followed by three pictures of a jar.

In a next stage of development, the Canaanites, a Semitic people settled along the eastern coast of the Mediterranean and inland, reduced fully syllabic signs to ones that stood primarily for consonants. One early form of such signs has been found in mines on the Sinai peninsula which were worked around 1300 B.C. This particular form may have been derived from Egyptian hieroglyphics. Another form was created, perhaps from Mesopotamian cuneiform, around 1000 B.C. in northern Canaan, the region later called "Syria," and probably at the important port of Byblos. The Canaanite signs for consonants still had a syllabic residue, since the reader was expected to supply with each consonant whatever vowel the context required. Since, however, the Canaanite signs, despite this syllabic quality, stood primarily for single consonants, they may properly be called "letters." In fact, in later Semitic writing, marks called "points" came to be added to the signs for consonants to indicate what vowels should be supplied. Among various forms of Canaanite writing, that found in northern Syria, particularly at Byblos, had the most lasting influence, since from it derived successively Phoenician and Greek writing.

After widespread piratical raids at the end of the second millennium B.C. had broken up the earlier states of the Canaanites, their descendants along the middle coast of the Mediterranean emerged as the Phoenicians, whose centers of maritime trade were Tyre and Sidon. The Phoenicians used and spread by commerce the north Canaanite set of letters, what is today called an "alphabet." This term is composed from the first two letters of the Greek alphabet, *alpha* and *bēta,* just as in English a child is said to learn his *ABC. Alpha* and *bēta* are in turn Greek pronunciations of the Phoenician letters *aleph* and *beth.* The originally pictorial character of the Phoenician (or Canaanite) letters appears in some of their names. For example, presumably a picture of a door was initially used to represent the sound *d* since its name continued to be the Phoenician term for door, *daleth.* This name became in Greek *delta.* The Phoenician alphabet, like the earlier Canaanite forms, still required that the reader had to supply with each sign for a consonant the vowel sound suggested by the context. The next step toward making the signs into proper letters was taken by the Greeks.

An ideographic form of writing was created in the Aegean area over a millennium before the Greek alphabet appeared. Although this form of writing vanished during the Greek Dark Age, between 1000 and 800 B.C., it may be described before discussing the Greek alphabet. By 2000 B.C., speakers of an Indo-European language that was a very early form of Greek were already occupying or had recently moved into the Hellenic peninsula and many of the Aegean islands. They came under the influence of the brilliant civilization that had been developed in Crete during the third millennium B.C. by its pre-Greek inhabitants. These are called "Minoans" from the name of the legendary king Minos. The mainland speakers of proto-Greek adapted the Minoan civilization to their own needs. They built strongly fortified palaces, in contrast to the unwalled ones that existed in Crete, such as Knossos. The best known of the mainland sites, Mycenae, has given its name to the mainland version of the Minoan civilization. Fortresses were also constructed at Tiryns, Athens, Thebes, and elsewhere. The latest of the mainland palaces, which emerged about 1200 B.C. at Pylos in the southwest of the Peloponnesus, was apparently undefended, like the earlier Minoan ones. The Minoans had also developed written signs that had passed from the pictographic to the ideographic stage. This form of writing is known as "Minoan Linear A," and so far no agreed upon interpretation of the language that it represents has been put forward. Sometime during the second half of the fifteenth century B.C. the Mycenaeans conquered Crete. Their success may have been facilitated by the weakening of Minoan power in consequence of the destruction caused by earthquakes and high waves after a tremendous eruption of the volcanic island of Thera (modern Santorin). This eruption occurred at a date still not surely determined but probably around 1450 B.C.

The Mycenaean conquerors of Crete adopted the Minoan Linear A writing for their own proto-Greek language. Their derivative form is called "Linear B." Careful analysis of Linear B texts on small clay tablets found both at Knossos in Crete and on the mainland at Mycenae, Pylos, and elsewhere has demonstrated that its signs stood for syllables of proto-Greek words, each beginning with a consonant followed by a vowel. This suggests the Semitic practice of indicating only the consonants and leaving the following vowels to be supplied by the reader. Linear B ideographs are followed by explanatory pictographs, such as the statement about jars being followed by pictures of the number of jars involved, or one about chariots being followed by pictures of wheels.

So far as has yet been discovered, Linear B was used only for records of objects, produce, animals, or even persons supplied to the Mycenaean palaces by their dependent territories. It was not used for literary works, such as hymns, laws, or poetry. These last may have been written on more perishable materials or transmitted orally. The small clay tablets that have survived were originally sun-dried and under normal circumstances would have dissolved during the centuries of burial in damp earth. Apparently only the tablets recording transactions during the final year of the existence of the palaces, particularly that at Pylos, have survived, and these were undoubtedly baked to a resistant hardness by the fires which destroyed the palaces.

During the Greek Dark Age, the two centuries or so after about 1000 B.C., and probably in consequence of the occupation of the Mycenaean territory by later, more barbarous Greek-speaking intruders, the ability to write Linear B was lost. The last wave of such intruders may have been the people known later as "Dorians," who finally occupied most of the Peloponnesos.

THE GREEK ALPHABET

At a date after 800 B.C., perhaps about 750 B.C., the Greeks, emerging from their Dark Age, adapted to their language the consonantal alphabet used by the Phoenicians. It is uncertain whether they got this from Phoenician traders who penetrated the Aegean, or whether Greek seamen, following the routes opened by their Minoan and Mycenaean predecessors, reached the coast of Canaan

(Syria) and there took over the Phoenician alphabet, or whether, less probably, the Phoenician alphabet, which seems to have passed overland through Asia Minor to Phrygia, moved down from there to the Greek settlements on the eastern shore of the Aegean.

Various Semitic alphabets had already begun attaching signs to their consonantal letters to indicate what vowels should be pronounced with them. But the Greeks made the crucial advance of assigning regular letters to express the five principal vowel sounds of their language. For this purpose they used some of the Phoenician consonantal signs for which Greek had no equivalent sounds. Thus the Greeks first definitely restricted signs or letters to the sounds of individual consonants or vowels rather than to syllables or to consonants implicitly followed by a vowel sound.

Initially, various parts of Greece applied the Phoenician signs somewhat differently to their own sounds. For instance, the inhabitants of the island of Euboea, whose early colonists took their alphabet to the Bay of Naples in Italy, used the sign X for a sound that can be represented in English writing by *ks* or *x*. But the people in Ionia, on the coast of Asia Minor, used the same sign for an aspirated hard sound which probably resembled the Scotch pronunciation of *ch* in "loch" and which is usually represented in English writing as *kh*. The Euboean or west Greek alphabet also preserved the sign *H* for full aspiration, whereas the Ionian dialects on the eastern coast of the Aegean early weakened aspiration. Rather than retain the whole *H*, they halved it to make two signs, to show either the presence of slight aspiration or its absence. These signs, known as rough and smooth breathings, were first written as ⊢ and ⊣ and later as ' and ' suspended before an initial vowel. The Ionians then used undivided *H* to distinguish long *ē*, called *ēta*, from short *e*, called *e-psilon* = bare *e*. In the earliest Greek writing the sign ϝ represented a sound approximately like English *w* and called *diagamma,* or double *G*, because the Greek *G* was written as Γ and called *gamma.* As the original sound represented by *digamma* passed out of currency, the sign may already have begun to be employed in Italy for the sound *F*, which it came to represent in Latin and still does today.

In 404 B.C. the Athenians officially adopted what they had

probably already been using in daily life for some time, the Ionian or eastern Greek alphabet. The classical Greek or Ionic/Attic alphabet contained twenty-four letters, of which seventeen represented consonants and seven vowels. There were seven for the five vowels *a, e, i, o,* and *u* because separate letters represented long *ē* (*ēta*) and long *ō* (*ō-mega* = great *o*). The Ionians apparently regarded the difference in length between short and long *e* and *o* as more marked than that between the short and long pronunciations of the other three vowels, for each of which one letter sufficed for both lengths.

So limited a number of signs achieved only an imperfect representation of the wide variety of consonant and vowel sounds that must have characterized spoken Greek, as it would almost any spoken language. The reduction of sounds to writing always tends to standardize pronunciation and to eliminate subtle differences of sound. But it should not be assumed that the sound represented by any given letter was always identical. In particular, for the vowels there must have been a wider range both of sound and of the length of time taken to pronounce them than is covered by the simple classification into short and long.

The Euboeans made their first western settlement about 754 B.C. at Cumae, just north of the Bay of Naples on the west coast of Italy. If the alphabet reached Greece proper only around 750 B.C., the Euboeans presumably introduced the west Greek version into their area of colonization only later, but how much later cannot be determined. In the late eighth century B.C., the Etruscans were beginning to develop their civilization north of the Tiber. It is disputed whether, if the Etruscans came from Asia Minor during the eighth century, they brought the west Greek alphabet with them or, as seems more likely, they adopted it from the Euboean colonies during the early seventh century. If they had migrated to Italy long before the eighth century, or if they were an indigenous people in contact with the eastern Mediterranean, then in all probability they would have adopted a Greek alphabet in use in southern Italy. In any case, their language came to be written in Greek characters. Hence its sounds can be determined approximately. However, the lack of extensive documents or of translations into

Latin or Greek has prevented scholars from determining the meaning of more than the simplest Etruscan words or from proving the affinity of Etruscan to any known major linguistic group.

INTRODUCTION OF WRITING AT ROME

The Roman scholar Varro, a contemporary of Cicero in the first century B.C., fixed the date of the founding of Rome as 754 or 753 B.C., at about the time both of the first Greek settlements in southern Italy and Sicily and of the emergence of the Etruscan civilization. Modern scholars argue on archaeological evidence that the urbanization of Rome began only in the early sixth century B.C., probably as the work of the last kings, the Etruscan Tarquins. Since archaeological evidence also shows the presence of earlier village settlements of Latins and Sabines on the hills surrounding the later Forum, one of these, on the Palatine, might have been regarded by the Romans as the proto-Rome. It is nevertheless unlikely that a scanty, backward, agricultural, or pastoral population had many outside contacts or any occasion to adopt an alphabet.

Perhaps by 500 B.C. the inhabitants of the by then fairly well urbanized Rome had direct relations with the Greeks of Campania, but it is more likely that they derived their alphabet, as they did so much else of their material urban culture, from their northern neighbors, the Etruscans. Although legend suggests that in the eighth century B.C. such early kings as Numa Pompilius, the traditional founder of Roman religious institutions, were able to write, perhaps the skill was only introduced by the Etruscan Tarquins during the sixth century B.C. Certainly when, two centuries and a half later, Latin literature began, writing must have been familiar at least to the educated class.

Nevertheless little evidence survives for the writing of Latin from the period before about 200 B.C. Such evidence appears on nonperishable materials like metal or stone; that is, it comprises inscriptions. The dates and sequence of the very few objects inscribed with archaic Latin texts that have so far been found is much disputed, since dating them depends on correlating the forms of their letters with the letters on inscriptions from Etruria or from

Magna Graecia, which are themselves not frequent or readily datable.

The first of these inscriptions is on the protecting catch of a gold safety pin or *fibula*. The provenance of this fibula is uncertain. It was long thought to have been among the contents of an Etruscan tomb excavated at Praeneste (Palestrina) southeast of Rome. If so, it would date from the seventh or sixth century B.C., as some scholars still hold. But since this provenance cannot be proved, the fibula may be of later date, and its very genuineness has been suspected, though a recent study endorses its authenticity. The inscription is in Greek letters running from right to left, or backward according to later practice. Transliterated into Roman letters, it reads *Manios med fhefhaked Numasioi,* which in later Latin would be *Mānius mē fēcit Numasiō* = Manius made me for Numasius.

If the fibula is indeed genuine, it may well be no older than an even more famous, and surely genuine, archaic inscription that was found buried in the Roman Forum under a small black pavement known to the Romans as the *lapis niger* = black stone. The letters of this inscription are tentatively dated, by comparison with Greek and Etruscan letters, to about 500 B.C. They lie, to modern eyes, on their sides, forming lines that originally ran alternatively up and down the four sides and one beveled corner of a stone now called the Forum *cippus* = marker. This fashion of inscribing lines was used in early Greek inscriptions, but generally ran alternatively from left and from right rather than up and down. It is called *boustrophedon* = as the ox turns (in ploughing). The Forum cippus was originally a small obelisk but the top half has been broken off. In consequence, the beginnings and ends of alternate lines have been lost and the meaning is obscure. It appears to be a religious prescription about a sacred place. Too long and fragmentary to be quoted here, it may be found, along with that of the fibula, in collections of early Latin inscriptions such as that by E. H. Warmington.

The rarity of inscriptions from the fifth, fourth, and third centuries B.C. suggests that the Romans wrote either only on perishable materials or very little. Roman historians do speak of documents of an early republican date, such as the treaty made by the Roman consul Spurius Cassius with the Latins in 493 B.C. or the laws drawn up by the decemvirs in 450–451 and published in the Roman Forum by the consuls of 449 on twelve placards (tables) probably of wood rather than of bronze. Many modern scholars have questioned whether these documents cited by later authors were really as early in date as the writers thought. Thus, on the one hand, Roman contact with the Etruscans renders it not improbable that the art of writing had been acquired by the Romans during the sixth century B.C., and this conclusion is supported by the existence of a few early inscriptions. On the other hand, if writing had been common before the middle of the third century B.C. more inscriptional (epigraphical) evidence might be expected to have survived from the centuries before about 250 B.C.

THE LATIN ALPHABET

The Romans adopted the alphabet which they derived from the Etruscans, or less probably directly from the west Greeks, to meet the needs of their own language. Many, if not most, of the changes found in the Latin alphabet actually represent adaptations first made by the Etruscans. In the following discussion of the Latin adaptation of the Greek alphabet, capital letters are used to represent the letters as found in ancient inscriptions. Lower case letters are used for the equivalent English sounds or letters or for Roman cursive forms as attested in mediaeval manuscripts.

Among the vowels, the Romans took over *A*, *E*, and *O* but not the Greek signs for *ēta* (long *ē*) and *ō-mega* (long *ō*). The Romans wrote Greek *Y* (*u-psilon* = bare *u*) as *V*, probably a quicker form. In the cases of *I* and *V*, the Romans used these signs for both the vowel sounds and their consonantal equivalents. In the later Republic they employed *Y* in its original Greek form to represent in borrowed Greek words a very short *u* sound, which was much less distinct than was the Latin *u* sound and closely resembled German *ü*. Thus the Roman vowel signs were originally only five, *A*, *E*, *I*, *O*, and *V*, to which they later added *Y*. In cursive, or running, script these became *a*, *e*, *i*, *o*, *u*, and *y*, though *i* was not dotted.

The Romans adopted most of the Greek consonantal signs.

Following the west Greeks, they used *H* to show aspiration rather than for long *ē*, and *X* for the *ks* or *x* sound represented in Attic Greek by Ξ, the name for which should properly be spelled *xei* rather than *xī*. The Romans had no sound corresponding to the Greek Θ (*thēta*), an aspirated *t-h* which was pronounced not like the *th* in English "the" but more like the *t-h* in English "at home" run quickly together. Similarly the Romans had nothing resembling the sound of Greek Φ, an aspirated *p-h*, the name for which should properly be spelled *phei* rather than *phī*. This was not the initial sound of English "physics," despite the derivation of that word from Greek, but rather the sound of the *p-h* in English "up-hold" run together. Nor did Latin have any sound like the Greek Ψ = *ps*, whose name should be spelled *psei* rather than *psī*. This is preserved in such English derivatives from the Greek as "psychology." These three Greek letters—*thēta*, *phei*, and *psei*—the Romans kept only for numerals.

The Romans also at first had no sound for, and discarded, the Greek Z (*zēta*), which was pronounced in different Greek dialects either as the *dz* in English "adze" or as *zd*. However, the Romans adopted it in the late republican period in words borrowed from the Greek. The Greeks had early abandoned the use of ϝ (digamma) for a sound rather like that expressed by English *w*. Whether or not this letter had already come to stand in Italy for an *f* sound, the Romans, using it for that sound, wrote it *F* and placed it in their alphabet after *E*. They did not need it for the *digamma* sound, which was adequately represented by their consonantal *V* (*u*).

The Romans kept the Greek *K* for the hard *c* (*k*) sound in only a few names, like *Kaeso* or *Karthago*, or the term for the first day of the month, *Kalendae*. At first they employed the Greek Γ (*gamma*) both for the hard *c* (*k*) sound and for the hard *g* sound. They wrote Γ quickly as *C* and eventually as cursive *c*. Later they distinguished the hard *g* sound from the hard *c* (*k*) sound by employing for the former a *C* with a finial added to make *G*. However, even classical Latin kept *C* for the hard *g* sound in abbreviations for the names *Gaius* and *Gnaeus*, namely *C*. and *Cn*.

The Romans borrowed an old Greek letter Ϙ (*koppa*) which had been written for the Greek *k* sound before the vowels *o* and *u*.

Koppa was later dropped by the Greeks and the sign *K* (*kappa*), originally used before the other vowels, was also used before *o* and *u*. The Romans kept the *koppa* sign in its original place in the Greek alphabet between *P* and *R* and wrote it as *Q*. In spelling they always followed it with a *V* in the form *QV* (*qu*) to represent an original single Indo-European sound.

The earliest Latin alphabet thus had fifteen consonantal letters— *B, C, D, F, G, H, L, M, N, P, Q, R, S, T,* and *X*— to which were later restored Greek *K* and *Z* for a total of seventeen consonants. These become in cursive script: *b, c, d, f, g, h, k, l, m, n, p, q, r, s, t, x,* and *z*.

GREEK AND LATIN ALPHABETS COMPARED

In sum, the alphabet of classical Latin, Greek in origin, was almost certainly derived through Etruscan and not directly from south Italy. Classical Latin used six vowel signs in all, five derived initially through Etruscan from Greek and one later introduced directly from Greek, namely Y, the sign that the Latins had originally received from Etruscan in the form *V* (*u*). Fourteen of the fifteen original Latin consonantal signs were also taken through Etruscan from Greek, although *F* (from the Greek sign for *digamma*) and *Q* (from the sign for *koppa*) were adaptations of signs that Attic Greek had dropped very early. The fifteenth Latin sign was *G*, introduced as a variant on *C* to differentiate the sound *g* from hard *c* (*k*). To these fifteen the Romans later added two more Greek signs, *K* and *Z*. Their final number of signs or letters was twenty-three, six for vowels and seventeen for consonants: *A, B, C, D, E, F, G, H, I, K, L, M, N, O, P, Q, R, S, T, V, X, Y,* and *Z*. This was one less than the classical Greek or Ionic attic alphabet of twenty-four letters.

The letters that the Romans used to represent the same sounds as in Greek, those that they used with changed sound significance, those that they dropped, and those that they added are shown in the accompanying comparative table of the classical Greek and Latin alphabets. In the Greek list, the two letters in parentheses

Classical Greek and Latin Alphabets

Greek	Latin	Latin adaptation
A	A	
B	B	
Γ	C	*Gamma* written quickly
Δ	D	*Delta* written quickly
E	E	
(F)	F	*Digamma* kept for sound *f*
Z		*Zeta* at first dropped but later introduced for borrowed Greek words and placed at end
	G	Variant of *C* to differentiate the sound of hard *g* from that of hard *c* (*k*)
H	H	*H* used not for long *ē* but for aspiration
Θ		*Thēta* dropped
I	I	
K	K	
Λ	L	*Lambda* on its side, as often inscribed in early Greek, and written hastily
M	M	
N	N	
Ξ		*Xei* dropped and its sound (*x*) represented by *X* (*kei*)
O	O	
Π	P	Probably *pei* written hastily
(Ϙ)	Q	*Koppa* written hastily; *Q* always appears with *V* (*qu*) to represent an original single Indo-European sound
P	R	Tail added to distinguish from *pei* (Latin *P*)
Σ	S	Hasty writing of *sigma* similar to the minuscule form (*s*) used at the end of Greek words
T	T	
Y	V	Tail of *u-psilon* dropped; the full sign *Y* later introduced at the end for use in Greek words
Φ		*Phei* dropped
X	X	Used for the sound *x*, not as in classical Greek for *kh* (hard *ch*)
Ψ		*Psei* dropped
Ω		*Ō-mega* dropped
	Y	*U-psilon* introduced later for use in Greek words
	Z	*Zēta* introduced later for use in Greek words
24 (plus *F* and Ϙ)	23	

(*digamma* and *koppa*) were dropped from classical Greek usage, presumably after they had been introduced into southern Italy and adopted by the Etruscans and Romans.

The achievement of first the Canaanite and then the Greek civilizations in evolving the alphabet, however this achievement was accomplished, was truly remarkable. The final result was an alphabet at once varied enough to represent reasonably well the consonantal and vowel sounds used in speech and at the same time brief and simple enough to be readily learned and recognized. This alphabet spread far beyond its original home in the Mediterranean. It has been adopted, and adapted, to express in writing a wide range of languages, many not belonging to the Indo-European family. Often its adoption has been at the cost of older locally evolved letters which were more elaborate and less easily recognizable than were those that passed from the Canaanites through the Phoenicians to the Greeks, Etruscans, and Romans.

LATER HISTORY OF THE LATIN ALPHABET

During the Middle Ages, the consonantal sounds *i* and *u* began to be distinguished from the corresponding vowel sounds by being written *J* and *V*. *J* had its beginnings in a high *I* (*i longa*) often used in Latin inscriptions to represent a long *i* sound. *V* and its lower case form *v* were distinguished in writing from *U* for the vowel sound, a capitalization of the Latin cursive letter *u*. In the alphabet, these new letters were placed after their respective vowel signs, *J* following *I* and *V* following *U*. Also in the Middle Ages a new letter was introduced, *W*, to represent a Germanic sound which in English is pronounced like the Latin consonantal *u* but in modern German like *v*. This was placed before *X*, *Y*, and *Z*. By the addition of *J*, *V*, and *W*, with their cursive forms *j*, *v*, and *w*, the alphabet employed to write modern English became twenty-six letters, as against the twenty-three of classical Latin. In words borrowed from Greek, English pronounces *y* either short, in the ancient manner, or long. For example, Americans usually pronounce "myth" with a short sound, like the *i* in "with," but "hydrangea" with a long sound, like the *i* in "high." Many English people also give "myth" the long sound.

Latin texts, from the invention of printing down to the late nineteenth century, preserved the mediaeval practice of writing the consonantal *i* and *u* sounds as *j* and *v*, reserving the letters *i* and *u* for vowel sounds. Modern texts have generally abandoned *j* and print both the consonantal and vowel *i* sounds as *i*, but many still keep the distinction between *v* and *u* for the consonantal and vowel *u* sounds. Consistently editors should return to the Latin practice of using the letters *i* and *u* (capitals *I* and *V*) for both consonantal and vowel sounds in each case, as is done in this book.

LATIN NAMES FOR THE LETTERS

In contrast to the sounds given by the Romans to the letters, which are known, it is very uncertain how they named them, that is, how they recited the alphabet. They did not use the Greek names *alpha*, *bēta*, and so on. These may already have been discarded by the Etruscans, but since evidence for the Etruscan letter names is lacking, it cannot be asserted that the Romans adopted the Etruscan names, although they probably did take over the Etruscan versions of the Greek letter forms.

The Romans appear throughout their history to have called the five vowels, apart from the tardily borrowed *y*, by their long sounds: *ā, ē, ī, ō*, and *ū*. During the Republic the Romans apparently used for names of the consonants the consonant itself followed by a long *ē*: *bē, cē, dē*, and so on, except that *h* and *k* were named *hā* and *kā*, and *q* was called *qū*. At some uncertain time during the Empire the Romans began to name the semivowels, those with a slight vowel sound—namely *f, l, m, n, r, s*, and *x*—by prefixing a short *e* to them: *ef, el, em*, and so on. Later, the name *ex* for *x* may have become *ix*.

In view of these uncertainties, beginning students of Latin should probably not attempt to spell Latin words or to recite the Latin alphabet by using Latin letter names as given in many systematic Latin grammars. They should simply seek to pronounce Latin words with the Latin pronunciations of the letters.

ROMAN NUMERALS AND CALENDAR

In both Greek and Latin, the signs used for numerals were originally letters. The Greeks employed letters, with some distinguishing mark like a line above them, for numbers running well above ten; that is, their system was not at all decimal in its signs. The Romans took from them the letters *thēta*, *phei*, and *psei* to signify numerals. Θ (*thēta*) represented a hundred and came to be written *C*, perhaps influenced by the spelling of the Latin *centum* = hundred. Φ (*phei*) stood for a thousand and came to be written first (|) and then *M*, perhaps because assimilated to the first letter of Latin *mille* = thousand. Ψ (*psei*) was used for fifty and came to be written ⊥ and then *L*.

The Romans used numerical signs that conformed much more closely to the decimal system than did the Greek. They represented numbers 1–4 by upright lines: *I, II, III, IIII,* and five by the open hand, written quickly as *V*. To *V* they added upright lines to represent 6–9 (*VI, VII, VIII, VIIII*) and then put two hands together as *X* for 10. They combined *I, V,* and *X* for numbers up to 50 (*L*). Similar combinations were made up to 100, or *C*, and from 100 to 500. This last was written by halving the sign for 1000, (|) = *M,* to make |) = *D*. Combinations were again made to express numbers from 500 (*D*) to 1000 (*M*).

The Romans often used a subtractive count for numbers one digit below a higher sign. For example, they wrote *IV* instead of *IIII* for 4, *IX* instead of *VIIII* for 9, *XL* instead of *XXXX* for 40, and so on. However 49 would be written *XLIX*, not *IL*. Occasionally subtraction was carried back two places, as *XIIX* for 18.

The Romans applied this subtractive count to the days in their month. They also reckoned any number of days inclusively of both the first and the last day. Similarly the French use *huit jours* = eight days for the English week of seven days. The Romans called the first day of any month the Kalends, or *Kalendae*. Varro connected this name with the verb *calō* = I call, because, he said, the king and later the pontiffs called the people together on the first of the month to announce the dates of the two other fixed days in the month and of any festivals. No better etymology has been suggested for *Kalendae*. English has taken over a derivative of *Kalen-*

dae to mean a list of days or dates, a calendar, and in spelling it has reverted to the Latin hard *c* instead of keeping the Greek *k*. In Latin, *kalendārium* means "an account book" because accounts were then as now generally settled on the first of the month. The Romans called a calendar *fāstī*. This is an adjective with which *dies* is understood, to mean "days which are *fās*, or religiously lawful, for doing business."

The days of the latter half of any month were numbered back inclusively from the Kalends of the following month. For instance, January 31 would be *prīdiē Kal(endās) Feb(ruāriās)* = the day before the Kalends of February. January 30 would be, reckoning inclusively, *a(nte) d(iem) III Kal(endās) Feb(ruāriās)* = the preceding day three from the Kalends of February, and so forth.

This count was carried back to a named day in the middle of the month, the Ides or *Īdūs (Eidūs)*, a word that Varro identifies as Etruscan but for which he gives no meaning. The Ides fell on the thirteenth of some months and the fifteenth of others, so that the number of days counted back inclusively from the following Kalends varied from month to month, depending on both the date of the Ides and the length of the month. In February, with normally twenty-eight days and the Ides on the thirteenth, the fourteenth was *a.d. XVI Kal. Mār(tiās)*, while in January, also with its Ides on the thirteenth but having thirty-one days in all, the fourteen was *a.d. XIX Kal. Feb.*

From the Ides nine days were counted back inclusively to the Nones or *Nōnae*, from *nōnus* = ninth. Thus there were always eight days inclusively between the Ides and the preceding Nones. But the Nones fell on the fifth of months in which the Ides fell on the thirteenth, and on the seventh of months in which the Ides fell on the fifteenth. In consequence, either four or six days were reckoned inclusively from the Nones back to the Kalends.

To find the equivalent of any English day of the month in Latin, one can either memorize the length of each month and the dates of its Ides and Nones or, more expeditiously, consult a calendar table in some systematic Latin grammar.

Only in the Middle Ages did western Europe adopt the concept of zero and the signs used today for the numbers 0–9 from the Hindus through the Arabs. These can readily be combined by place to represent higher numbers. It might appear that even simple mathematical procedures, like addition and subtraction, not to mention multiplication, division, and more complicated mathematical calculations, would be difficult with the Roman signs for numbers, and even harder with the Greek letter numerals. But as far as the basically decimal Roman system goes, persons familiar with it can perform quite elaborate calculations rapidly and accurately. Moreover, the ancients, like the Chinese, used a frame called an abacus in which balls on strings represent digits, tens, and so on. A skilled user can calculate very quickly on an abacus.

VI

PRONUNCIATION

Latin is a dead language in that it is no longer spoken as an active, native tongue, even in the Roman Catholic Church. Moreover, throughout its long history the pronunciation of Latin has changed constantly, first during the centuries when Latin itself was regularly spoken and later when it survived as the language of learning, diplomacy, and the church, and when speakers of the various European tongues adapted the pronunciation of Latin in greater or lesser degree to the pronunciations of their own languages. Even today, Italians and many Roman Catholic priests trained in Italy or under her influence pronounce Latin like Italian. The French give it a French sound. Until recent years the English had their particular manner of speaking it, and legal Latin still preserves a pronunciation somewhat similar to the older English one.

In Germany and the United States today, however, and for the most part in England, a uniform pronunciation has been adopted, based on a scholarly effort to recreate the way in which the Romans of the late Republic and early Empire spoke their language. This effort began as part of the intense philological study that flourished during the late nineteenth century. The countries with Romance tongues have been somewhat less ready to change their pronunciations of Latin to this so-called "reformed method."

To determine how the Romans of the classical period spoke

61

Latin, linguistic research has drawn on various sources: comments by Roman authors; the reproduction of animal sounds, like the bleating of sheep, which presumably have remained constant over the ages; puns, alliteration, assonance, and similar literary devices that depend on similarity of sounds; confusions of spelling that result from like sounds; the eventual convergence of two originally distinct sounds into one, which attests to an originally close similarity; transliteration of Latin words into other languages, especially into Greek, and vice versa, which show that given letters in one language were used for certain sounds of the other; analysis of parallel sounds in the Romance languages, which permits the reconstruction of the original sound that gave rise to them; and sound changes, conventions of spelling, and metrical practices in Latin itself.

Such intensive study has resulted in recovery of the probable sounds represented by the various letters and combinations thereof in classical Latin. The placing of the word accent in classical Latin is also known, although there is dispute as to whether it was a tonal change, a stress, or a combination of the two. Yet the sounds represented by individual letters and written syllables, and the accents of words represent only two of the various elements that make up any speech. The rhythm of phrase and sentence, the intonation of the voice, the speed of delivery, the slurring of unimportant sounds, and many other subtleties are almost impossible to recover. In particular, speakers of Germanic languages, such as English, lack the rapid and varied delivery that still characterizes Italian. Thus their spoken Latin is likely to be too slow, monotonous, and ponderous. Even with all the improvements that have been made during the past century in the pronunciation of classical Latin, Cicero or Vergil would probably have difficulty in understanding a modern reading of one of their own works. This inability to recreate fully all the nuances of sound in spoken Latin is a particular handicap to the full appreciation of Latin poetry.

The plays of Plautus afford some impression of the liveliness and excitability of spoken Latin about 200 B.C. Such a passage as the opening of Cicero's first speech against Catiline, delivered in 63 B.C., shows that rhetorical Latin was not always composed in an elaborate and complex style. In moments of intensity a Roman orator was capable of rapier-sharp thrusts of incisive speech. Petronius, who lived in the middle of the first century A.D., reproduced in his highly original comic novel, the *Satyricon*, the colloquial and elliptical speech of the lower classes of Italy. The list could be much extended.

Despite the difficulty of recapturing the sounds and tempo of spoken classical Latin, teachers and students should constantly keep in mind that the language was primarily oral and that writing served principally as an aid to reading aloud or as a prompt for reciting. An oral approach, therefore, however much it may fall short of the original, contributes greatly both to understanding the meaning, through the effect of verbal phrasing and emphasis, and to literary appreciation, since sound was as important a literary characteristic as were sense or style.

The importance of an oral appreciation of Latin justifies giving attention to the way in which individual units of sound, whether written as letters or as syllables, were pronounced. Linguists classify the units of sound represented by letters into categories based on the physical processes involved in their pronunciation. The first classification is that into consonants and vowels.

CONSONANTS

A consonant is so called from the Latin present participle *cōnsonāns*, with *littera* understood, to mean "a letter sounding with another." Consonants are conditioners of vowel sounds, so much so that in certain circumstances they cannot even be pronounced in isolation from vowels. They are called either "voiceless," when the vocal chords are simply held apart in one position so that no sound is produced until the following vowel is pronounced, or "voiced," when the vocal chords vibrate to give to the consonant a certain sound. For example, when in English the consonant written as *s* is uttered, there is no vibration of the vocal chords; *s* is therefore voiceless. In uttering the consonant represented by *z*, however, the vocal chords vibrate; *z* is therefore voiced. The difference can readily be perceived by closing the ears and uttering the two.

Consonants may also be classified according to the vocal organs involved in uttering them. For instance, *p* is called a "labial" (from *labium* = lip) because it is uttered by employing both lips. The sound represented in English by *th* is called a "dental" (from *dēns, dentis* = tooth) because the tongue is pressed against the teeth. Simple *t* is an "alveolar" because it is uttered by pressing the end of the tongue against the upper gum (*alueolus*). And *k* is a "velar" because the back of the tongue is pressed up against the rear of the soft palate (*uēlum*, literally a sail, or veil).

Besides these four categories based on the parts of the mouth used in uttering consonants, there are further categories according to the manner in which air passes from the mouth in articulation. Consonants in whose articulation the mouth is completely closed are called "stops," either nasal stops if the mouth is closed but the nasal passages are open, as in uttering the sound represented by *m*, or plosive stops if the mouth and nasal passages are both closed, as in uttering *p*. "Plosive" is the simple form of the more common "explosive." Both derive from the passive perfect participle *plōsus, -a, -um* of *plōdō*. This in turn is a popular pronunciation with a long *ō* of *plaudō* = I clap, or applaud. *Explōdō* meant intensively, "I drive off the stage by excessive clapping," and then metaphorically ,"I force out violently." A plosive stop is therefore one in which the breath is forced out through the closed passages. Plosive stops are further divided into aspirated and unaspirated. In aspirated stops the vocal cords are open and a slight sound of *h* follows the plosive consonant. In unaspirated plosive stops, although the vocal chords are also open, there is no following sound of *h*.

If the mouth is not closed, or stopped, completely to produce a plosive, it may be only slightly open. The resulting consonantal sound is called a "fricative" (from *fricō* = I rub) because the air rubs or presses past the tongue and lips. Fricatives in English are *f* or *v*. If the mouth is slightly open but the tongue is pushed forward to form a closure against it, the air flows past the tongue on either side and produces a consonantal sound called a "lateral" (from *latus* = side). In English *l* is a lateral.

Linguists classify the sounds represented by the seventeen consonantal letters of the Latin alphabet in accordance with these categories. Four consonantal sounds, represented in writing by *p*, *t*, hard *c*(*k*), and *qu*, are voiceless plosives, that is, in pronouncing them, the vocal chords do not vibrate and the air is driven through the closed mouth and nasal passages. Of them, *p* and *t* were pronounced in Latin much as they are in English "pink toes." However, in Latin they may have been conditioned by a slight aspiration, a suspicion of *h* following them, as is suggested by two phenomena. Roman grammarians found *p*, *t*, and hard *c*(*k*) difficult to distinguish in certain circumstances from the parallel voiced plosives *b*, *d*, and hard *g*, which suggests that the former were not wholly without some contribution of the vocal chords, presumably a light aspiration. Moreover, when the Romans borrowed Greek words containing voiceless plosives, they changed them to voiced plosives. For instance, Greek *puxos* became in Latin *buxus* = the box-tree, and Greek *kubernō* became in Latin *gubernō* = I steer. This also indicates an approximation of sound in Latin between the voiceless and the voiced plosives.

Latin *c* was always a hard sound, a velar plosive like *k* in English "kin." Thus the Romans pronounced the name of their greatest orator *Kikero*, and not, as its pronunciation has become in English, *Sisero*, or in Italian *Chichero*. English has softened the Latin hard *c* to a soft *c*, or an *s* sound, before *e* and *i*. Italian has reduced it to a sound like the soft *ch* in English "church" before the same vowels. The Romans gave their rarely written *k* the same hard sound as they did to their *c*. Finally *qu* (*q* appears in written Latin only in this combination) represented by two letters a single sound, a labiovelar as in English "queer." Latin *qui* was presumably pronounced as a monosyllable, as if written in English "kwi" rather than "k-u-i."

When the voiceless plosives *p*, *t*, and *c* were fully aspirated, they were written in Latin with a following *h* but did not really become double consonantal sounds. Such genuinely double aspirated consonants occur in Latin only in words derived from Greek, and probably even these were pronounced, except by well-educated Romans, without any marked aspiration.

Parallel to the voiceless plosives are the three voiced plosives *b*, *d*, and *g*, plus the combination *gu*. Of these, *b*, *d*, and *g* sounded like their English counterparts in such a phrase as "badly damaged gun." Latin had no sound to correspond to the soft sound of the *g* in English "damaged" but only the hard sound of the *g* in "gun." Before a following consonant, *b*, *d*, and *g* became voiceless. That is, such words as *urbs* = city or *obtineō* = I obtain were pronounced *urps* or *optineō*. Quintilian, a writer of the late first century A.D., noted in his book on teaching oratory the *Institūtiō Ōrātōria* I 7.7, that in *urbs*: "logic requires the letter *b*; the ears hear rather *p*," *b litteram ratiō pōscit*; *aurēs magis audiunt p*. Apparently *g* was nasalized in Latin before the dental nasal sound written *n*, so that *gn* in such a word as *agnus* = lamb sounded like *ngn* in English "hangnail." Before a vowel *gu* was a voiced plosive corresponding to voiceless *qu*. But before a consonant *gu* constituted a full syllable. For example, *sanguis* = blood contained only two syllables, pronounced as if written in English "sangwis." The meter shows that its ablative has only three syllables, one long and two short, to form a metrical unit called a "dactyl," as in Vergil, *Aeneid* I 19, *Trōiānō ā sănguĭnĕ dūcī* = to be derived from Trojan blood. But in such a word as *gustō* = I taste, the *gu* is a full syllable. Also *g*, unlike *q*, appears regularly with the other vowels to constitute syllables.

The plosives, whether voiceless, namely *p*, *t*, *c* (*k*), and *qu*, or voiced, namely *b*, *d*, and *g*, with the aspirated forms of the former, namely *ph*, *th*, and *ch*, are called "mutes" because they are pronounced with the lips together so that they have no sound (are silent) except insofar as they condition the sound of a following vowel. Latin metrical practice shows that in pronunciation the combination of a mute consonant followed by a liquid one (*l* or *r*) might count either as a single consonant sound or as two together. That is, the genitive *patris* = of a father might be pronounced as *pa-tris* or as *pat-ris*.

The two Latin nasal consonants are *m* and *n*. The pronunciation of both probably corresponded to that of the equivalent English letters.

Latin had only two liquids, *l* and *r*. They are so called because they are pronounced smoothly, often with a slight vocal thrill. The lateral liquid *l*, pronounced by forcing air either side of the tongue, had two sounds in Latin, as it does in English. Before a vowel it was clear, as in English "law," while before a consonant or when final it was thickened, as in English "gold" or "animal." Latin *r* was more rolled on the tip of the tongue than it is in English; it approximated the Scotch pronunciation of *r*.

The two Latin fricatives *f* and *s* had the same sounds as they do in English "fine soap." Latin *s* always had this voiceless sound and never the voiced articulation which English gives to it in such words as "rose" or "miser."

Full aspiration, expressed in writing by the letter *h,* was weak in Latin, as is shown by the phenomenon in versification known as "elision." This term, from *ēlīdō* = I squeeze out, refers to the fact that in Latin verse, and presumably in ordinary pronunciation, a final vowel or vowel plus -*m* was run together with an initial vowel to form a single syllable, that is, the final vowel or vowel plus -*m* was "elided." For instance, in Vergil, *Aeneid* I 3, *multum ille et* = and he much should be read as only three syllables: *mult' ill' et*. When the first vowel of a word is preceded by an initial *h-,* elision also occurs, as in *Aeneid* I 125, *ēmissamque hiemem* = winter let out must be read *ēmissamqu' hiemem*. Similarly *h* does not make position, so that in *Aeneid* I 63, in the phrase *dāre iussus habēnās* = ordered to give rein, the second syllable -*us* is short despite the following consonant. Clearly *h* was not strongly enough pronounced to prevent elision or make position. Also such words are *nihil* = nothing or *mihi* = to me were often written and probably commonly pronounced as *nīl* and *mī* with internal elision and combining of the two short vowels to make one long.

Of the two Latin double consonants, rare *z* was introduced into Latin late and only in borrowed Greek words. It was normally pronounced by the Romans like the *dz* in English "adze." The Latin letter *x* represents the double sounds *ks*. It occurred where an *s* was added after a *c* or *g*, as in the perfect form *dīxī* = I said, in which to a stem *dīc*- was added a past tense ending -*s*- plus a past personal ending -*ī*. The same occurred in the nominative singular noun *rēx* = king, where to a stem *rēg*- was added a nominative ending -*s*.

Two letters represent both consonantal and vowel sounds, though in Latin they are listed among the vowels. Consonantal *i* had a sound much like *y* in English "yes" and consonantal *u* had a sound like English *w*. Because they were regarded as vowels having also a consonantal function, they are often called "semivowels." In Latin verse, and presumably in pronunciation, when consonantal *i* and *u* follow another consonant, they render the preceding syllable long. Latin syllables have quantity, as well as do individual consonants. A syllable is long not only when it contains a long vowel but also when a short vowel is followed in the same syllable by a consonant. Since two successive consonants are pronounced separately, unless they are a mute and a liquid, the first concludes the preceding syllable. Consonantal *i* and *u* count as full consonants for thus "making position," except that *qu* regularly and *gu* before a vowel represent single consonant sounds and do not make position.

VOWELS

The term "vowel" comes through French *voyelle* from the Latin adjective *uōcālis*, which derives from *uōx* = voice. With *uōcālis* is to be understood *littera* = letter so that a vowel as written represents a full sound, or a spoken vowel sound. The voice is modified differently by resonance in the oral passage to give the different vowel sounds. Vowels are classified as front, mid, and back, according to the position in which the tongue is placed in the mouth in order to pronounce them. They are also classed as closed or open, according to whether they are pronounced with the mouth relatively closed or open. Thus the sound represented by the English letter *i* is a front closed vowel because it is pronounced in the front of the mouth, which is almost entirely closed. English *a* is pronounced in the middle of the mouth, which is open, so that *a* is a mid open vowel.

Latin vowels had quantity; that is, they required a shorter or longer time for their pronunciation. To represent the wide variety of vowel sounds that must have characterized Latin, like any other language, by only five letters, or at most six including *y*, was a simplification of speech in writing. Not only did vowels presumably vary in sound, but they must also have had a considerable range of pronunciation time. Thus the formal limitation to two quantities, short or long, was an oversimplification. Yet the fact that the limitation of quantity to only two types was taught in schools may well have encouraged educated speakers to restrict variation of length in their pronunciation of vowels.

Difference of quantity was accompanied by a slight difference of sound. Short *a* had the sound of the final *a* in English "idea," while long *ā* had that of the *a* in standard English "father." Short *e* resembled *e* in English "get," but long *ē* came close in sound to the *a* in English "date." Short and long vowel *i* differed as do the *i* in English "ship" and that in "machine." Short and long *o* may be paralleled to the *o* in English "hot" and that in "holy." Short and long vowel *u* had the respective sounds of *u* in English "put" and "crude." The Greek *upsilon*, taken late into Latin as *y*, always had a short sound, that of German *ü* and almost that of the short *i* sound in American "myth," never that of the long *ī* sound in "hydrangea." In this book, short vowels are left unmarked except when the placing of a short mark (˘) above them is desirable for clarity. If a short vowel stands alone, it is generally preceded by the word "short." Every effort has been made to mark all long vowels with the long mark (¯) above them, even when they stand alone and are preceded by the word "long."

The Romans themselves sometimes had difficulty in recognizing the quantity of a vowel in a written word, and some of their scholars suggested differentiating long from short vowels in script. Accius (170–c. 85 B.C.), a distinguished philologian as well as a tragic poet, doubled long vowels in writing, while Sulla, the dictator of Rome from 82 to 79 B.C., wrote long vowels larger than short ones. This practice is attested in inscriptions, where long *ī* is often written with a taller letter than is short *i*. The taller letter, *i longa*, was adopted in the Middle Ages as the sign for consonantal *i* and eventually became in English the letter *j*.

Occasionally ancient grammarians or others state that the quantity of a vowel in a given word was long or short. For instance, the length of vowels in the various endings of nouns or verbs is often mentioned by ancient writers. In Latin meter the basis of rhythm is the quantity of syllables, rather than word accent, as in English. When a syllable ends in a vowel, the quantity of the vowel determines that of the syllable. In consequence metrical requirements will show the true quantity of any vowel final in a syllable. Such a syllable, ending with a vowel that determines its quantity, is called "open."

A syllable which ends in a consonant, that is, one whose vowel is followed by two or more consonants which have to be separated in pronunciation, is called "closed." A closed syllable is in any case long because of the added time necessary to pronounce its final consonant. In consequence the long metrical quantity of a closed syllable does not show that of its vowel, which may be either long or short. Vowels in closed syllables are therefore said to have "hidden quantity." The length of such a vowel may be stated by an ancient author, or it may be discovered from linguistic derivation or from development in the Romance languages, or it may be attested by transliteration into some other language, particularly Greek. However, the hidden quantity of some vowels in closed syllables is still uncertain and is marked differently in dictionaries. Such occasional uncertainty does not seriously handicap the proper pronunciation of Latin.

A vowel before *ns*, whether final or internal, is always pronounced as long, even though in origin, or by nature, it may be short. This causes confusing changes of quantity in stem vowels. For example, nouns, adjectives, and participles ending in -*ns* have the preceding vowel pronounced long. But when in the oblique cases the -*ns* becomes -*nt*-, the preceding vowel is pronounced short, even though the syllable retains a metrically long quantity because of the following two consonants. Thus in the nominative masculine singular *dēns* = tooth, the -*ē*- is long, but it reverts to the naturally short -*e*- of the stem in other cases, as in the genitive *dentis*. The same difference of quantity appears between the nominative and other cases of adjectives or participles ending in -*ns*, as in *prūdēns* = prudent, or wise, genitive *prūdentis*, or *amāns* = loving, genitive *amantis*. Another case of the lengthening of a short vowel before -*ns*- is afforded by the prefix short *in*-, which may have a negative force or be the preposition, since the two became assimilated in spelling though different in origin. The initial *i*- is lengthened in pronunciation when the *in*- is prefixed to a word beginning with *s*-, as in *īnsomnia* = sleeplessness, or *īnspīrō* = I breathe into, or I inspire, as against *indūcō* = I lead into, or *inūtilis* = not useful, or useless. Although in the first two examples the *i-* is pronounced long before the *-ns-* while in *indūcō* it is pronounced short, in all three the syllable *in-* remains long metrically (by position) because the *i-*, whether pronounced long or short, is followed by two consonants. The marks of quantity placed here above the *i-* refer only to its pronounced quantity, not to the metrical quantity of the syllable *in-*.

In this book, except in the discussion of meter, the quantity of syllables as such is not considered. That is, a long mark, or a short one when given, applies only to the vowel over which it stands, not to the whole syllable in which the vowel occurs.

When two vowels in Latin occur in immediate succession, they may be pronounced separately. For example, such a word as *fīō* = I become is pronounced as two syllables. This is particularly true of words borrowed from the Greek, such as *āēr* = air. In both these words the first vowel is long, contrary to the usual Latin practice of pronunciation, that a vowel before another vowel is short, as *-ĕ-* in *aenĕus* = of bronze, brazen.

However, certain successions of vowel sounds were regularly merged. For example, *ae* was pronounced like the *-igh* in English "high"; *au* was pronounced like the *ow* in English "how"; *ei* was pronounced like the *ay* in English "day"; *eu* was perhaps pronounced somewhat like the French "eu" meaning "well"; and *oe* was pronounced like the *oy* in English "boy." The combination *ui* became merged in only two words, *huic* = to this, and *cui* = to whom. In these, the *u* had almost its consonantal value, so that the sound might be approximately represented if written in English *hwic* and *cwi*; compare the pronunciation of *qu* and occasionally of *gu* as single sounds. Such a merger of two successive vowels is called a "diphthong," from a Greek adjective meaning "having two sounds." Many diphthongs originated from two separate vowel sounds. For instance, the genitive singular ending of the first declension was originally two syllables: *-āī*, but became the diphthong *-ae*. It is probable that most diphthongs, if not all, were pronounced as two sounds slurred together. But diphthongs count in meter as single syllables and are always long in quantity. Hence they are not marked with a long mark in this book except when this seems desirable for clarity or in presenting meter.

ACCENT

Recognition of spoken words depends not only on the proper enunciation of the sounds composing them, represented by letters, but on the correct stressing of a given syllable, namely on word accent. Although Latin words had only one main accent, it is probable that longer words had other accented syllables since speech tends toward an alternation of accented and unaccented syllables. In early Latin the word accent appears to have consisted in laying a greater stress or vocal emphasis on a given syllable in a word. It was also recessive, that is, it fell either on the first syllable or soon thereafter. Ancient sources indicate that in classical Latin the word accent consisted in a change of tone, presumably a raising of the voice, on a given syllable. Most modern scholars feel however that these sources simply repeated a statement about the Greek accent, which was a change of tone, and that the Latin accent continued to be one of stress in the classical period, as it almost certainly was in late Latin. In this book the Latin accent is regarded as one of stress, not of tone.

In classical Latin the accent, whether stress or tonal or both, had become fixed to one of two syllables: either the third from the last, called the "antepenult" (before the penult); or the one before the last, called the "penult" or almost last, from Latin *paene* = almost and the superlative adjective *ultimus* = last. The antepenult bore the accent if the penult was an open syllable ending in a short vowel. The penult was accented if it was an open syllable ending in a long vowel or a closed syllable, one that ended in a consonant and therefore was itself long whether its vowel was long or short. The place of the accent depended entirely on the quantity of the penult, the syllable before the last. The quantities of the antepenult, the second syllable from the end, and of the ultimate, the last syllable, did not influence whether the penult or the antepenult was accented. Furthermore the quantity which determined the placing of the accent was that of the whole penultimate syllable, not merely that of its vowel.

The effect of the quantity of the penult on the word accent is illustrated by contrasting examples. The feminine noun *cupīdō* = desire has a long penult which is accented. But the masculine or neuter dative or ablative singular of the adjective *cupidus* = desirous is *cúpidō* with a short penult and therefore stressed on the antepenult. The fact that the -*u*- of the stem is in both cases short and the final -*o* of the two endings is long has no bearing on the placing of the word accent. In the present participle *éducāns* = educating, the -*u*- is short and the accent falls on the first syllable; in the oblique cases, as in the genitive *ēducántis*, the penult is accented because the -*a*-, whatever its own quantity (here short), is followed by two consonants and the syllable is therefore long. The short -*u*- in the stem of *éducō, -āre*, suggests that it does not derive from *ēdúcō* = I lead out, or at least that it contains an early variant of the stem *dūc*-.

FURTHER SIGNIFICANT PHENOMENA

In languages, habits of speech affect pronunciation and ultimately written spelling. For example, in Latin, words of two syllables comprising a short syllable followed by a long one tended to be uttered with a shortened final syllable when its long quantity was not necessary to show its syntactical relation to other words. This phenomenon is called *breuis breuiāns* = a short (syllable) making (the following long syllable) short, or more commonly in English "iambic shortening" since the sequence of quantities, a short followed by a long, constitute a metrical foot called an "iamb."

Iambic shortening is not widely represented in written Latin. The nominative singular of nouns of the first declension should end in long -*ā*, but this must early have been shortened in disyllabic nouns with a short first syllable, such as *toga* = a toga. This short -*a* was then generalized for all nominative and accusative singulars of the first declension, but not for the ablative singular, where the long -*ā* was necessary to distinguish the case from the nominative.

Iambic shortening also operated to shorten the final long -*ē* of a few common adverbs from adjectives of the first/second declension, such as *bene* = well and *male* = badly. A more uncertain case is the nominative of the first person singular personal pronoun *ego* = I. In Latin, the final -*o* of this word is short, but in the closely parallel Greek form it is long and bears a rising tone accent, namely *egó*. It is uncertain how far the rise in tone indicated in Greek by this "acute" accent also involved a stressing of the syllable, but if it did, Latin put the vocal stress (word accent) on the first syllable, and this may have led to the shortening of the final *-o* in Latin by iambic shortening.

Iambic shortening must have been much more common in actual speech than these few permanent results would suggest. Latin verse down to Cicero's day shows that metrically a long syllable preceded by a short one and either preceded or followed by the word accent, or by the verse stress called "ictus" (a blow), might be treated as short. Nor need the sequence of short and long be only in a disyllabic word; any such sequence either within a longer word or between the last syllable of one word and the first of the next might be subject to iambic shortening if the accent or ictus fell either on the opening short syllable or on the syllable, short or long, following the long syllable. In particular, poets writing after the time of Augustus (d. 14 A.D.) might treat as short the final long *-ō* of the first personal singular active indicative of verbs when it was preceded by a short syllable and preceded or followed by the ictus. Similarly, Juvenal once gives *dēclāmātiō* = a declamation a final short *-o* when the ictus follows.

A second phenomenon concerns *-s-* between vowels within words, or intervocalic *-s-*. In the century roughly from 450 to 350 B.C. a single intervocalic *-s-* came to be pronounced as *-r-*. However, once this change had been completed, any single intervocalic *-s-* which either occurred later as a result of linguistic changes or appeared in a word borrowed from another language did not change to *-r-*. Thus classical Latin shows an active future participial ending *-ūrus* (*-a*, *-um*) for an original *-ūsos*, as in the future participle *futūrus*, *-a*, *-um* from the verb *sum* = I am. But it retains *ūsus*, *-a*, *-um*, as the perfect participle of *ūtor* = I use, because this participle was, down to a period after 350 B.C., pronounced *ūtsus*.

Latin also retained a single intervocalic *-s-* in *causa* = cause because this was pronounced, and in early inscriptions written, *caussa*, as in an epitaph probably of the early second century B.C. which reads in line 2, *honōris uirtūtisque caussa* = on account of (that is, to recognize his) honor and bravery, or virtue. The double sound of -*ss*- here resisted change to -*r*- even though it came ordinarily to be written as single -*s*-.

In this same epitaph, *honōris* shows the change from an original *honōsis*, the genitive singular of the third declension masculine noun *honōs* = office, or honor. The -*r*- was later adopted into the nominative singular and the -*o*- shortened to yield *honor*. The change of intervocalic -*s*- to -*r*- also occurred in the ending of the genitive plural of the first declension, which from -*ā-som* became -*ārum*, with a reduction of short -*o*- to short -*u*-. From this first declension ending was formed a similar one, -*ōrum*, for the genitive plural of the second declension.

If the safety pin (*fibula*) once supposed to have come from a tomb in Praeneste is not a fake, the dative name *Numasiōi*, with an ending -*ōi* that later became long -*ō*, would have a nominative *Numasios*. This is apparently the early form of the later gentile (family) name *Numerius*, which shows not only the change of intervocalic -*s*- to -*r*- but the weakening of -*a*- to -*e*- and of the ending -*os* to -*us*. The Roman historian Livy, who died in the early first century A.D., says in his *History of Rome from Its Foundation* (*Ab Urbe Conditā* II 50.5) that a certain Marcus Valerius, *Volesī filius*, became dictator, or single emergency commander of the army, in 494 B.C. Undoubtedly the name of the dictator had been modernized in Livy's source, but that of his father remained in the earlier form *Volesios*. *Valerius* shows a shift of the first -*o*- to -*a*-, a change of the intervocalic -*s*- to -*r*-, and a weakening of the final -*os* to -*us*. If Livy correctly preserves the father's name and the date of the dictatorship, this constitutes evidence that the change of intervocalic -*s*- occurred after 494 B.C.

Some words in which intervocalic -*s*- appears in classical Latin were presumably adopted by the Romans after the change was completed. For instance, the -*s*- appears in *rosa* = a rose, probably because this Greek dialectical word was adopted into Latin when the Romans first met the flower during their expansion into Campania in the second half of the fourth century B.C. The word therefore constitutes evidence that the change was complete by about 350 B.C. and that intervocalic -*s*- in words introduced later was not affected by it.

The change of intervocalic -*s*- to -*r*- also did not occur when the

-*s*- was the initial consonant of a simple stem to which a prefix ending in a vowel had been added, as in *dēsinō* = I cease. Presumably at the period when the change occurred such prefixes were still regarded as relatively independent words.

The Romans apparently had difficulty in pronouncing *cl* together and in speech inserted a light transitional vowel sound, which came to be written as -*u*-. Thus *perīculum* = risk or danger is composed from the root of *pereō* = I perish and a suffix indicating means or instrument, which appears in Greek as -*tlon* and must originally in Latin have been -*clom*; thus original *perīclom* = something by which one may perish. When in 273 B.C. the Romans were suffering from a plague, they are said to have imported from Epidaurus in Greece a serpent sacred to the Greek god of healing *Asklēpios*. The serpent swam ashore on an island in the Tiber, where the Romans built a temple to the new god. Since around Epidaurus the name appeared in a dialectical form *Aisklapios*, the Romans first used this but later inserted a -*u*- to make their form of the name *Aesculapius*.

The Romans had earlier adopted many of the Greek anthropomorphic gods from the Etruscans and these latter tended to drop syllables in borrowed Greek words, so that the god *Apollo* appears in Etruscan as *Aplu* and *Hēraklēs* as *Hercles*. Plautus has a regular expletive *hercle* = by Hercules, or often *me hercle*, in which the *hercle* is probably a nominative that has lost its final -*s* and the *me* the accusative singular of the first personal pronoun with the -*e* shortened in rapid speech. If so, the expletive probably implies a verb: "(may) Hercules (help) me." In classical Latin the form *Hercules* with -*u*- inserted between *c* and *l* is regular. Whereas the Romans borrowed the original shortened form *Hercles* from Etruscan, they apparently derived *Apollo* directly from Greek, since it does not show the Etruscan shortening.

Latin verse gives evidence of other phenomena of speech. In speech a syllable ending in a vowel, a diphthong, or a final -*m* was absorbed into a following initial syllable beginning with a vowel, a diphthong, or an *h*-. In verse such slurring or elision (squeezing out) eliminates metrically the final syllable of the first of the two words involved. How the two syllables were actually merged in speech is uncertain. Their sounds may have been pronounced rapidly together or, as is the modern practice in reading Latin verse, the first may have been wholly dropped. Initial *h* does not function as a consonant to prevent elision or, indeed, to make position. Similarly the aspirated consonant sounds *ph* and *th* do not count as double consonants to make position but simply each as one. More difficult to explain is the fact that final *-m* permitted elision; that is, a preceding vowel sound would be run into a following initial one, perhaps with some nasalization. But *m* before another consonant, whether at either end of or within a word, makes position.

Down to Cicero's day, final *-s* was also lightly pronounced. It might or might not make position before an initial consonant. And when followed by *es* or *est* = you are, or he is, the final *-s* and the initial *e-* could be dropped and the *-s* or *-st* of *es* or *est* be pronounced directly with the vowel preceding the final *-s*. This phenomenon, called "prodelision," occurs most frequently when a masculine nominative singular past participle is combined with *es* or *est* in a passive perfect second or third personal singular. For example, *amātus es* or *est* = you are, or he is, loved might be pronounced *amatu's* or *amatu'st*. Vergil does not employ prodelision.

In conclusion, it cannot be assumed that the pronunciation of Latin was ever fixed; it varied from period to period, from social class to social class, and from area to area. When, under the Empire, Latin spread widely through the Mediterranean, it became more and more diverse.

Despite the various pronunciations of spoken Latin, once there began to be a considerable body of written Latin, whether official records, public laws, or particularly literary prose and verse, there emerged an accepted standard of spelling and pronunciation. The first recognition of such a norm may date back to the middle of the third century B.C. when Latin literature is traditionally regarded to have begun. By the end of the first century B.C., with the full flowering of Latin prose and verse in the Ciceronian and Augustan ages, a norm was well established, at least for the educated classes. For written Latin this norm continued to be accepted until the end of the Roman Empire and even in the Middle Ages.

The recovery of Latin authors in the Renaissance restored the written styles of the Ciceronian and Augustan ages to their earlier primacy. However, as spoken Latin changed in pronunciation both during and after the Roman Empire, literary words were read aloud with the pronunciation that would be understandable. Only in the late nineteenth century was a serious effort made to reconstitute for spoken Latin the pronunciation that had characterized the Ciceronian and Augustan ages.

VII

THE MORPHOLOGY OF NOUNS, PRONOUNS, AND ADJECTIVES

"Grammar" is the term applied to the systematic description of a language. The earliest grammarians in the European tradition were Greeks. Thus the terminology of grammar either preserves Greek terms, such as the word "grammar" itself, or these terms are translated into the later European languages, especially Latin. More important, since Latin closely resembled Greek in its general structure and behavior, it was natural for Roman grammarians to seek to fit the linguistic phenomena of their language into the system already established by the Greeks and to apply to them Greek concepts. By and large, this adaptation did not represent inaccurately the linguistic phenomena of Latin, but in some cases in which Latin differed from Greek, the use of Greek system and concepts tended to obscure the original nature of the Latin form or construction. English in turn took its grammar from Latin, but since English differed from Greek considerably more than did Latin, and also differed considerably from Latin, the application to English of the Greco-Roman grammatical system and concepts has sometimes obscured the original character of English forms and constructions.

The three chief subdivisions of grammar are: phonology, the study of the sounds of a language and the changes of sound that occurred in its history; morphology, the description of the nature and development of the forms that its words adopt to show their relation to other words or to the general thought; and syntax, the analysis of the constructions or ways in which the appropriate forms of words are put together in larger correlated sequences to express complex thoughts. Phonology, or the study of sounds and sound changes, is a complicated topic, which is relevant mainly to an advanced understanding of classical Latin grammar. It is therefore discussed only incidentally in this book. Since the details of Latin morphology and syntax can readily be found in any standard grammar, the treatment of these subjects is here restricted to generalities and to illustrations such as may show that behind the variety of form and the complexity of construction in classical Latin lay an original consistency and coherence which were in part preserved and in part altered during the long development of the language.

Latin words may be somewhat arbitrarily divided into those which are inflected and those which are uninflected. The word "inflect" comes from the verb *inflectō* = I bend. Inflected words are bent, or altered, from their simplest form either by stem changes or by the addition of prefixes or suffixes so as to show a meaningful relation to other words or to the entire thought being expressed. Uninflected words express a single relationship, either by a single ending, as in the case of adverbs, or by their own form, as in the case of conjunctions, prepositions, and interjections. Inflected words may be subdivided into those that are declined, namely nouns, pronouns, and adjectives, and those that are conjugated, namely verbs. The word "decline" comes from the verb *dēclīnō* = I bend away from, that is, the oblique cases bend away from the nominative. The word "conjugate" comes from *coniugō* = I unite together and means putting into order the related forms of the verb.

These classifications are not absolute. For example, such a word as *plūs* = more may serve as noun, adjective, or adverb. Cardinal numbers are generally adjectives, and those from one through three are declined as such: *ūnus, -a, -um; duo, -ae, -o;* and *trēs, tria*. From *quattuor* = four through *centum* = hundred cardinal numbers are indeclinable. *Mille* = thousand is adjectival in the singular, but its plural, *milia*, is a noun. Adjectives may be used as

80

nouns, like *amīcus* = friend as well as friendly; and nouns may be used as adjectives, like *uictor* = conquering as well as victor. Verbs have forms that serve as nouns, like the infinitive, gerund, and supine, or as adjectives, like the participle or gerundive. The same word may serve as an adverb or a preposition, such as *circā* = about. Declined forms of nouns or adjectives may be used adverbially, like *uērum* and *uērō* alongside the adverb *uērē* to mean "truly," or may even be used prepositionally, like *secundum* = following, which came to mean "according to." New words may be formed by adding endings to a stem and then putting inflectional endings on these. For example, from the noun *studium* = study was made an adjective *studi-ōs-us, -a, -um* = studious. Compounds may be formed from two words, which in the simplest type retain their original forms. For instance, the adverb *magnōpere* = exceedingly shows elision from the ablative of manner *magnō opere* = with great labor; and the verb *animadvertō* = I notice is similarly combined from *animum advertō* = I turn my mind to. Despite such overlaps, the relations expressed by declension and conjugation on the whole differ from one another and from those denoted by uninflected words.

The term "noun" derives from the Latin neuter noun *nōmen* = name and translates the Greek *onoma* with the same meaning. Noun signifies a word which denotes or names a person, place, or thing, whether material or immaterial, such as English "friend," "city," "book," or "virtue." Noun also covers proper names like *Marcus* or *Rōma*.

A pronoun, from Latin *prō* = instead of and *nōmen*, stands in place of a noun. Its reference may be clear from its own meaning, as with the personal pronouns *ego* = I, *tū* = thou, and so on. Or the context may explain what the pronoun stands for, which is commonly the case with demonstrative and interrogative pronouns, as in the question *ille quis est?* = that (man), who is he? or who is that? Or a noun may stand to a pronoun as its antecedent, a term derived from the Latin verb *antecēdō* = I go before, meaning that to which the pronoun refers. This is frequently the case with demonstrative pronouns and always with relatives, as in *ueritās, haec est quam requīrō* = the truth, this is (all) that I require, or *uir quem uideō* = the man whom I see.

An adjective, from the passive perfect participle *adiectus* of the Latin verb *adiciō* = I add to, adds some qualification, or modifies, a noun or pronoun. It therefore takes on endings to show that it agrees with its noun or pronoun in gender, number, and case.

DECLENSION

In an inflected language like Latin, the relation of nouns and pronouns to other words or to the whole thought being expressed is shown by the addition of endings. These may cause slight changes in final vowels or consonants of the basic stem, that is, of the original, uninflected form. Thus the position of nouns and pronouns, and indeed of verbs, in the correlated sequence of words is of less importance in conveying meaning than is their form. Hence it is of the highest priority in the study of Latin to be thoroughly familiar with inflectional forms, especially the endings, and with the relationship or relationships that they define for the word in question in the particular sequence where it appears.

Nouns, pronouns, and adjectives are said to be declined when they assume different case endings in their singular and plural to indicate different relationships. The term "case" comes from the Latin noun *cāsus* = a falling, which translated the Greek *ptōsis* with the same meaning. The nominative case is called in Latin the *cāsus rēctus* = the upright or straight case, and the remaining cases are called *cāsūs oblīquī* = sloping or oblique cases. It is not clear what *rēctus* and *oblīquī* signified. Possibly in examples of declensions, the nominative of the noun was written on its side upward, like a clock hand pointing to twelve, and the other cases were written sloping away from it like a minute hand sloping away from the hour hand. An alternative possibility is that the nominative was written on a straight line at the top and the other cases on lines beneath it but successively indented to produce a sloping or oblique left margin beneath the nominative. In either pattern the oblique cases could be said to "decline" from the nominative and the word itself to be "declined." *Dēclīnō* originally meant "I bend away from (a straight path)."

Latin nouns are divided into five declensions on the basis of differences of stem and of added case endings. The stems of Latin nouns end in vowels save in one class of the third declension. The stem vowels for the five declensions are as follows: in the first declension long -ā, in the second short -o, in the third either a consonant or a short -i, in the fourth short -u, and in the fifth long -ē. This order is not one of priority; the first, second, third, and probably fourth go back to Indo-European; the fifth seems to have been evolved in Latin. Moreover, the first, second, and partially the fourth show a regularity that reflects the tendency of a developing language to devise new consistencies to meet new challenges and to drop former consistencies when they no longer fulfill linguistic needs. In the third declension, a great variety of stems and many irregularities of declension suggest that the declension preserves older practices that were still useful and thus resisted alteration.

In the first, second, fourth, and fifth declensions both the stem endings and those added thereto to show case relationships correspond to some extent, but by no means uniformly, to what is known as "grammatical gender." Latin inherited from Indo-European a classification of nouns into three types, which Greek grammarians called "masculine," "feminine," and "neuter." In fact these types have sexual significance only in some obvious instances; for the most part grammatical gender seems quite arbitrary and many nouns for things that have no gender, or are neuter, show either masculine or feminine stem and case endings. Thus "masculine," "feminine," and "neuter" are misnomers which have become enshrined in grammatical tradition.

Nouns of the first declension with their nominatives ending in short -a are in general classified as feminine even though most of them indicate things. In agreement with such first declension nouns signifying things, adjectives that have masculine endings of the second declension, feminine of the first, and neuter of the second use the feminine endings of the first, such as *toga pulchra* = a beautiful toga. Nouns of the first declension that denote persons engaged in various activities, such as *nauta* = sailor or *agricola* = farmer, are, despite their short -a ending, masculine, and adjectives with the first/second declension endings that modify them use the masculine endings of the second declension, as in *agricola bonus* = a good farmer.

The second declension contains primarily masculine nouns with their nominative ending in *-us* or *-er* and neuters in *-um*. But names of trees are feminine, such as *myrtus* = myrtle, a word taken over from Greek.

In the third declension there is only occasional correspondence between endings of the nominative and genders.

Nouns of the fourth declension whose nominative ends in short *-us* (genitive in long *-ūs*) are generally masculine, but there are a few feminines, of which *domus* = home and *manus* = hand are the most common. Nouns of the fourth declension whose nominative ends in long *-ū* (lengthened from the short *-u* of the simple stem) are neuter.

Nouns of the fifth declension, whose nominative ends in long *-ēs*, are regularly feminine. However *diēs* = day is masculine except when used to denote a specific day.

In short, Latin shows only a partial equating of stem or case endings with gender, whether gender indicates sex or simply defines the general class of nouns. For instance, *equa* = mare and *equus* = stallion are shown to be respectively feminine and masculine by their endings of the first and second declension. The third declension noun *uictor* = victor is distinguished by its ending as masculine whereas *uictrix* is the feminine, and both may be either noun or adjective. Also in the third declension, *mēns* = mind is feminine but *dēns* = tooth is masculine, though both are declined alike.

CASE

Indo-European used different endings to indicate possibly eight different relations in the singular and plural between nouns or pronouns, with their modifying adjectives, and other words or the general thought being expressed. Probably each of these primary cases had already been broadened in Indo-European to cover more than one simple relationship. Latin reduced the number of its case endings to five ordinarily, with occasionally two more to indicate address (vocative) and place where (locative). But it had to use these case endings to cover an even more varied range of relationships than presumably had the cases of Indo-European. Hence the term "case" can be applied in an external, morphological, sense to the forms that the stems assume by the addition of the case endings. Or it may apply more broadly to the different relationships thus expressed. Often a given case form expresses several relationships.

The normal five Latin cases did not in all declensions show different endings. Examples given in grammars of declensions, conjugations, and other morphological sequences of forms are called "paradigms" from Greek *paradeigma* = a pattern or an example. American grammars, in their paradigms of declensions, present the cases in the order nominative, genitive, dative, accusative, (vocative), ablative, and (locative). The vocative and locative are given only when they have distinct endings. English grammars more logically have the sequence nominative, (vocative), accusative, genitive, dative, ablative, and (locative). The vocative is normally the same in form as the nominative; only in the singular of masculine nouns of the second declension in -*us*, and usually when these are proper names, does the vocative have its own ending of short -*e*. For example, *Cicero* = Cicero or O Cicero, but *Marcus* has the vocative *Marce* = O Marcus. Place where is usually indicated by an ablative, but for certain nouns, primarily the names of cities, the first and second declensions have separate endings, respectively -*ae* and long -*i*, as in *Rōmae* = at Rome and *Corinthī* = at Corinth.

In the development of Latin case forms, a number of linguistic processes operated to obscure the original system of declensions and endings and to produce variations that make the classical paradigms seem often inconsistent and arbitrary. Some of the general processes will serve to indicate how the declensions and endings crossfertilized.

FIRST AND SECOND DECLENSIONS

Although Latin generally ends the nominative singular in -*s*, it inherited from Indo-European a class of nouns whose stem ends in long -*ā* and which are usually feminine. For these a nominative ending also in long -*ā* was used. Added to the long -*ā* of the stem, this should have combined to produce a nominative ending in a single long -ā. However, the phenomenon of Latin speech called "iambic shortening" operated to shorten the final long -ā in disyllabic nominative singulars with a short first syllable. This short -a was then generalized not only in all nominative singulars but also in all accusative singulars of first declension nouns.

Iambic shortening did not, however, shorten the long -ā of the ablative singular of the first declension, either because it was necessary to show the case or because the ablative singular of the first and second declensions and of the first and second personal singular pronouns originally ended in -d. An inscription of 186 B.C. preserves a *senātūs cōnsultum de Bacchānālibus* = a senatorial decree (restricting assemblies) of worshipers of Bacchus. In line 9 occurs the phrase *dē senātūs sententiād* = in accordance with the opinion of the senate, and in line 15, *nēue in pōplicōd nēue in preiuātōd nēue extrād urbem* = neither in public nor in private nor outside the city. The first phrase shows the -d after the long -ā- of the ablative of the first declension and the second shows it after the long -ō- of the ablative of the second declension and after the long -ā of the preposition *extrā* = outside, which could also be an adverb and which, whether or not in origin an ablative, is here treated as such. Incidentally, an original -ei- for long -ī- may be observed in *preiuātōd* = private. The presence of the long -ā- before the -d in *sententiād* = opinion and *extrād* seems to show that the shortening of the original final long -ā in the nominative of the first declension occurred before the loss of the final -d in the ablative; otherwise the final ablatival long -ā might also have been shortened by iambic shortening. However its length may have been preserved to distinguish the case ending of the ablative from that of the nominative.

The metrical practice of the comic poet Plautus, whose later years were contemporary with this inscription, indicates that he might or might not regard the final -d as pronounced. Although the surviving manuscripts of his plays, derived from copies made long after his death, never show a final -d, the ablatival endings long -ā and long -ō must frequently be pronounced before a following initial vowel or *h* in order to satisfy the requirements of his meters. That is, he felt free to elide or not to elide these ablatival endings, and when he did not, it may be assumed that he expected a *d* to be pronounced after them. The inscription therefore illustrates the conservatism of official legal language in the early second century B.C., while the verse of Plautus proves that in ordinary speech there was already established an option whether or not to pronounce the -*d*.

In early Latin the final -*d* appears also on the ablative singular of the fourth declension after long -*ū*, but not after the long -*ī* of the ablative of *i*-stem nouns of the third declension or the long -*ē* of the ablative of the fifth declension. However, the final -*d* does appear on both the ablative and the accusative singular of the first and second singular personal pronouns; that is, *mēd* and *tēd* occur as well as *mē* and *tē* for both cases. A verse preserved from a tragedy entitled *Alexander* written by a younger contemporary of Plautus, an outstanding early Latin poet named Ennius, reads *mēd obesse, illōs prōdesse, mē obstāre, illōs obsequī* = that I should hinder, they help, I oppose, they obey. In this verse the accusative, used as subject of the infinitive, occurs as both *mēd* and *mē*. In the first occurrence, the -*d* was probably added to prevent elision; in the second it was omitted to permit elision. In these pronominal accusatives, the -*d* was probably transferred from the ablative because of the identity of form in the two cases.

In the classical first declension, four endings are the same: the diphthong -*ae* of the genitive, dative, and occasional locative in the singular, and of the nominative plural. But each represents the result of a different development. In the genitive singular, the earlier ending, including the long -*ā* of the stem, was long -*ās*, which survived in the legal phrase *pater familiās* = father of a family. But in general the genitive of the first declension was assimilated to that of the second declension by adding long -*ī* to the long -*ā* of the stem. Even in Cicero's day, the archaizing poet Lucretius still wrote this as two syllables: -*āī*. But in speech it was reduced to the diphthong -*ae*. In the dative, an ending long -*ī* combined with the long -*ā* of the stem also to yield the diphthong -*ae*. The original locative ending was short -*i*, which similarly joined the long -*ā* of the stem to give -*ae*. Finally, in the nominative plural, there was substituted for an original long -*ās* an -*āī* on the model of the ending of the nominative plural of the second declension, which was originally the short -*o* of the stem plus a short -*i*. The result in the first declension was a fourth ending in -*ae*, whereas in the second declension disyllabic -*oi* became long -*ī*.

There were other interactions between the closely similar and generally regular first and second declensions. In the plural, the first declension might add to the long -*ā* of the stem in the dative and ablative an ending -*bus*, found regularly in the third, fourth, and fifth declensions. This survived in words that used the same stem for feminines in the first declension and for masculines in the second declension, when it was necessary to distinguish the gender, such as *filiābus* from *filia* = daughter compared to *filiīs* from *filius* = son. But generally the first declension nouns used the short -*is* of the second declension, which with the stem vowels long -*ā* and short -*o* yielded respectively disyllabic -*āis* and -*ōis*. Both of these endings were then reduced in speech to long -*īs*.

The first declension originally had a special ending -*som* for the genitive plural, instead of the -(*u*)*m* found in the other declensions. However, in the century roughly from 450 to 350 B.C., *s* between vowels, or intervocalic *s*, came to be pronounced as *r*. Also by Cicero's day short *o* was usually reduced to short *u*. Thus an original -*ā-som* became -*ārum*. In the second declension, the original genitive plural ending -*m* survived in words of common use, like *nummum* = of coins or *deum* = of the gods. Perhaps because the -*um* ending for the genitive plural resembled that of the accusative singular, nouns of the second declension for the most part adapted the -*ārum* of the genitive plural of the first declension to yield -*ōrum*. Thus *deōrum* became as common to mean "of the gods" as was *deum*.

In the second declension, the original ending of the nominative singular was -*s* for masculines and -*m* for neuters. When these combined with the short stem vowel -*o*- of the second declension, the resulting endings were -*os* and -*om*. In masculines, except those whose stems ended in -*ro*-, and in all neuters, the short -*o*- was reduced to short -*u*-, to yield the classical endings -*us* and -*um*. However, Quintilian (*Inst. Ōr.* I 7.7), writing in the late first century A.D., says that his teachers, presumably early in the century, still wrote *seruos* = slave or *ceruos* = stag; that is, short -*o*- after

88

consonantal -*u*- was still pronounced, and therefore written, as short -*o*-. In Quintilian's own day the spelling -*uu*- had become established. He adds that neither spelling exactly expressed the sound that was heard.

In the case of masculine nouns whose stems ended in -*ro*- the usual -*os* was dropped, and regularly in the nominative singular and occasionally in the other cases, a short -*e*- appear before the -*r*-. For example, from the stem *agro*- = field the nominative is *ager*, the genitive *agrī*, and so on. From the stem *puero*- = boy the nominative is simple *puer* and the -*e*- of the original stem is retained in the other cases, as in *puerī*. Some stems ending in -*ro*- have a regular nominative; such as *erus* = master, *erī*, and so forth, or *taurus* = bull, *taurī*, and so on.

In nouns of the second declension whose stems ended in disyllabic -*io*-, writers through the Augustan era combined the short -*i*- of the stem with the long -*ī*- of the genitive singular to yield a single long -*ī*-, which presumably represented the pronunciation. The accent of the nominative is retained, as *ingénī* = of genius. In post-Augustan authors and inscriptions the two tended to be kept as disyllabic -*iī*, though a single long -*ī*- continued to appear. Thus during the Republic the genitive singular of *filius* = son was written *filī*. During the Empire, such nouns in -*ius* and -*ium* tended to show in the genitive singular -*iī*; for instance the genitive of the neuter *imperium* = rule would be written *imperiī*. Even under the Republic, however, -*iī* seems to have been retained in the nominative plural and -*iīs* in the dative and ablative plural. In the vocative singular of such nouns, -*i*- plus -*e* combined into long -*ī,* with the same accent, as *Vergilī filī* = O son Vergil.

The ending of the dative singular in the second declension was originally -*o-ī*. These merged into the diphthong -*oi*. Plautus in the early second century B.C. still used *quoi* for the dative singular of the masculine and neuter of the relative pronoun *qui, quae, quod* = who, which, and of the interrogative pronoun *quid, quid* = who, what. In classical Latin *quoi* was reduced to *cui*. In nouns of the second declension the -*o*- of the stem combined with the ending -*oi* to yield long -*ōi*. Unlike the ending of the first declension, in which the long -*āi* was reduced to the diphthong -*ae*, in the second declension the final -*i* was lost, leaving the dative ending as simple long -*ō*. Thus this dative ending, though different in origin, resembles the second declension ending of the ablative, also long -*ō*.

THIRD DECLENSION

In the third declension, both borrowing and sound change occurred widely. The nominative plural of consonant stems should have added short -*es* to the final consonant, but long -*ēs* became regular under the influence of the *i*-stems. In these the original stem ending was -*ei*, in which the -*i* was consonantal. When the case ending short -*es* was added to this, the resulting combined ending became first -*ees* and then long -*ēs*. Similarly in the dative and ablative plural consonant stems should have added -*bus* directly to the final consonant, but perhaps because it was difficult to pronounce -*b*- after consonants, -*ibus* was taken over from the *i*-stems. Again, in the *i*-stems the genitive singular ending short -*is* was employed on the model of the consonant stems. A few *i*-stems show the proper accusative singular in short -*im*, like *turrim* from *turris* = tower, but most changed to short -*em* under the influence of the consonant stems.

Alterations of sound under the influence of endings occurred most commonly in the consonant stems of the third declension. For instance, the nominative singular ending -*s* could combine with some consonants, as with -*t*- or -*d*-, to form a single consonantal sound written as simple -*s*. Thus the nominative *mīles* = soldier represents an original *mīlets*, of which the genitive, with change of the stem -*e*- to -*i*-, is *mīlitis*. In some cases the loss of the -*t*- or -*d*- led to the lengthening of the stem vowel, as in the nominative *pēs* = foot, with genitive *pedis*. When the nominative -*s* combined with certain other consonants, the two consonantal sounds were preserved, without change in the preceding vowel, but were written with a single letter as a double consonant, as in *rēx*, *rēgis* = king. Finally the -*s* might simply be added to the stem consonant, as in *urbs*, *urbis* = city. While a short stem vowel might be lengthened only in the nominative, due to the combination of the stem consonant with the final -*s*, as in *Cerēs, Cereris* = (the goddess) Ceres, the lengthening was frequently extended throughout the paradigm, as in *uōx, uōcis* = voice, from an original stem with a short -*o*- preserved in the verb *uocō* = I call.

In the third declension, certain masculine stems originally were in long -*ōs* and certain neuters in short -*os*, the second of which became by Cicero's day short -*us*. These stems in origin kept the -*s*- when terminations were added in the oblique cases. But the change of intervocalic -*s*- to -*r*- introduced the latter in the oblique cases before the case terminations. In due course the -*r*- was taken over in the nominative of the masculines but not in that of the neuters. Likewise in the masculines, the long -*ō*- was shortened. Quintilian (*Inst. Ōr.* I 4.13) remarks that the masculine nominative singular forms in long -*ōs* once existed. Indeed, into the early Empire such a nominative as *honōs* = honor, or office, continued in use alongside *honor*, both with the genitive *honōris*. Clearly by Quintilian's time the masculine nominative singular in short -*or* had become regular. In the case of neuters, however, the -*s* remained in the nominative and accusative singular, so that original *corpos, corposis* = body became *corpus, corporis*. Some neuters reduced the short -*o*- to short -*e*- in the oblique cases; for example, original *genos, genosis* = race, or class, became *genus, generis*.

In the third declension the stem is found most readily by dropping the genitive singular ending -*is*, subject to these sound changes.

FOURTH AND FIFTH DECLENSIONS

The fourth declension originally added the case endings quite regularly to the short -*u*- of the stem. But some nouns, notably *domus* = home, tended to adopt endings from the second declension because of the close similarity of the nominative singular forms. The dative and ablative plural regularly show -*ibus* instead of the -*ubus* that should represent the addition of -*bus* to short -*u*-. Presumably, since short *u* closely approximated in sound short *i*, the short -*u*- here was assimilated in writing to the short -*i*- in the ending of the third declension.

The fifth declension was a late development in Latin. In it, only *diēs* = day and *rēs* = thing, or matter, show complete paradigms, and there was much assimilation to the first declension, as in the shortening of the accusative singular to *-em*, in the ending of the genitive plural *-ērum*, or in words that may be declined in either the fifth or the first declension, such as *materiēs* or *materia* = matter. In the fifth declension the long *-ē-* of the stem is usually shortened before a following vowel in a case ending, as in *rēs, reī*. However *diēs* regularly retains long *-ē-*, as in *diēī*, and *fidēs* = trust, or faith, shows *fidēī* until the Empire, and even *rēs* occasionally shows *rēī*.

NEUTER NOUNS

In the three declensions where neuters occur, namely the second, third, and fourth, they show certain special case endings. Their nominative and accusative have the same endings, though different as between singular and plural. In the second declension these add in the singular *-m* to the short *-o-* (becoming short *-u-*) of the stem, whereas in the third and fourth declensions the simple stem affords the nominative and accusative singular. In *i*-stems of the third declension, the short *-i-* of the stem becomes short final *-e* in the nominative singular, and this may be dropped. Thus *mare* = sea and the neuter of adjectives, such as *leuis, leue* = light, show the short final *-e*, whereas *animal* = animal has lost it. In the fourth declension neuters, the nominative and accusative singular have lengthened the short *-u-* of the stem to a final long *-ū*. The neuter dative uses an old locative form in *-ū*, and the ablative of both masculines and neuters lost a final *-d* after a long vowel (*-ū*), as in the first and second declensions. Thus in the singular, neuters of the fourth declension show the same form except in the genitive: *cornū, cornūs, cornū, cornū, cornū* = horn.

In the nominative and accusative plural, neuters of the second, third, and fourth declensions adopted what was apparently in origin a long *-ā* ending of generalizing feminine singulars of the first declension and shortened it to the familiar short *-a*, added in the second declension with the loss of the short -*o*- of the stem, but in the third and fourth declensions attached to the final consonant or vowel of the stem. Examples of the nominative and accusative plural forms are: in the second declension, from *monumentum*, *monumenta* = monuments or from *gaudium, gaudia* = joys; in the third declension, from *corpus,* genitive *corporis, corpora* = bodies or from *mare, maris* (an *i*-stem), *maria* = seas or from *animal, animalis* (also an *i*-stem), *animalia* =animals; and in the fourth declension, from *cornu, cornua* = horns.

PRONOUNS

Pronouns are among the oldest and most commonly used words, particularly the first and second personal pronouns. These last have very irregular declensions, in which not only do the singular stems differ from the plural, but in the first person the nominative singular has a different stem from the oblique cases. Also, particularly in the singular, the case endings correspond only partially to those for the nouns. These declensions must therefore be studied by themselves. The demonstrative, and in general the relative, pronouns tend to conform to the first and second declensions, but with the intrusion of special endings, such as the genitive and dative singular endings in -*īus* or -*ĭus* and -*ī*, or the neuter nominative singular in -*d*. The interrogative pronoun, though sharing such forms, generally follows the third declension in its endings.

ADJECTIVES

Adjectives fall into two classes: those that are declined with the endings of the first declension for feminine agreement and the endings of the second declension for masculine or neuter, and those that are declined with the endings of the third declension. Among the latter, some show in the singular different endings in the nominative for all three genders, that is, are adjectives of three terminations; some have the same form in -*is* (accusative -*em*) for masculine and feminine but show -*e* in the neuter, that is, are adjectives of two terminations; and some show the same nominative form throughout all three genders, that is, are adjectives of one termination. Except in the nominative and accusative singular and plural, adjectives of the third declension have the same terminations for all genders.

Adjectives have a characteristic not shared by nouns and pronouns, that of comparison, of indicating by special terminations three degrees of intensity: simple or positive, greater intensity than some other condition or comparative, and the utmost intensity or superlative. Positive adjectives of the third declension use certain *i*-stem endings: long -*ī* (for short -*e* of the consonant stems) often in the ablative singular of all genders, long -*īs* (for long -*ēs*) often in the masculine and feminine accusative plural, -*ia* (for short -*a*) regularly in the nominative and accusative neuter plural, and -*ium* (for short -*um*) in the genitive plural of all genders. The comparative suffix of adjectives has two endings, -*ior* for masculine and feminine and -*ius* for neuter. These are added to the stem with the loss of any vowel ending it. They are declined with the regular case endings of consonant stems of the third declension. The superlative suffix is usually -*issimus*, -*a*, -*um*, which is added to the last consonant of the stem. However, adjectives ending in -*er* double the -*r* and add -*imus*, -*a*, -*um*, and a few adjectives ending in -*ilis* have superlatives in -*illimus*, -*a*, -*um*. Examples of the comparison of adjectives are: *dūrus* = hard, *dūrior*, *dūrissimus*; *tristis* = sad, *tristior*, *tristissimus*; *fēlīx* = happy, or fortunate, *fēlīcior*, *fēlīcissimus*; *pulcher* = beautiful, *pulchrior*, *pulcherrimus*; *asper* = rough, *asperior*, *asperrimus*; and *facilis* = easy, *facilior*, *facillimus*. According to Quintilian, *Inst. Ōr.* I 4.8, the short -*i*- preceding the -*mus* in the superlative suffix represented a sound intermediate between short *i* and short *u*. It was in fact often written by early authors and in inscriptions with *u*, for example *optumus* = best.

In conclusion, the variation in case endings shown by the five declensions of nouns resulted in part from the use of somewhat different sets of endings in each declension but also from the way in which the same endings combined differently with the stem vowels or consonants. These combinations and the resulting sound changes occurred in speech, which the written forms simply sought to reproduce. There is also a tendency in any language for endings that have become inconsistent to be replaced by ones more consistent with the current practice of the language in order to increase intelligibility. This trend leads to greater homogeneity of endings between the declensions or even within them.

What is commonly called the case ending may truly be such, as is the short -*is* added to the consonant stems of the third declension in the genitive singular, or the short -*a* added to the short -*u*- of the stem of neuters of the fourth declension in the nominative and accusative plural. The case ending is often, however, a combination of a stem vowel and an ending, like the diphthong -*ae* in various cases of the first declension, or the long -*ī* of the genitive and locative singular and nominative plural of the second declension. It may also represent an ending added with the loss of the stem vowel, like the nominative and accusative plural of neuters of the second declension, where short -*o*- has vanished without any compensating lengthening of the final short -*a*.

Although the number of cases was recognized by ancient grammarians as five (or seven), the endings that distinguish them had in fact become fewer in every declension by assimilation. The feminine singular of the first declension shows only four different forms: nominative and vocative in short -*a*; genitive, dative, and locative in -*ae*; accusative in short -*am*; and ablative in long -*ā*. Moreover the ending -*ae* reappears in the nominative plural. Aside from such instances as the identity in form of the dative and ablative plural in all declensions, the singular of neuters of the fourth declension is an extreme example of reduction since in only two different forms appear: nominative, dative, accusative, and ablative in long -*ū*; and genitive in long -*ūs*. The speaker of Latin therefore had to grasp the meaning of such similar forms from the context in which they appeared. Those Romans who, under the guidance of Greek scholars, reduced the declensions and cases to a system for teaching purposes probably had little or no knowledge of the linguistic processes by which the declensions and cases had developed or the endings become similar or different. They elaborated their system in part from differences of form, as in case endings, and in part from differences in the relationships expressed. Once they had decided that five (or seven) such primary relationships were expressed by the different case endings in at least some of the declensions, they set up a uniform pattern for all, dividing forms that showed the same ending according to the relationships that they were used to express.

VIII

THE MORPHOLOGY OF VERBS

The morphology of the Latin verb derived from Indo-European but developed its own peculiar features to an even greater extent than did the morphology of nouns. The derivation of "verb" from the Latin *uerbum* = word might suggest that the Romans regarded terms denoting action as words par excellence. In fact, however, just as the Latin *nōmen* translates the Greek *onoma* = name, so *uerbum* renders the Greek *rhēma* = word, or saying, which indicated that the verb is essential to what is said about the subject, that is, to the predicate of a sentence. The verbal concepts are either of action or of existence. Action may proceed from the subject either absolutely (active intransitive) or to affect an object (active transitive). Action may also react upon its subject (middle) or affect it from some outside source (passive).

The morphology of verbs requires that a distinction be drawn which was not so necessary in the case of nouns, that between root and stem. A root is the simplest functional element in a word, the sound that stands for the barest meaning. The stem is that part of an inflected word which remains relatively unchanged throughout inflection. Certain sound changes do sometimes result from the adaptation of a stem by prefixes, inner vowel changes, or the addition of endings to express the various relationships in which the inflected word may stand to other words or to the whole idea being expressed.

A root may itself serve as a verbal stem, or it may have some element added to form a stem. Thus the root $(g)n\bar{o}$-, found in most Indo-European languages, as in English "know," appears in Latin in the perfect passive participle *nōtus* = known. However the addition of an inceptive suffix -*sc*-, denoting the beginning or undertaking of an action, gives the present stem $(g)n\bar{o}sc$- = know. This in turn may be extended by the addition of prefixes, usually prepositional, and personal endings, to yield *cum-gnōscō* or *co-gnōscō* = I know with, I understand, or simply I know; *ad-gnōscō* = I recognize; or *in-gnōscō* or *i-gnōscō* = I examine into, and hence, by justifying an action, I pardon. A root may be used to form other parts of speech besides verbal stems. For instance, the root *do-* = give appears in the verb *dō, dare* = I give, in another verb *dōnō, dōnāre* = I make a gift, in the noun *dōnum* = gift, and in another noun *dōs* = dowry, as well as in numerous derivatives and compounds of these words. Latin developed its vocabulary by building on relatively few roots rather than by using a wide number of them. Particularly is this true of the formation of verbs; Latin verbal formations on simple roots show great variety and complexity.

Vowels either in roots or in suffixes may change their intensity in different derivatives. Such a change is called by the German term *ablaut* = off-sound, or sound away from. In English, for instance, the vowel of the present verb "sing" changes in the past to "sang" or "sung." The commonest form of ablaut in Indo-European was one in which the three grades or stages were: a short -*e*-, a short -*o*-, and an absence of vowel sound between consonants called the zero grade. Latin shows the -*e*- and -*o*- grades in the stems of *pendō* = I weigh as against *pondus* = weight, or in *tegō* = I cover and *toga* = a toga. The -*e*- and zero grades appear in *genus* = kind as against *gi-gn-ō* = I produce, or I bear, in which the initial *g*- is reduplicated with a transitional sound written as short -*i*- and the final long -*ō* is the ending of the first person singular active present indicative, so that the root is the simple -*gn*- without a vowel sound (zero grade). Greek shows in addition the -*o*- grade in *gonos* = child. Some philologists hold that ablaut was a continuing force still operative to produce sound changes in at least early Latin; others think that it had been operative at a very early stage of the language but that its surviving instances are simply residues of a linguistic mechanism no longer operative even in preliterary Latin.

Indo-European verbal stems were of two types. In one the verbal endings were separated from the stem by a connecting vowel sound later written as short -e- or short -o-. This vowel sound is called "thematic" from the Greek *thema* = a primary form, or stem (of a word), that is, it became part of the stem. The other type, in which the endings were added directly to the original stem without any connecting or thematic vowel, was called "athematic," in which a Greek negative prefix *a-* is added to thematic. Latin preserved from Indo-European very few athematic verbs and even those that did survive were largely assimilated in conjugation to the thematic verbs.

Thus in the conjugation of the verb *ferō* = I bear, the athematic active and passive present infinitives *ferre* = to bear and *ferrī* = to be borne are formed by adding the active and passive endings for the infinitive -*re* and -*rī* directly to the stem *fer-*, without inserting the thematic vowel -*e*- between stem and ending. In the active present indicative, *ferō* shows athematic forms in the second person singular *fers* = you bear, the third person singular *fert* = he bears, and the second person plural *fertis* = you bear. However the same tense, the active present indicative, has thematic forms in the first person singular *ferō* = I bear, the first person plural *ferimus* = we bear, and the third person plural *ferunt* = they bear. The passive present indicative shows only athematic second and third persons singular: *ferris* = you are borne and *fertur* = he is borne. The remaining tenses (imperfect and future) of the active and passive present systems are wholly thematic, as are the active and passive present subjunctives. But the imperfect subjunctives, active and passive, are athematic: *ferrem* = I might bear and *ferrer* = I might be borne. The imperatives are athematic in the active present second person singular *fer* and plural *ferte*, which both mean "bear," and in the passive second person singular *ferre* but not in the passive second person plural *ferimini* which both mean "be borne." Similarly the so-called future imperative has in the active second and third person singular and second person plural the athematic forms *fertō, fertō,* and *fertōte,* but a thematic third person plural *ferunto,* all used in legal or solemn language to mean "bear." In the passive future imperative, the first and second persons singular are athematic, *fertor, fertor*; there was probably no distinct second person plural, and the third person plural is thematic, *feruntor*; all these are likewise used in solemn or legal language for "be borne."

While the active present second person singular imperative *fer* is an original athematic form, three other similar imperatives often learned with it, namely *dic* = say, *duc* = lead, and *fac* = do, have simply lost the original thematic ending short -*e* through the attrition of constant use; these three verbs are otherwise fully thematic.

Another verbal stem that shows in itself and in its compounds some athematic forms is *uol-ō* = I wish. This verb exists only in the active. In its present indicative, the third person singular is *uult* = he wishes, and the second person plural is *uultis* = you wish. The present infinitive is *uelle* = to wish, and the imperfect subjunctive is *uellem* = I might wish. As these forms suggest, the present system of *uolō* shows various peculiarities in addition to athematicism. In classical Latin, the stem -*o*- changed to -*u*- before -*lt* (or -*lt*-), as in the above forms. It changed to -*e*- before -*ll*- and also before a final syllable containing -*i*-, as in the present subjunctive *uelim* = I may wish. The present subjunctive also shows an optative -*i*- rather than the usual vowels indicative of the subjunctive, long -*ā*- or -*ē*-. The most difficult form to explain morphologically is the present indicative second person singular *uīs* = you wish. In early Latin this appears to have been written either *ueis* or *uois*; in classical Latin the -*oi*- yielded long -*ī*-, as in the nominative plural of masculines of the second declension. The form *uois*/*ueis* does not seem to have been contracted from *uol-is*/*uel-is* but perhaps to be derived from another root *uei-*/*ue-* = strive for, aspire to. This root may probably also be recognized in the adjective *in-uī-tus, -a, -um* = unwilling. The verb *sum* = I am exists only as active and intransitive. Its present system displays an intricate mingling of ablaut from a root (*e*)*s*- and both thematic and athematic endings. *Sum* also uses the optative -*i*-, as does *uolō*, in its present sub-

100

junctive *sim* = I may be. Apart from a few old, common, and irregular verbs like these, Latin conformed its verbal morphology to the thematic conjugations.

The inflection of a Latin verb is called its "conjugation," from the Latin verb *coniugō* = I unite; that is, a conjugation unites in systematic order all the forms built upon a given verbal stem. Just as declension may mean the actual inflection of a given noun or one of the five types of inflections of nouns, so conjugation may mean the actual inflection, that is, the full schematic arrangement or paradigm, of all the forms of a given verb. Or it may denote the one of the four or five types of inflection to which the verb belongs. In Latin verbal forms, the thematic vowels short -*e*- or -*o*- were generally absorbed into the final vowels of the verbal stem.

Verbs are grouped into four conjugations, or five if the short *i*-stem verbs of the third conjugation are regarded as forming a separate one. The verb stems in each conjugation end in a vowel appropriate to the conjugation and which has absorbed into itself the thematic vowel. To the final vowel of the stem are added the various endings that indicate the relationships into which the verb enters with other words in a sentence. The four conjugations, counting the two types of the third as one, are arranged in an arbitrary rather than a historical sequence. They are: the first or long -*ā*-; the second or long -*ē*-; the third with either short -*e*- or, only in the present system, short -*i*-; and the fourth, whose stems end in long -*ī*- except before a following vowel and in the third person singular active present indicative. The short -*i*- verbs of the third conjugation may originally have been conjugated like the long -*ī*- verbs of the fourth conjugation but early became assimilated to the short -*e*- verbs. Thus despite an apparent resemblance to the distinction between consonant and *i*-stems in the third declension nouns, the distinction in the third conjugation has no real connection with that in the third declension.

Indeed, there is no general or significant relation between the conjugations and declensions. Yet verbs of the third conjugation, like nouns of the third declension, show a much wider range of morphological changes than do those of the other declensions. This suggests that they represent an older level of formations which, because of frequent use, never became conformed to a regular pattern as much as did the other conjugations. This variation appears in changes of stem vowels, in reduplication of initial vowels in the perfect system, and in the tense suffixes of the active perfect system. Latin also has a number of irregular verbs, such as the partly athematic ones, which do not fit into the pattern of any of the four conjugations and whose forms must be learned specially.

Within the four conjugations, the inflection of Latin verbs expresses an even more elaborate variety of relationships than do the declensions of nouns; and the only relationships shared between verbs and nouns are those of number and, in compound tenses, of gender and case. The relationships in which a verb may stand to its context were inherited from Indo-European. They are voice, mood, tense, person, number, and occasionally gender and case. These apply only to the forms of the verb subject to conjugation. Such forms are called finite, from the perfect passive participle *fīnītus* = delimited of the verb *fīniō* = I delimit. That is, the meaning of the verb form is delimited in respect to voice, mood, tense, person, and number by either stem changes or the addition of endings, or both.

The principal verbal form that shows minimal changes, restricted to those of voice and tense, is called the "infinitive," from the adjective *īnfīnītīuus* = not delimited. This adjective is formed from a simpler one, *īnfīnītus*, in which a negative prefix *in-*, in origin different from the prepositional prefix *in-*, is combined with the passive perfect participle of the verb *fīniō*. Thus the infinitive is a verbal noun whose meaning is not delimited by mood, number, or person, although it does show different endings according to whether it is active or passive in voice and present or perfect in tense. The infinitive functions in fact as a noun, that is, as a name for the action or state of being denoted by the verb.

Other noun and adjectival forms of the verb, such as the supine, gerund, gerundive, and participle, vary in the extent to which they show stem changes and add endings to indicate voice, tense, number, gender, or case. They do not, however, show mood or person and, because they are restricted in their indications of the other characteristics, they may also be regarded, like the infinitive, as forms not fully delimited and therefore not finite.

VOICE

The word "voice" derives through French *voix* from Latin *uōx*, a term that does not appear to have been used by Latin grammarians for what the Greeks called *diathesis* = disposition, function, or voice. Priscian, a grammarian of the early sixth century A.D., wrote a still surviving work on teaching grammar, *Institūtiōnēs Grammaticae*. In book VIII 7 he discusses voice in a section entitled *de significātiōne*. He begins the section, "*significātiō* or *genus*, which the Greeks call the *affectus* of the verb." *Affectus* here translates the Greek *diathesis*. Later, in section 11, he writes *in uerbīs etiam sunt quaedam uōce actīuā*. In this sentence *uōx* does not, however, mean "voice" but, as elsewhere in his work, "word" or "form of the word." The sentence should be translated "among verbs also, some are active in form," and not "in the active voice." Possibly mediaeval grammarians, understanding this or some similar passage to mean active in voice, adopted *uōx*, *voix*, and "voice" for the disposition of the verb as regards its subject.

There are at least three possible relations of the verb to its subject, or three voices. The verb may express an action proceeding from the subject and be called "active," a term derived from the passive perfect participle, *āctus*, *-a*, *-um*, of the verb *agō* = I lead, or I do. An active verb may be transitive, an adjective formed from the passive perfect participle, *trānsitus*, *-a*, *-um*, of the verb *trānseō* = I go across, in which case the action proceeds from the subject to a person or thing directly affected, called the direct object. Or if the action is sufficient in itself and does not affect an object, the active verb is intransitive, as in *eō* = I go. An active intransitive verb may also express a state of being or becoming, as do *sum* = I am or *fīō* = I become. In the case of verbs meaning "become" or the like there may be a predicate nominative in agreement with the subject, as in *rēx fīō* = I become king. Second, the action may both proceed from the subject and affect the subject itself, in which case the verb is called "middle" because the action was thought of as lying between active and passive. Third, the action may affect the subject, either of itself or as proceeding from some outside source, an agent or an instrument, in which case the verb is called "passive," an adjective derived from the passive perfect participle, *passus, -a, -um*, of the deponent verb *patior* = I suffer, because the subject suffers the action.

The phrase *auis cantat* = the bird sings is active intransitive; *uir equum dūcit* = the man leads the horse is active transitive. Neither Latin nor English has special forms for the middle, but in Latin the passive occasionally has a middle force, probably as a direct inheritance from Indo-European, though this use was extended in Latin poetry under Greek influence. Thus *exercētur currendō* may mean "he exercises himself by running," rather than "he is exercised by running." Generally, however, Latin, like English, uses an active verb with a reflexive pronoun to express the middle, as in *sē currendō exercet* = he exercises himself by running. Finally, *hasta iacitur* = the spear is thrown is passive in Latin; English has to express the passive by forms compounded with the auxiliary verb "to be."

The active and passive voices are not always clearly distinguished in Latin. For instance, the verb *fīō* = I become is active present intransitive in form but came to be used as the passive present for *faciō* = I make, that is, I am made. Or an active or passive verb may have no expressed subject; that is, it may be impersonal. Though some scholars think that *pluit* = it rains implies the sky or the sky god Jupiter as subject, the action probably stands by itself to express a natural phenomenon. An impersonal passive may similarly express an action without a subject; for example, *curritur* = there is a running, or, with the English indefinite, people run.

Such true impersonal passives must be distinguished in Latin from passives in which the subject is an infinitive or subordinate clause, as in *trāditum est Homērum caecum fuisse* = it is (or has been) said that Homer was blind. In the latter case, English uses the same construction with "it is" that it uses for impersonal concepts, but the subject of *trāditum est* in Latin is the infinitive clause *Homērum caecum fuisse*. This pseudoimpersonal construction is common in the passive perfect system, but in the present a more personal construction with the nominative is used, *Homērus trāditur caecus fuisse* = Homer is said to have been blind. Verbs that in the active take as objects *ut* clauses of purpose regularly have these clauses as subject in the passive, in both the present and the perfect, as *mihi persuādētur ut eam* = it is persuaded to me that I should go, or persuasion is (applied) to me that I should go, that is, I am persuaded to go. Such passives with clauses as subjects are not truly impersonal, though the English rendering often makes them appear so.

Some verbs exist only in the passive inflection though they are active transitive or intransitive in meaning. These are called "deponents," from the present active participle, *dēpōnēns* (stem *dē-pōnent-*) = laying down, from the verb *dēpōnō* = I lay down, or put off, because they have laid down or put off their active forms. Examples are the transitive *sequor* = I follow, the intransitives *cōnor* = I try, or *morior* = I die, and the transitive or intransitive *patior* = I suffer, or I endure. A few verbs are semideponent; that is, they are deponent only in the perfect system. For example, *audeō* = I dare has an active present system, including the active present infinitive *audēre* = to dare, but becomes passive in the perfect: *ausus sum* = I dared, or I have dared.

Again, a passive verb may occasionally take an object, particularly in poetry, as *galeam induitur* = he puts on (himself) a helmet. This is a middle use, either native or more probably borrowed from the Greek, in which language the middle voice often takes a direct object.

The active and passive voices in Latin are distinguished by different sets of personal endings in the moods and tenses and by different suffixes in the infinitives, participles, and other nonfinite forms. Moreover the perfect system of the passive appears to have been a late development. It was supplied by combining the passive perfect participle as a predicate adjective with forms of the present system of *sum* = I am. It therefore properly expresses a present state resulting from a past action. For example, *amāta est* = she is (one who has been) loved came to mean "she was loved." Such a compound form is often called by the Greek term "periphrastic," meaning "roundabout," or "circumlocutory." In time, the connotation of past time was shifted from the participle to the auxiliary verb so that such forms as *amāta fuit* are found, which means equally "she was loved," but reduces the participle to a timeless predicate adjective.

MOOD

The character of the action expressed by a verb is called its "mood," from the noun *modus* = measure, or manner. If the verb simply states or denies a fact, its mood is said to be indicative, from the passive perfect participle *indicātus* = shown, of the verb *indicō*; that is, the indicative simply points something out. *Indicō* has a short *-i-* in its stem as against the long *-ī-* in simple *dīcō*. If the verb expresses any form of uncertainty, whether doubt, possibility, potentiality, wish, or will, its mood is said to be subjunctive, from the passive perfect participle *subiunctus* = subjoined, or dependent on, of the verb *subiungō*. The term indicates that the uncertainty of the statement arises from its dependency on, or subordination to, some other statement; indeed a dependent subjunctive is usually connected to the verb of the main statement by a subordinating conjunction. In Europe this mood is called the conjunctive, because the uncertain statement is conjoined to the main statement by a conjunction. Neither term serves to describe independent subjunctives, which express uncertainty in a main statement. However, in the United States subjunctive is applied to the mood, whatever its use. The Latin subjunctive combines two Indo-European moods: the subjunctive proper, expressing uncertainty, and a mood expressing wish, called the optative from the passive perfect participle *optātus* = desired, of the verb *optō*.

Verbal forms denoting injunction or command are put in the imperative mood, a word derived from the passive perfect participle *imperātus* = commanded, of the verb *imperō*. Since commands are seldom addressed to oneself and normally to others present before one, this mood has only the second person singular and plural in the active and passive present. There is also a so-called future imperative, which is actually a solemn legal or religious form of command. Such solemn commands may be directed toward a third person or action, as in English "let it be done." The future imperative has therefore in the active a second and third person singular and plural. In the passive, it is uncertain whether the second person plural existed apart from the second person plural of the passive present imperative, which in turn is the same in form as the second person plural of the passive present indicative.

To these three true moods is generally added the infinitive. The infinitive simply names the action indicated by the verb, without restriction of qualification. The simple forms of the infinitive are therefore indeclinable verbal nouns. The forms show changes of stem and ending to indicate tense and voice. In infinitives compounded with participles, namely the active future and the passive perfect, the participle, being essentially a predicate adjective, agrees with the subject of the infinitive in gender, number, and case. The infinitive, being a verbal rather than a simple noun, may have a subject or an object, and may be modified by adverbs as well as by adjectives. The case of the subject of an infinitive is the accusative except when the infinitive is historical.

The indicative, subjunctive, and imperative moods add endings, and the vowel or syllable connecting them to the stem may differ in the three moods. For instance, a final long -$\bar{o}$ indicates the first person singular of the active present indicative; verbs that form their future indicatives with an inserted -b- have -$\bar{o}$ in the active future first person singular; and all verbs have it in the first person singular of the active future perfect indicative. Otherwise the active first person singular ending is normally -m in both indicative and subjunctive. However the active perfect indicative has its particular set of personal endings, of which the one for the first person singular is long -$\bar{\imath}$. The imperative also has special endings except for the passive second person plural.

TENSE

Latin developed a temporal significance for those verbal forms that in Indo-European had indicated the character or aspect of the action. Latin grammarians applied to these categories of forms the term *tempus* = time, which became, through old French *tens*, the English designation "tense." From the aspect of action continuing or vividly present to the speaker, Latin developed a tense to denote action contemporary with the speaker's utterance, whether the action is simple, continuing, or even prospective, that is, looking forward to an immediate future. Thus Latin uses one form, such as *iaciō*, to cover what English distinguishes as simple present, "I throw," or as continuing or repetitive present, "I am throwing," or as prospective, "I am going to throw."

On the present stem, Latin formed two new tenses. One indicates immediate past and normally a continuing, repeated, or customary past action. It is called the "imperfect" from an adjective *imperfectus* = incomplete, which was formed by adding the negative prefix *in-* to the passive perfect participle of the verb *perficiō* = I complete. The imperfect thus stands in contrast to the perfect, the tense of completed action.

To distinguish the imperfect, Latin inserts (infixes) a *-b-* after the stem vowel and a thematic vowel *-a-* between the *-b-* and the consonantal personal endings. Thus the active imperfect indicative first person singular of two verbs of the first and second conjugations respectively are *amābam* = I was loving and *dēlēbam* = I was destroying. In the third conjugation the short *-e-* of the stem is lengthened before the *-b-a-* to yield as active imperfect indicative first person singulars *regēbam* = I was ruling or *capiēbam* = I was taking. Verbs of the fourth conjugation ordinarily insert a long *-ē-* between the long *-ī-* of the stem and the infix *-b-a-*. The long *-ī-* of the stem is shortened before the following vowel. Thus the fourth conjugation verb *audiō* = I hear has the active imperfect indicative *audiēbam* = I was hearing. This long *-ē-* was probably introduced by analogy with the short *i*-stems of the third conjugation, in imitation of such a form as *capiēbam* = I was taking. However some verbs of the fourth conjugation may add the *-b-a-* directly to the long *-ī-* of the stem. Thus the active imperfect indicative first person singular of *sciō* = I know is both *sciēbam* and *scībam* = I was knowing.

The second tense created on the present stem is one to indicate true futurity, which had not been adequately differentiated in Indo-European. In the first and second conjugations, and occasionally in the fourth, Latin characterized this tense also by an infixed *-b-* and a thematic vowel *-i-* before the consonantal endings. In the first person singular active and passive, the *-i-* does not appear before the respective personal endings long *-ō* and short *-or*. In the second personal singular of the passive the thematic *-i-* becomes *-e-* before the personal ending *-ris* or *-re*. In the third person plural the respective active and passive endings after the *-b-* are *-unt* and

-untur. Thus the active and passive futures of the verbs of the first and second conjugations just given as examples for the imperfect are *amābō, amābis, amābit* . . . *amābunt* = I will love, etc., and *amābor, amāberis* (*-re*), *amābitur* . . . *amābuntur* = I will be loved, etc.; *dēlēbō, dēlēbis, dēlēbit* . . . *dēlēbunt* = I will destroy, etc., and *dēlēbor, dēlēberis* (*-re*), *dēlēbitur* . . . *dēlēbuntur* = I will be destroyed, etc.

In the third conjugation and normally in the fourth, the future indicative shows alternative forms of the subjunctive endings without the infixed *-b-*; the first person singular has as its thematic vowel long *-ā-* and the other persons have long *-ē-*. Thus the first person active and passive of the future indicative in these conjugations is indistinguishable from the first person singular of the present subjunctive, but the other persons differ. For example, the future of the third conjugation verb *regō* = I rule runs *regam, regēs, reget* . . . = I will rule, etc., and *regar, regēris* (*-re*), *regētur* . . . = I will be ruled, etc., but the subjunctive goes *regam, regās, regat* . . . and *regar, regāris, regātur* . . . = I may rule, etc. Similarly in the fourth conjugation, *audiam, audiēs, audiet* . . . = I will hear, etc., and *audiam, audiās, audiat* . . . = I may be heard, etc. However, some verbs of the fourth conjugation may show both the subjunctive forms for the future and those with the infix *-b-i-* added directly to the long *-ī* of the stem. For example, from *sciō* = I know come both *sciam* and *scībō* = I will know, but in contrast to the imperfect, not *sciēbō*.

It may well be that in the first and second conjugations a generalization of the thematic vowels long *-ā-* and *-ē-* for both the subjunctive and the future would have led to confusion not only between these two tenses but also with the present indicative. If so, this would explain why in these two conjugations the imperfect infix *-b-* was adopted to characterize the future as well, with the substitution of the thematic vowel *-i/e-* for the imperfect long *-ā-*. The extension of *-b-i-* to some verbs of the fourth conjugation would then have occurred by analogy since, like the first and second conjugations, the fourth is regular, in contrast to the third.

The origin of the infixed *-b-* is uncertain. A somewhat similar formation of the future is found in Celtic, and it is argued that both Latin and Celtic may have combined with the verb stem forms from the old root of the verb "to be," *bhu-*. To this were added the endings that appear in the imperfect and future of the verb *sum* = I am, namely *eram, erās* . . . = I was, etc., and *erō, eris* . . . *erunt* = I will be, etc. On this hypothesis, these first, second, and occasionally fourth conjugation imperfects and futures began as compound forms. For example, *amābam* would originally have been the stem *amā-* plus an imperfect *bhuam*, which meant respectively "to love" and "I was." This is, however, only a possible derivation of the imperfect infix *-b-*.

The Indo-European aspects of simple action, usually past, and completed action were combined by Latin into one tense, which took its name "perfect" from the passive perfect participle *perfectus* = completed of the verb *perficiō*. Although Latin combined into one tense simple past action and completed past action, Greek maintained the distinction between a tense of simple past time, called the "aorist" or undefined tense, and the perfect. During the late Empire, popular (vulgar) Latin restored this distinction, so that, for instance, *dīxī* = I said (aorist) and *dictum habeō* = I have said. In *dictum habeō* the passive perfect participle is an invariable neuter accusative singular modifying what one has said. This differentiation survived in the Romance languages, as in French between *je dis* (called preterit) and *j'ai dit*.

The active perfect system was differentiated from the present system in various ways, more than one of which may serve to differentiate a given perfect. The initial consonant of the verbal stem may be repeated, or reduplicated, with the introduction between the new initial consonant and the similar one of the original stem of either the vowel *-e-* or the stem vowel. In those verbs where reduplication is found in classical Latin it had been inherited from an earlier stage of the language in which it was an operative method of forming the perfect. In classical Latin it had become inoperative as a formalized survival in a few verbs; it was not used to create active perfects of other verbs than these.

Another way in which active perfects were indicated was by a change in the nature or quantity of the stem vowel. Or a special ending might be inserted, or infixed, between the stem and the personal endings. Finally, the active perfect indicative has its own set of personal endings. The active pluperfect and future perfect indicative and the active perfect and pluperfect subjunctive used the regular active personal endings appropriate to the two moods but had characteristic syllables infixed between the perfect stem and these personal endings. The passive perfect system, both indicative and subjunctive, was compounded from the passive perfect participle and appropriate forms of the verb *sum* = I am.

To give some examples of the formation of perfect stems, the active present indicative verb *dō* = I give has as its active perfect indicative *dedī* = I gave, or I have given. This shows both reduplication of the initial *d*-, with an intervening -*e*- before the stem *d*-, and the ending of the first person singular of the active perfect indicative, long -*ī*.

Such an active perfect indicative as *didicī* from the present *discō* = I learn shows a variety of sound changes. In the present, a suffix -*sc*- was inserted between the stem and the personal endings to indicate the action as beginning. This suffix, called "inceptive" from *inceptus*, the passive perfect participle of *incipiō* = I begin, has absorbed the -*c*- which originally ended the stem. In the perfect, the -*sc*- has been dropped so that the -*c*- reappears before the special ending for the first person singular of the active perfect indicative, long -*ī*. At its beginning, *didicī* shows reduplication of the original initial *d*- with the repetition also of the stem vowel -*i*-.

Tetulī = I have lifted, or raised up, is the original form of the first person singular of the active perfect indicative of the verb *tollō* = I lift, or I raise up. In classical Latin it was used in a shortened form *tulī* as the perfect of *ferō* = I bear and therefore meant "I have borne." The original *tetulī* shows reduplication, ablaut of the stem -*o*- to -*u*-, loss of one stem -*l*-, and the same special perfect ending -*ī*. The passive perfect participle of both *tollō* and *ferō* is *lātus*, -*a*, -*um* = raised up, or carried, which seems at first wholly unrelated to the roots of either of these verbs. However it derives from the simpler root *tul*- reduced to the zero grade of ablaut *tl*-. A form of this root is preserved in Greek, where the *tl*- is followed by a long -*ā*-, and the same form was used in Latin to make the original passive perfect participle *tl-ā-tus*. Since the Latins found *tl* difficult to pronounce together, the *t*- was dropped to leave *lātus*.

To continue with the formation of active perfect stems, *cēpī* = I took, from *capiō* = I take, has lengthened its stem vowel and changed its tone from short -*a*- to long -*ē*- and affixed to the stem the special ending -*ī*. *Rēxī* = I ruled, from *regō* = I rule, has lengthened its stem vowel, added an infixed -*s*- to the stem -*g*- to yield the double consonant -*x*-, and affixed the special ending -*ī*. An infixed -*s*- is often found in the Greek aorist, the tense of simple past action, and was therefore presumably one of the Indo-European signs of this aspect, adopted in many Latin verbs into the perfect. One of the most common infixed terminations in Latin to characterize the active perfect is a consonantal -*u*-, which may appear between the stem vowel and the personal endings, as in *laudā-u-ī* = I praised, or may be added directly to the stem consonant and be vocalized, as in *uetuī*, from *uetō* = I forbid, or in *monuī*, from *moneō* = I advise.

Reduplication to show an active perfect stem is generally lost in compounds. Thus the simple verb *cadō* = I fall has as its active perfect indicative *cecidī* = I fell, but its compounds have only -*cidī* without reduplication. For example, *incidō* = I fall has as its active perfect indicative *incidī* = I fell into. The perfect system also has simple forms only in the active. Presumably the passive was a late development, since it is supplied by compound, or periphrastic, forms in which the passive perfect participle is combined with the present system of *sum* = I am, and in Ciceronian and later Latin occasionally with its perfect system.

The infixed consonantal -*u*-, used as a sign of the active perfect system regularly in the first and fourth conjugations, frequently in the second, and occasionally in the third, tended to vanish. Possibly its occurrence between two vowel sounds meant that it was passed over in speech. Or possibly the forms without the consonantal -*u*- were in fact the more archaic. In any case, *amāstī* is found as an alternative, if not as a shortened, form for *amāuistī* = you have loved. Instead of *petīuit* = he has asked, or sought, *petiit* is regular, with the long -*ī*- shortened before the now immediately following short -*i*-. *Petiit* in turn may be shortened to *petīt*, where the two short -*i*-s combine into one long -*ī*. This last is distinguishable from the third person singular active present indicative *petit* only by the long -ī-. Such an active pluperfect as *audīueram* = I had heard regularly appears as *audieram*, in which the long -ī- has been shortened before a following vowel. Other perfect forms without the -*u*- are common.

Upon the perfect stem, as upon the present, were created in the indicative two new tenses: a tense of action that had occurred previously to a past action, called the "pluperfect" or more than completed; and a tense called the "future perfect," used for action occurring in past time but future in relation to another past action, whether or not the main action had been completed at the moment of speech. In the active voice these tenses were formed by the addition to the perfect stem of endings -*era*- and -*eri*-. In the passive voice they were, like the perfect, compounded from the passive perfect participle and the imperfect and future forms of *sum* = I am. The active personal endings were added to the -*era*- and the -*eri*-, and in the first person singular of the active future perfect the -*i*- of -*eri*- vanished before the final long -*ō*.

Also in early classical Latin, for example, in Plautus and Terence, the -*i*- of the endings of the active future perfect indicative was generally short, in contrast to the active perfect subjunctive in which it was usually long. In Ciceronian Latin and thereafter, the -*i*- might be either short or long in either tense. Thus Ovid uses *dederīs* = you will have given, or you might have given, as second person singular of the active future perfect indicative and the perfect subjunctive, while Horace has *dīxerīs* = you will have said in the second person singular of the active future perfect indicative and *accēperīs* = you might have received in the active perfect subjunctive.

Since the subjunctive itself expresses uncertainty, it did not develop a future tense. It did, however, form on the present stem an imperfect tense and on the perfect stem a pluperfect. Thus it shows only four tenses rather than the six found in the indicative. The active present subjunctive uses the vowels -*ē*- in the first conjugation, -*ā*- in other conjugations, or -*i*- in irregular verbs (an optative ending) to connect the personal endings to the consonant or vowel of the stem. The active imperfect subjunctive uses an infixed -*re*- between the stem vowel and the personal endings. The active

113

perfect subjunctive adds to the perfect stem an infixed *-eri-* before the personal endings. This produces forms like those of the active future perfect indicative except in the first person singular, where the future perfect indicative has long *-ō* and the perfect subjunctive *-m*. The active pluperfect subjunctive adds to the perfect stem an infixed *-isse-* before the personal endings.

It is often said that the active imperfect and pluperfect subjunctives may be formed by adding the personal endings to the active present and perfect infinitives. For example, *amāre* = to love yields *amārem* . . . = I might love, etc., and *amāuisse* = to have loved yields *amāuissem* . . . = I might have loved, etc. Though this is a convenient way of remembering the formation, in fact the infixes are of different origin from the endings of the two infinitives and have only come to resemble them by phonological development. The same is true of the infixes *-eri-* in the active future perfect indicative and the perfect subjunctive: their origins were distinct. As in the indicative, the passive perfect and pluperfect subjunctive are compound tenses, using the passive perfect participle and the appropriate subjunctive forms of *sum* = I am.

Another confusing similarity of endings arises from the varied uses of the suffix *-re*. In its different occurrences this ending had different origins, though the resulting forms in classical Latin often appear identical. The suffix *-re* is regular on the active present infinitive. But it also may appear as an alternative to *-ris* on the second person singular of the passive, regularly in the imperative, commonly in the present subjunctive and future indicative, and occasionally in the present and imperfect indicative. Thus *amāre* may = to love, be loved, or less commonly, you are loved. *Regere* may = to rule, be ruled, or you are ruled. The *-re* forms of the second person singular in the passive present subjunctive are identifiable by the vowel of the endings: *amēre* or *regāre*. The suffix *-ēre* is also a common alternative for *-ērunt* in the third person plural active perfect indicative. The usual ending may originally have had a short *-e-*, *-erunt*. If so, the short *-e-* became lengthened by contamination with the long *-ē-* of *-ēre*. The short *-e-* survives occasionally in verses in the dactylic hexameter meter. When quantities are unmarked, the perfect ending *-ēre* may well cause confusion, particularly in authors who use the so-called historical infinitive for actions in past time. For example, without marked quantities, *incidere* = to fall upon, or into, resembles *incidēre* = they fell upon, or into. Ordinarily the context indicates which of the two forms has been used by the author.

NUMBER AND PERSON

Finite verbs show by their endings the number and person of their subjects, whether expressed or not, and in compound forms, their gender and case. The subject may be one or many, namely singular or plural; Latin did not perpetuate the Indo-European dual for two persons. The subject may be identical with the speaker or speakers, that is, be the first person. Or the subject may be the person(s) or object(s) whom the speaker addresses, that is, be the second person. Or the subject may be the person(s) or thing(s) about whom or which the speaker is talking, that is, the third person.

The term "person" is derived from the Latin *persōna* = mask, as customarily worn by an actor to represent the character whom he was playing. Thus "person" does not mean, as usually in English, a separate individual but rather the character that an individual assumes on a given occasion. In grammar, "person" means the relation or condition of the subject vis-à-vis the speaker and hence the verb form indicating the person of the subject, whether expressed or not. The first and second persons are generally animate individuals, though inanimate objects are frequently personified and imagined as either speaking or addressed by the speaker. The third person may be either animate or inanimate.

The sets of six personal endings, to indicate whether the subject is first, second, or third person and singular or plural in number, differ in the active and passive voices and to some extent in the various tenses, particularly in the active perfect indicative. These endings are single vowels, single consonants, or syllables. They are added to the stem vowel or to an infixed syllable or consonant when such is added to the stem vowel to indicate tense. The personal endings occasionally overshadowed a preceding vowel, as did the ending long -*ō* of the first person singular active indicative, as in *amō* = I love and *regō* = I rule. It did not do so in *moneō* = I advise, *capiō* = I take, or *audiō* = I hear. Before *-ō* the short *-i-* of the future infix *-bi-* and of the active future perfect infix *-eri-* vanishes, as in *amabō* = I shall love and *amāuerō* = I shall have loved, both from *amō* = I love. Before the endings *-nt* and *-ntur* of the third person active and passive plural, a preceding short *-e-* or short *-i-* was reduced to short *-u-*, as in *regunt* = they rule, or *amābuntur* = they will be loved, in contrast to *amant* = they love or *monentur* = they are advised. Verbs whose stems end in short or long *-ī-* apparently borrowed this *-u-* from consonant stems of the third conjugation and added it after the stem *-ī-*, as in *capiunt* = they take from *capiō*, a short *i*-stem of the third conjugation, or *audiuntur* = they are heard from *audiō*, a long *ī*-stem of the fourth conjugation.

The imperative is usually addressed directly to other persons or things. It therefore has basically only the second persons singular and plural, active and passive. In legal and religious language, however, a special form of imperative was used that might be directed toward somebody or might enjoin certain procedures. Hence this tense has both second and third persons singular and plural. It is actually little more future in connotation than the present imperative, since any command implies future performance of the action enjoined. However in legal and religious prescriptions validity is envisaged for any future occasion, and to that extent the name "future imperative" for this tense may be justified.

The present imperative shows four separate personal endings, that is, for the second persons singular and plural both active and passive. The future imperative has in the singular one ending each for active and passive, serving for both second and third persons. In the active future plural imperative there are two endings, for the second and the third person. In the passive future plural, grammars normally give a third person only and omit the second person plural passive future form, presumably because it does not occur in extant Latin writings. If it was employed, it had the same ending *-minī* that is used in the second person plural passive present imperative and also in the second person plural passive indicative. For example, *regiminī* might have any of three meanings: "you are ruled," "(you) be ruled (now)," or "(you) be ruled" in a solemn or legal sense of "on any occasion." In the other moods and tenses of the passive present system, appropriate connecting vowels or syllables distinguish the forms ending in *-minī* from the passive present indicative or imperative. This *-minī* may have originated as a participial ending, though it is not easy to see how it became personal.

NONFINITE FORMS: VERBAL NOUNS

The infinitive, though classed as a mood, is in fact a neuter verbal noun, indeclinable in its three simple forms. In the active present infinitive it is thought that originally a dative or locative ending *-si* was added to the stem vowel. If so, the final short *-i* would early have reduced to short *-e*, to yield *-se*. In the fifth to fourth centuries B.C. the intervocalic *-s-* would have changed to *-r-*. In the active perfect infinitive, the ending *-se* was added to the perfect stem ending *-is-*, which is preserved in the second person singular active perfect indicative, as in *fu-is-tī* = you have been. In the resultant form, the *-s-* of the infinitive ending was not intervocalic and therefore did not change to *-r-*; indeed the double *-ss-* did not reduce to a single *-s-* as it did in such a word as *caus(s)a* = cause. In the passive present infinitive, an ending long *-ī* was added to the *-r-* of the active form in the first, second, and fourth conjugations. But curiously, in both consonant and *i*-stem of the third conjugation it is attached directly to the consonant of the stem, as in *regī* = to be ruled or *capī* = to be taken. The origin of this ending long *-ī* is uncertain, as is also that of an alternative ending *-ier*, which is likewise added after the *-r-* in the first, second, and fourth conjugations, but to the consonant of the stem in the third. These three infinitives, the active and passive present and the active perfect, were presumably the oldest and show simple forms.

The passive perfect infinitive, like the passive perfect finite tenses, is compounded from the passive perfect participle and the present, or sometimes the perfect, infinitive of *sum* = I am, namely *esse* or *fuisse*, as in *amātum* (*-am, -um*) *esse* = to have been loved. Since the subject of an infinitive is usually in the accusative case the participle of compound infinitives is normally also given in the accusative. If a compound infinitive is historical, standing for a main verb, its subject and the agreement of its participle are in the nominative.

Since the tense of futurity was slow to develop in Latin, the future infinitives are also compound forms. The active uses the active future participle with *esse*, to indicate that the subject is a person or thing, or persons or things, about to become characterized by the activity denoted by the verb. For example, *amātūrum* (*-am*, *-um*) *esse* basically = a person (or thing) to be about to be loving. Latin devised a whole finite conjugation to denote prospective or immediate futurity, which it formed by using the active future participle and forms of *sum*. It is difficult to determine whether this arose from the active future infinitive or whether the latter was borrowed into the regular conjugation from this so-called first periphrastic (circumlocutory) conjugation.

The passive future infinitive was an even more roundabout formation. It combines the accusative singular of a verbal noun called the "supine" with *īrī*, which is the passive present infinitive of *eō* = I go not used elsewhere. Thus *amātum īrī* = to be going toward a loving, and hence to be about to be loved. Since the supine is a noun, there is no agreement in gender or number with any subject; the ending *-um* does not change. Early Latin had idiomatically used forms of *eō* with the accusative of the supine, in which the accusative indicates the action as the limit of motion in a construction called "place to which without a preposition." Thus *mercātum it* = he is going marketing, not to market, though the form might equally be the accusative of the fourth declension noun *mercātus* = market. The original literal meaning of "to go" became, as in English, prospective of intention or purpose, and the passive present infinitive *īrī* was invented to supply the need for a passive connotation. These three infinitives, the passive perfect and the active and passive future, developed as periphrastic compounds to express ideas more complex than those with which preclassical Latin was dealing when it shaped the simple finite and nonfinite forms of the verb.

Latin had two other verbal nouns besides the infinitive. The supine derives its name from the Latin adjective *supīnus* = lying back on. The justification for this term is not clear, but perhaps it meant that the supine, though showing declined forms like a noun, lay back on, or returned to, a verbal connotation, to convey, like the active present infinitive, the concept simply of the action. The supine is formed by adding the suffix -tū- to the final consonant or vowel of the stem, often with a change in the internal stem vowel or final consonant. Hence the supine resembles in stem the passive perfect participle, though the suffix for the latter is -to-, which became -tu- in the nominative and accusative singular.

The supine occurs only in the accusative and ablative singular, which have the endings of fourth declension nouns, namely -tum and -tū. Since the same termination -tū- is used to form fourth declension nouns from verbal roots or stems, it is usually held that supines are simply specialized verbal functions of the accusative and ablative of the corresponding fourth declension nouns. However fourth declension nouns based on verbal roots or stems seem to be late formations, and not all verbs that have supines have corresponding fourth declension nouns. It may well be that the supine forms were the earlier, made, like the simple infinitives, by adding noun endings to verb stems or roots. If so, the fourth declension verbal nouns were developed from supines.

Of the two cases of the supine, the accusative is used with īrī as an accusative of place to which in the passive future infinitive and in idioms like *mercātum it* = he goes marketing. The ablative of the supine is used as an ablative of specification, chiefly with adjectives, in such phrases as *horribile dictū* = horrible to relate. Since the supine does not take a subject or object or have adjectival or adverbial modifiers, its gender cannot be determined. Its accusative would suggest masculine, but its character as a verbal noun would suggest neuter, parallel to the infinitive and gerund.

The third Latin verbal noun is called the "gerund." This term represents a late Latin noun *gerundium*, derived from the verb *gerō* = I bear, or I perform. The exact relevance in meaning of *gerundium* to *gerō* is not clear. Perhaps it indicates that the gerund denotes an action as simply performed, without qualification of subject, mood, tense, and so forth. The gerund is active in voice and neuter in gender. Since the infinitive serves as the nominative verbal noun, the gerund is found only in the oblique cases. The infinitive may serve as a direct object of a verb, but the accusative of the gerund is regular after prepositions.

NONFINITE FORMS: VERBAL ADJECTIVES

In form, the verbal noun, or gerund, closely resembles a passive verbal adjective, called the "gerundive," in Latin *gerundīuus* (*modus*), an adjective derived from *gerundium*. As an aid to remembering the difference between the two forms, the gerundɪᴠᴇ is a ᴘᴀssɪᴠᴇ adjectɪᴠᴇ, and the gerund is the opposite, an active noun. Both are formed by adding a termination *-nd-* to the vowel of the present stem and attaching to this for the gerund the endings of the oblique cases of neuter nouns of the second declension and for the gerundive the endings of first/second declension adjectives. The gerund and gerundive may not be as closely related in origin as their similarity of form and name would suggest; the shared termination *-nd-* may have developed phonologically from originally independent endings.

In gerundives of verbs of the third conjugation, early Latin shows a variation between *-e-* and *-u-* before the *-nd-*. For instance, the deponent *sequor* = I follow has a regularly formed gerundive *sequendus, -a, -um* = following and also an older form *sequuundus*, in which, as was often the case, the *-qu-* became *-c-* before the following *-u-*, so that the form was written *secundus*. This form likewise meant "following" and became specialized as "second." Because a following wind was favorable, *secundus* might also mean "favorable." Such forms as *faciundus* = making, from *faciō* = I do, or I make, are common.

Besides the gerundive, Latin has three other verbal adjectives, called "participles." The English term represents the neuter of the Latin adjective *participiālis, -e*, with which *uerbum* should be understood, to signify any word that participates in, or partakes of, two functions, such as a verbal noun or a verbal adjective. *Participiālis* is derived from the Latin noun *participium*, represented by the French term *participe*. *Participium* in turn derives from the Latin adjective *particeps* = having a part in, or sharing. *Par-*

ticipium, like *participiālis,* was applied to any word that participates in two functions. Eventually, however, both the noun *participium* and the adjective *participiālis* became restricted in Latin grammatical writings to only one class of such words, the common verbal adjectives called in English "participles."

The active present participle was the only Latin participle inherited from Indo-European. It is formed by adding *-nt-* to the vowel of the present stem and then the case endings of third declension adjectives of one termination, for example, *amā-ns, ama-nt-is* = loving, from *amō* = I love. There is no passive present participle.

The perfect participle, on the contrary, exists only in the passive; it is often called simply the past participle. It adds to the stem, whether this ends in a vowel or a consonant, an adjectival termination *-to* (*tu,* or *t*)- and to this the case endings of the adjectives of the first/second declension, for example, *amā-tu-s, -t-a, -tu-m* = having been loved, or simply loved.

When the termination *-to-* is added directly to the consonant of a stem containing before the consonant a long vowel, that vowel is shortened, though this shortening remains a hidden quantity, since a syllable is always long when its vowel, whether long or short, is followed in the same syllable by a consonant, that is, when the vowel is followed in all by two or more consonants. Thus *dīcō* = I say has the passive perfect participle *dictus, -a, -um* = said, in which the *-i-* is shortened but the syllable *dic-* is nevertheless long.

Often a long stem vowel is shortened or changed before the *-to-,* usually in verbs in which the stem vowel has been lost in the active perfect system. For instance, *amō* = I love preserves the long stem vowel *-ā-* in both the active and the passive present infinitives, in the active perfect system, and in the passive perfect participle. These are respectively *amāre, amārī, amāuī,* and *amātus* (*-a, -um*). However *uetō* = I forbid has the long *-ā-* in both the present infinitives, *uetāre* and *uetārī,* but not in the active perfect system *uetuī,* where the *-u-* is added directly to the stem consonant *-t-.* The passive perfect participle is therefore *uetitus* (*-a, -um*). Similarly in the second conjugation, *dēleō* = I destroy, whose principal parts continue *dēlēre, dēlēuī, dēlētus* (*-a, -um*), may be contrasted with *moneō* = I advise, *monēre, monuī, monitus* (*-a, -um*). In the fourth conjugation, *audiō* = I hear, *audīre, audīuī*, has the passive perfect participle *audītus* (*-a, -um*), but *aperiō* = I open, *aperīre, aperuī*, has *apertus* (*-a, -um*). In the third conjugation, the stem changes and manner of adding to *-to-* vary considerably, and changes of vowels within the stem or of final consonants are common; indeed all conjugations contain verbs showing irregularities from the norm.

The third participle is the active future. This is formed on the supine stem in *-tū-*, which resembles the stem of the passive perfect participle except that the *-u-* is long. To the supine stem is added an infix which was originally *-so-* but which became *-ru-* by the change of intervocalic *-s-* to *-r-* and the weakening of *-o-* to *-u-*. To the resulting form are joined the endings of adjectives of the first/second declension. Thus for *amō* = I love the active future participle is *amā-tū-ru-s, -tū-ra, -tū-ru-m* = going, or about, to be loved. The gerundive is in some grammars included as a passive future participle, but its connotation and use are such that it is better regarded as distinct from the participles. There is therefore no passive future participle.

Deponent verbs, namely those that in the finite tenses show only passive forms but have active meanings, nevertheless have the compound future active infinitive as well as the passive present and compound perfect infinitives. They also have active present and future participles as well as the passive perfect participle, and the active gerund and supine as well as the passive gerundive.

PRINCIPAL PARTS OF VERBS

In dictionaries of the English language a verb is listed under its simple present stem form, followed by its past form or forms and its present participle; for example, "love, loved (preterit and past participle), loving," or "sing, sang (preterit), sung (past participle), singing." From these forms the full conjugation may be derived. In Latin four forms are normally given: the first person singular of the active present indicative, which is the form under which the verb is listed, the active present infinitive, the first person singular of the active perfect indicative, and the passive perfect participle, usually only in the masculine nominative singular. From these four so-called principal parts the full conjugation may be derived. When there is no stem change from the present to the perfect systems, dictionaries frequently list merely the appropriate endings for the principal parts.

Some verbs do not show all four principal parts. For verbs that do not have a passive perfect participle, either the supine or the nominative masculine singular of the active future participle is given. Deponents show the first person singular of the passive present indicative, the passive present infinitive, and either the masculine nominative singular of the passive perfect participle or the first person singular masculine of the passive perfect indicative, in which the passive perfect participle is compounded with *sum* = I am. Semideponents show a first person singular of the active present indicative, an active present infinitive, and either the masculine nominative singular of the passive perfect participle or the first person singular masculine of the passive perfect indicative. Defective verbs show the appropriate forms of the voice, tense, or person to which they are limited. Some examples of principal parts are:

Regular of the first conjugation: *amō* = I love, *amāre* = to love, *amāuī* = I loved, or I have loved, *amātus* = loved.

Irregular, with no passive perfect participle: *eō* = I go, *īre* = to go, *īuī* or *iī* = I went, or I have gone, either *itum* (supine) = a going or *itūrus* (active future participle) = about to go.

Irregular, with no passive perfect participle or supine: *sum* = I am, *esse* = to be, *fuī* = I was, or I have been, *futūrus* = about to be.

Deponent of the third conjugation: *sequor* = I follow, *sequī* = to follow, either *secūtus* = followed or *secūtus sum* = I followed, or I have followed.

Semideponent of the second conjugation: *audeō* = I dare, *audēre* = to dare, either *ausus* = dared or *ausus sum* = I dared, or I have dared.

Defective, limited to the present system: *fīō* = I become, or I am made, *fierī* = to become, or to be made. Usually a third principal part is given, the first person singular masculine of the passive perfect indicative of *faciō* = I make, namely *factus sum* = I was made, or I have been made.

123

Defective, limited to the perfect system: *coepī* = I begin, *coepisse* = to begin, either *coeptus* = begun or *coeptus sum* = I began, or I have begun.

Defective, limited to the perfect system and with no passive perfect participle: *meminī* = I remember, *meminisse* = to remember.

Defective, limited to the third person singular: *licet* = it is permitted, *licēre* = to be permitted, either *licuit* or *licitum est* = it was permitted, or it has been permitted.

In conclusion, Latin preserved very slight traces of the classification of verbs in Indo-European into thematic and athematic. Instead it developed a classification into four or five conjugations, distinguished by the final vowels of their stems. These conjugations show many irregularities and cross-influences in their methods of deriving various stems and forms from roots. There are also a number of wholly irregular verbs. Latin, along with the other Italic languages, kept the Indo-European active voice but eliminated the Indo-European middle, which appears also to have served as a passive. Instead Latin developed its own special forms with a true passive significance. Latin also reduced the four moods inherited from Indo-European to three: indicative, subjunctive (which absorbed the optative), and imperative. The infinitive is ordinarily, but improperly, counted as a fourth mood.

Latin gave to the three Indo-European aspects of action, namely immediate, single, and completed, temporal significances and combined the last two so that Latin has two main tense systems, the present and perfect. In the indicative mood, the present and perfect tense systems each contain three tenses: beside the present were created the imperfect and future, and beside the perfect the pluperfect and future perfect. The subjunctive shows only two tenses in each system, present and imperfect, and perfect and pluperfect. In the passive, the whole perfect system seems to have developed late, since it has compound forms. The imperative has only the present tense and, for legal and religious injunction, a tense called "future."

The verbal nouns and adjectives have both voice and tense, but incompletely. The infinitive shows present, perfect, and future active and passive forms, some formed as compounds. But the participle has only the active present and future and the passive perfect, while the supine and gerund have an active present meaning and the gerundive a passive present one.

Within the various tenses of the two voices, the indicative and subjunctive show three persons in the singular and in the plural. The imperative shows in the present only the second person singular and plural active and passive and, in the so-called future, second and third persons in both numbers of the active, but in the passive it lacked a distinct form for the second person plural. Latin did not retain the Indo-European dual in verbs or in nouns.

Verbs, apart from their compounded passive forms, show gender and case only in verbal nouns and adjectives. Of the verbal nouns, the infinitive and the gerund, and probably the supine, are neuter. Simple infinitives change their stem or endings only to show voice and tense. Though they serve as nouns, they are not declined. Compound infinitives, except the future passive, show endings for case, number, and gender on their participles, which are essentially predicate adjectives with infinitives of *sum* = I am. The supine has only an accusative and ablative singular of the fourth declension. The gerund has the case endings of the oblique cases of the second declension neuter singular. The verbal adjectives, namely the gerundive and the passive perfect and active future participles, have full declensions. They agree in gender, number, and case with the nouns or pronouns that they modify, whether they themselves are used purely adjectively or as components of compound verbal forms. In compound forms a participle or gerundive is still adjectival in the predicate with forms of *sum* = I am and agrees in gender, number, and case with the subject of the verb. While the subjects of compound verbs are ordinarily in the nominative, they may be in the accusative with compound infinitives, as they are with most infinitives.

A full description of a verb form should take account of conjugation, voice, mood, tense, person, number, gender, and case, though not all of these are found in every form. For instance, finite simple forms do not have gender and case. Verbal adjectives—participles and the gerundive—do not have person or mood but may have tense and do show number, gender, and case; their voice

125

is given by their particular form. The verbal nouns do not have mood, if the infinitive is not reckoned as such. Of them, both the gerund and supine are presumably present, or undefined, in tense, singular in number, and probably neuter in gender. The gerund is passive in voice and has the oblique case endings; the supine is active and shows only accusative and ablative endings. Simple infinitives show by their endings only voice and tense. Compound verb forms, both finite ones and infinitives, show in their component participles voice and tense, namely passive perfect and active future. They also show gender, number, and case in agreement with their subjects. Their component finite forms of *sum* = I am are active in voice and show mood, tense, person, and number. The component infinitives *esse* and *fuisse*, likewise active, show only tense.

Usually the description of a finite verb is given approximately as follows, using for an example *amāuistī* = you have loved: second person singular active perfect indicative of the first conjugation verb *amō* = I love, *amāre, amāuī, amātus*. In the phrase *alea iacta est* = the die is, or has been, cast, the compound verb *iacta est* is the third person singular passive perfect indicative of the third conjugation *i*-stem verb *iaciō* = I throw, or I cast, *iacere, iēcī, iactus*. The passive perfect participle *iacta* is singular feminine nominative in agreement with the subject *alea* = a die, a singular feminine noun of the first declension. The compound verb is in the indicative in a simple statement and in the perfect to indicate either simple past time or more probably completed past time, to show the finality of a decision. Plutarch, a Greek author of the late first and early second centuries A.D., wrote a Greek life of Caesar in which he gives this famous phrase, attributed to Caesar when he was about to cross the Rubicon in 49 B.C., in a form that would translate into Latin as *alea iacta esto*. If this is the correct wording, *iacta esto* is an unusual compound passive "future perfect" imperative in the third person singular. It means "let the die have been cast," that is, "let the decision have been made," with the implication "let the decision stand, come what may." This meaning seems more in accord with Caesar's fatalism than the simple statement of fact *iacta alea est*, the form in which it is given by Suetonius, a Latin biographer contemporary with Plutarch.

IX

THE MORPHOLOGY OF
ADVERBS AND OTHER
PARTICLES

The term "particle," from the Latin *particula*, a diminutive of *pars* = part, is applied to subordinate words that are not inflected, namely prepositions, conjunctions, and interjections. It may also be extended to cover adverbs, though these show inflectional endings for comparison.

Particle also covers words that appear only as attached to the ends of other words to give intensity or emphasis. Examples are *-pte* on pronominal adjectives in the ablative, as in *meōpte ingeniō* = by my very own ingenuity; *-met* on personal pronouns, as in *nōsmet* = we ourselves, and on pronominal adjectives, as in *suāsmet* = their very own; *-ce* on demonstrative pronouns, which came to be permanently attached to some forms of the demonstratives, as *hīc* (earlier *hic*) = this, from *hi-ce*, or *hunc* from *hum-ce*, but not to *hūius*, *hōrum*, or *hīs*; *-dum* on adverbs, as in *interdum* = meanwhile, or from time to time, and on imperatives, like *agedum* = come now. Two conjunctions also appear only as attached to the second of two words that they connect, namely *-que* = and, and *-ue* = or. Likewise the interrogative particle *-ne* is attached to the first word of a direct or indirect question. Occasionally the preposition *cum* is attached to an ablative pronoun with which it goes, as in *pāx uōbīscum* = peace (be) with you. Such attached particles are called "enclitics" from a Greek adjective meaning "leaning back on."

ADVERBS

An adverb, from *aduerbium* = (a word attached) to (another) word, is an indeclinable modifier of a verb or adjective. Adverbs in Latin are formed by adding endings to the stems of adjectives. In the positive degree, adjectives of the first/second declensions change the final *-us* of the nominative masculine singular to long *-ē*. For example, from the adjective *lātus, -a, -um* = broad the positive adverb is *lātē* = broadly, or widely. Adjectives of the third declension usually form their adverbs in the positive degree by adding *-iter* to the stem, which may most readily be arrived at by dropping the ending *-is* of the genitive singular. For example, from *celer, celeris, celere* = swift, genitive *celer-is*, the positive adverb is *celer-iter* = swiftly; from *ācer, ācris, ācre* = sharp, genitive *ācr-is*, it is *ācr-iter* = sharply; from *fortis, forte* = strong, genitive *fort-is*, it is *fort-iter* = strongly; and from *atrōx* = fierce, genitive *atrōc-is*, it is *atrōc-iter* = fiercely. But adjectives with stems ending in *-nt-* add simply *-er*, as from *prudēns* = prudent, genitive *prudent-is*, the positive adverb is *prudent-er* = prudently.

Some adjectives of the first/second declensions have positive adverbs either with long *-ē* or with *-iter*, as from *miser, misera, miserum* = miserable the positive adverb may be either *miser-ē* or *miser-iter* = miserably. In a few common adverbs of the first/second declensions the final long *-ē* has become permanently shortened by iambic shortening. Two such adverbs are *bene* from *bonus, -a, -um* = good, which also shows ablaut in its stem of *-o-* to *-e-*; and *male* from *malus, -a, -um* = bad. Such second declension adverbs in short *-e* should be distinguished from an adverb like *saepe* = often, which was probably in origin the neuter of a third declension adjective no longer used.

The neuter accusative singulars of adjectives are often used adverbially, frequently to the exclusion of the regularly formed adverb, such as *multum* from *multus, -a, -um* = much, or many; and *parum*, the neuter of *paruus, -a, -um* = little, or small. In this last adverb the consonantal *-u-* has been combined with the following vowel *-u-* in ordinary speech. Similarly *nihil* = nothing, or not at all, which was originally a neuter nominative or accusative *nihilum* which lost its final syllable in speech and was itself frequently shortened to *nīl*, serves as both a noun and an adverb. Occasionally the neuter accusative singular of a pronoun is so used, such as *quid* = why, from the interrogative pronoun *quis, quid* = who, what.

The ablative singular of adjectives, pronouns, or occasionally nouns may be used adverbially. Thus, although the adjective *uērus, -a, -um* = true has a regular adverb *uērē* = truly or really, the accusative and ablative singular of its neuter, *uērum* and *uērō*, are also used to mean "in fact" or "certainly." Other ablatives similarly employed adverbially are *forte* = by chance, from the noun *fors*, not from the neuter accusative singular of the adjective *fortis, -e* = strong; or *sponte* = of (one's) own accord, from an obsolete noun that occurs only in the genitive *spontis* and in this adverbial ablative. Examples of pronominal ablative adverbs from the relative pronoun are *quā* = where, *quō* = whither, and *quī* = how, the last of which shows the original *i*-stem ablative.

Many adverbs are accusatives, ablatives, or locatives of nouns that have ceased to be used otherwise, such as *iterum* (neut. sing. acc.) = a second time, *statim* (fem. sing. acc.) = immediately, and *forās* (fem. plur. acc.) = out of doors, whose noun is usually the feminine plural or singular of the third declension *forēs* (genitive *-ium*), or *foris* (genitive *-is*) = door. Adverbs ending in long *-ā* are often regarded as petrified adverbial ablatives of the first declension, as some in long *-ō* would be of the second declension. It may be that this adverbial long *-ā* is in fact an independent adverbial ending. Some such adverbs are *rectā* = straight, or straightway, with which is usually supplied the feminine ablative singular noun *uiā*, as it is also with *ūnā* = along with; *intrā* = within; and *ultrā* = beyond, which also shows *ultrō*. This last adverb may also mean "of one's own accord," from the implication "beyond other people's help." Locative forms used adverbially are *uesperī* = in the evening, from *uesper* = evening, from which an old ablative *uespere* is also used adverbially; and *humī* = on the ground, from *humus* = earth.

Dumtaxat = to this extent, or so far, combines the particle (conjunction or enclitic) *dum* = while, or up to the time that, and *taxat*, the third person singular of the active present subjunctive of an otherwise unused third conjugation form of *tangō* = I touch, namely *taxō, -ere*, which has the desiderative meaning of "I seek to touch" and should be distinguished from a similar first conjugation form *taxō, -āre*, which has the frequentative or intensive meaning of "I touch often" or "I touch firmly." Thus *dumtaxat* literally = up to the time (or point) that one can touch.

Latin adverbs had varied origins, and, as in the case of final long *-ā*, the source of their endings is sometimes disputed or unknown. The *-tus* of such an adverb as *fundi-tus* = from the bottom seems to correspond to a Greek adverbial ending *-then*, which indicates place from which. The *-dem* in *quidem* = indeed and the *-dam* in *quondam* = formerly may be accusative endings. The source of *-dō* in *quandō* = when is not clear. Some adverbs are phrases that have coalesced into words, like *dēnuō* = anew, or freshly, contracted from *dē nouō* = from the new; and *uidēlicet* = namely, or to wit, from *uidēre licet* = it is possible to see. This last was abbreviated during the Middle Ages to the familiar *viz.*, in which the last sign is not the letter *z* but a mediaeval symbol for the abbreviation of most of the word that looks enough like *z* to be written or printed as such. Systematic Latin grammars give the derivations of adverbs and classify them according to their functions as adverbs of place, time, manner, degree, or cause. Interrogative and negative particles are also functionally adverbs.

Adverbs are inflected in that, like adjectives, they change their endings from the positive to indicate two degrees of comparison with some other stated or implied condition, namely the comparative and superlative degrees. Unlike adjectives, they do not decline their forms in any of the three degrees. For the comparative, the neuter accusative singular of the comparative adjective is used. For example, from the adjective *leuis, -e* = light the positive adverb is *leuiter* and the comparative *leuius*. The superlative is formed on the superlative of the adjective according to the method in the first/second declensions, namely by changing the final *-us* of the nominative masculine singular to long -*ē*. For example, the superlative of *leuis, -e* is *leuissimē*.

The word "preposition" represents the noun *praepositiō*, formed from the passive perfect participle *praepositus* of the verb *praepōnō* = I place before. These particles are so called because they are generally placed before the word or phrase which they govern, that is, which they put into relation with other words or phrases. The relationship given by a preposition is ordinarily adjectival, as in English "a bridge *of iron*," or adverbial, as in English "he goes *into the city*." In Latin, because the cases, particularly the genitive, generally suffice to indicate the adjectival relation between two nouns, prepositional phrases tend to be adverbial. However, in such a phrase as *templa circum forum* = temples around the forum the prepositional part is adjectival, as perhaps also in *ūnus ex hominibus* (an alternative for *ūnus hominum*) = one of (literally from) the men.

The use of prepositional phrases developed when cases alone became inadequate to express complex or new thoughts. Thus, while some prepositions in Latin may have been inherited as such from Indo-European, most, and perhaps all, were adverbial in origin, and frequently in Latin the same form is used as either adverb or preposition.

Simple prepositions such as *ā* (*ab*) = away from, *ad* = to, or toward, *dē* = down from, *ē* (*ex*) = out from, and *ob* = in front of, or on account of, may always have been such. But such possibly ablatival forms as *extrā* = outside, *infrā* = below, and *suprā* = above serve as either adverbs or prepositions. Similarly *circum* = around and *coram* = in the presence of are isolated accusative singulars, respectively neuter and feminine, employed as adverbs or prepositions. *Circiter* = around is an adverbial formation from the root found in *circā* and *circum*; like them, it may be used both adverbially and as a preposition. Other prepositions in -*ter*, such as *inter* = between and *praeter* = beyond, or besides, show a suffix that may have been the original from which the positive adverbial ending -*iter* derived. *Versus* and *uersum* = toward seem in origin to have been the nominative masculine and accusative masculine or neuter singular of the passive perfect participle of *uertō* = I turn, which originally qualified something as "turned toward" and then came to be an adverb and finally a preposition. It is held more dubiously that *trāns* = across was in origin an active present participle of the verbal root that survives in *intrō, -āre* = I enter.

Prepositions, therefore, except possibly for a few simple ones, were late in developing in preliterary Latin. They were of varied origin but normally closely allied to adverbs. Although in general they precede the noun or phrase that they govern, some are always postpositive, a term derived from the passive perfect participle *postpositus* of the verb *postpōnō* = I place after; that is, they followed their noun. Examples of postpositive prepositions are *tenus* = up to, or as far as, and *uersus* = toward when used as a preposition; *cum* = with may not only be postpositive but is also regularly attached to a pronoun that it governs, as an enclitic, for example, *mēcum* = with me. *Cum* is also regularly put between an adjective and the noun that it governs, as in *magnā cum celeritāte* = with great speed. Occasionally other prepositions are so placed, as in *quam ob rem* = for what or which reason. The nouns governed by prepositions are usually in either the accusative or the ablative case; some prepositions may be followed by either with differing connotations. Occasional phrases combining an ablative and a genitive came to have the significance of adverbial prepositional phrases, as did *exemplī gratiā* = for example, which is usually abbreviated to *e.g.*

CONJUNCTIONS

The term "conjunction" derives from the verb *coniungō* = I join. Conjunctions join or connect words, phrases, or clauses without affecting their grammatical form. Some are original, like *et* = and or *sed* = but. Many are petrified cases of nouns, etc., as *quod* = because, which is the neuter accusative singular of the relative *quī* = who; *dum* = while, which is possibly an accusative singular, as were perhaps the preposition *cum* = with and the

adverb *tum* or *tunc* (originally *tum-ce*) = then; and *uērum* and
uērō = but indeed, which are adverbial uses of the accusative and
ablative neuter singular of the adjective *uērus, -a, -um* = true.
Other conjunctions are stereotyped phrases, like *nihilōminus* literally = the less by nothing, and hence nonetheless, and *proinde*
literally = forward from there, and hence thereafter.

Conjunctions are classified either as coordinate, from Latin *cum*
= with plus the passive perfect participle *ordinātus* of the verb
ordinō = I put in order, or as subordinate, or ordering beneath
(*sub*). Coordinate conjunctions connect parallel or equal independent words or phrases. They may show connection, such as *et*
and *-que* = and; separation, such as *uel* and *aut* = or; contrast,
such as *sed* = but; cause, such as *nam* = for; or consequence, such
as *ergō* = therefore. Some of these have negative equivalents; for
example, for *et* there is *nec* (or *neque*) = nor. Many conjunctions
occur in pairs or in longer sequences, as correlatives, a term that is
apparently a modern Latin formation combining the preposition
cum = with (combining as *cor-* before initial *r-*) and the passive
perfect participle *relātus* of the verb *referō* = I refer (one thing
to another). Correlative conjunctions are therefore repetitions of
the same conjunction to balance or contrast successive words or
phrases, such as *et . . . et* = both . . . and, *uel . . . uel* =
either . . . or, and *cum . . . tum* literally = when . . . then,
and hence both . . . and.

Subordinate conjunctions introduce clauses that they render
dependent on some main thought. The subordination may be conditional, as with *si* = if; comparative, as with *quasi* = as if; concessive, as with *quamquam* = although; temporal, as with *cum* =
when; final (purpose), as with *ut* and *nē* = that and that not; consecutive (result), as with *ut* and *ut nōn* = that and that not; or
casual, as with *quod* = because.

The confusing use of *cum*, either as a conjunction to mean
"when," "since," or "although," or as a preposition to mean
"with," is an instance in which phonological development has
produced from different originals two words sounding, and therefore written, alike. *Cum* the subordinating conjunction is derived
from the relative stem *qu-*. *Qu-* preceding a following *-u-* (reduced
from an original *-o-*) came to be pronounced and written as *c-*, as

it was in the genitive and dative singular of the relative *cūius* and *cui*, originally *quōios* and *quōi*. Hence the conjunction *cum* was originally *quom*, later *quum*, an accusative singular neuter of *quī* = who. The preposition *cum*, earlier *com* and in compounds *con-*, *col-*, *cor-*, or even *co-*, always had the *c-*. It may have been either an original preposition or an isolated accusative. The preposition *cum* seems to have been peculiar to the Italic languages, including Latin, since parallels in other Indo-European languages are rare and questionable. The relative/interrogative root *qu-* appears in various forms in other Indo-European languages, as in English "who."

INTERJECTIONS

The term "interjection" comes from the passive perfect participle *interiectus* of the verb *intericiō* = I throw into. An interjection is a word thrown into a sentence without any grammatical change of its own form or syntactical relation to the rest of the sentence. Its use is to express emotion or to attract attention.

Some interjections merely represent sounds expressive of emotion, such as *Ō, heu*, or *eho*. Others are inflected parts of speech, such as the second person singular present active imperative *age* = come, and *em* = hey, or hey there, if this was in fact shortened from *eme* = take. Names of deities may appear in shortened form, as do *hercle* or *mehercle*, from *Herclēs* (later *Herculēs*), or *pol* from *Pollux*. Many were borrowed from the Greek, such as *euge* = well and *euhoe*, a drunken cry.

There is no sharp line between a sound that has no real significance but is simply an emotional interjection and a word which, originally used parenthetically, became an interjection. For instance, the use of *age* = come as an interjection may be compared with the frequent parenthetical use in Plautus of *amābō* = I will love, in the sense of "I will love (you if)," equivalent to the English "please."

Interjections may be used with cases of nouns, as in the familiar *uae uictīs* = woe to the conquered. In this phrase *uictīs* is the dative plural, probably masculine rather than feminine or neuter, of the passive perfect participle of *uincō* = I conquer; the thought implied is "(let there be) woe to (or for) the conquered." In the phrase *prō pudor* = for shame, *prō* is an interjection, not the familiar preposition = for, or on behalf of. It may take the nominative (vocative) as here, or the accusative, or occasionally in later Latin even the genitive. The various interjections and the sense of emotion or the meaning that they convey are best learned as they occur in reading.

In conclusion, the origins of adverbs, prepositions, conjunctions, and interjections in Latin are varied, but the predominant source was adverbial, apart from a few that may have originated as prepositions and conjunctions, and those interjections that merely represented an emotional sound. Many words are used in more than one of these classes.

X

THE FORMATION OF
COMPOUNDS

The union of two or more words to form one is called a "compound," from Latin *componō* = I put together; English has introduced in pronouncing its derivative a superfluous final -*d*. Compounds are here considered to be the creation of new stems by the
union of roots or stems of words that exist, or presumably once
existed, independently. Creating stems or forms by adding to roots
or stems prefixes or suffixes that never had their own existence as
separate words does not strictly constitute making compound words.

Compounds have a wide range in their methods of formation.
They may result simply from the joining of two words, as in
English "shipmate" or Latin *animaduertō* = I notice. In the latter,
the final -*um* has been dropped or elided before the preposition
ad- = to, or toward, which is prefixed to the verb *uertō* = I turn,
so that the word literally means "I turn (my) mind towards." In
other compounds the union is no longer readily recognizable, as in
dēnuō = anew, which was originally *dē nouō* = out of (something) new. It is often hard to know whether to write one class of
compounds, called "syntactic" from a Greek adjective meaning
"put together," as two words or as one, like English "week end"
or Latin *senātūs cōnsultum* = decree of the senate, or *iūris prūdēns*
= (a person) learned in the law. Indeed such a word as *iūs iūran-
dum* = a sworn right, or oath, though often written as one word,

is declined in both parts. However *duouirī* = two men (serving as magistrates of an Italian town) developed two singular forms: *duouir* and, using the genitive plural of *duo*, *duumuir*. Adverbs like *magnopere* = very much and *tantopere* = so much are simply ablatives of manner, which have suffered loss or elision of the final long *-ō-* of the adjective. At the other extreme, it is hard to know when more closely joined compounds like *dēnuō* ceased to be regarded as two words and became one.

PREFIXING PREPOSITIONS AND OTHER PARTICLES

The particles that appear in classical Latin as prepositions are also the most frequent prefixes used in compounds, generally to form compound verbs from simple ones or to form compound verbal derivatives. It may be that the use of these particles as prefixes went back to a period in the development of Latin when their character as prepositions was not yet distinguished from that as adverbs. Thus from the simple verb *colō* = I cultivate derive, among other compounds, *incolō* = I cultivate in or on, and hence I inhabit, and a parallel first declension masculine noun *incola* = an inhabitant. The common adjective *incultus* might be taken as the passive perfect participle of *incolō* but is in fact formed by adding not the prepositional but a negative prefix *in-*, so that *incultus* = uncultivated, either literally or in terms of mind or behavior.

A careful distinction should be made between these two prefixes *in-*, the prepositional and the negative. Here, as in the case of the preposition and conjunction *cum*, phonological development has produced forms of similar sound and spelling from different originals. The preposition *in* (or *en*) is common in the Indo-European languages. The negative prefix *in-* represents the zero grade of ablaut of the negative *ne*, namely a vocalic *n*, that is, *n* with a vowel sound. It appears in Greek as the so-called "alpha privative (taking away from)," namely the *a-* or *an-* in such words as *a-thanasia* = not death, or immortality, and *an-aisthēsia* = not feeling, or insensibility. It also appears in other Indo-European languages, for instance, in English and German as the negative prefix *un-*, as in "unknown."

Prepositional particles as prefixes may retain their prepositional sense and govern cases, particularly the dative or accusative. Frequently, however, they have their original adverbial connotation. For instance, verbs compounded with *circum-* = around, or about, may be followed by various types of accusative or be used absolutely. For example, *circumeō* = I go about, or I encircle, is followed in Plautus by an accusative, as in his *Menaechmi* 231, *omnēs circumīmus īnsulās* = we go about all the islands. In this phrase, since the simple verb *eō* is intransitive, the feminine accusative plural *īnsulās* is presumably in origin not a direct object but governed by the prepositional force of *circum*. Yet *circumcīdō* = I cut around, or trim, takes a direct object of the verb, as in *arbōrēs circumcīdunt* = they trim the trees, where the *circum-* is adverbial. Verbs compounded with *super-* = above are likely to be used absolutely, as *supersum* = I am above, hence I survive, or I remain. Nouns that follow such compounds are generally in the ablative or dative, not in the accusative. *Super-* may therefore be regarded as primarily an adverbial prefix.

Compounding a verb with a prepositional prefix may lead to a change of force or meaning. For instance, *ineō* = I enter upon originally took an accusative after the preposition *in-* = into compounded with it, but as with *circumeō*, the accusative came to be regarded as a direct object and the verb as transitive, as in *cōnsulātum iniit* = he entered (upon) the consulship. Most compound forms of the intransitive verb *eō* = I go thus acquired a transitive force, as in *mortem obeunt* = they undergo death.

Animaduertō = I notice illustrates a similar development. Originally *animum* was the direct object of *aduertō*, and a second accusative indicated the direction toward which the mind is turned; that is, it was governed by the preposition *ad-* = to, or toward, prefixed to the verb. But eventually *animaduertō* came to be regarded as a single verb and the second accusative as its direct object, the thing noticed.

Similarly, such a verb as *trādūcō* = I lead across takes in classical Latin a pseudo double accusative, one of which is the direct object of *dūcō* = I lead, and the other is governed by the preposition prefixed thereto, *trāns* (becoming *trā-*) = across, as in *mīlitēs pontem trādūcit* = he leads the soldiers across the bridge. This use of the accusative is not parallel to a real double accusative, such as appears in *mē sententiam rogat* = he asks me (for my) opinion.

Although most particles that appear as prefixes in compounds also are used by themselves as adverbs or prepositions, there are some prefixes which are not found in classical Latin as independent particles. One such is *ambi-* (*amb-, am-, an-*) = on both sides of, rather than around (*circum*), though it comes to have the second meaning, as in *ambeō* = I go around. A fourth declension noun *ambitus* from this verb originally meant "a going around," then "a going around to seek for votes," hence "a canvassing," and from this the feminine abstract *ambitiō* came to mean "ambition." The root in *ambi-* is the same as that in *ambō* = both, but they are parallel rather than formed either from the other. *Anceps* = double shows the most cut-down form of *ambi-* compounded with the root of *caput* = head. This latter root appears also in the similar adjective of one termination *praeceps* = forward on the head, or headlong. Another particle that occurs only as a prefix is *re-* (*red-*) = back, as in *reficiō* = I make again, or remake, and in *redeō* = I go back.

COMPOUNDING NOUNS, ADJECTIVES, ADVERBS, AND SUFFIXES

In compounds of which the first parts are stems of nouns or adjectives, any final vowel of the stem appears as short *-i-* before any initial consonant of the second part, as in *armiger* = armor bearer, from the noun stem *armo-* = arms and the root *ger-* = carry; and *agricola* = farmer, from the noun stem *agro-* (nom. sing. *ager*) = field and the root *col-* = cultivate. Before a vowel, the stem vowel is lost, as in *magnanimus, -ā, -um* = magnanimous, from the adjectival stem *magno-* = large and the noun root *animo-* = spirit, or mind. Consonant stems of the third declension occurring in the first part of a compound usually add a short *-i-* before an initial consonant of the second part, on the analogy of *i*-stems, as in *particeps* (an adjective of one termination) = sharing, from the noun stem *part-* = part and the verb root *cap-* (with ablaut to *cep-*) = taking. With *particeps* should be contrasted *anceps* = double, which both lacks the connecting *-i-* and derives its second half from a different root.

In general, the relationship between the components of such compounds may be of several types. In some compounds, the parts are simply added one to another, as in *suouetaurīlia* = a sacrifice of a swine, a sheep, and a bull, in which are run together the stems of *sūs* (genitive *suis*), *ouis*, and *taurus*, with the change of the *-i-* of *oui-* to *-e-*, the loss of the *-o-* of *tauro-*, and the addition of the adjectival suffix *-īlis* (*-e*) with a neuter plural ending to indicate that the adjective serves as a collective noun. This suffix, which indicates "pertaining to," is different from the adjectival suffix *-ilis*, *-e*, with a short first *-i-*, which gives the meaning "having the quality of," as in *frag-ilis* = having the quality of breaking, or breakable.

The cardinal numerals in the tens are, as in English, simply additive compounds. They merely combine the digits with "ten," as in *quattuordecim* = fourteen, where the final *-em* of *decem* has been reduced to *-im*.

Often the first part of a compound defines or modifies the second, like an adjective or adverb, as in *duouirī* = two men (magistrates); *lātifundium* = a wide estate, from the adjectival stem *lāto-* = wide and the noun stem *fundo-* = bottom, or piece of land, with a neuter abstract suffix *-ium*; and *beneuolēns* = well wishing, or benevolent, which simply combines the adverb *bene-* well and the present active participle of *uolō* = I wish. Or the first half stands in a quasi case relation to the second, as in the compounds *agricola* and *particeps*, in which the noun stems meaning "field" and "part" are in an objective relation to the verbal roots meaning "cultivate" and "take."

Compounds in which the main (second) part is a noun stem often become adjectives, denoting possession of the quality concerned, as does *magnanimus, -a, -um* = magnanimous and *anceps* = double, whose second parts are noun roots for "mind" and "head." So also do *ālipēs* = wing-footed, from *āla* = wing and *pēs* = foot; and *ūnoculus, -a, -um* = one-eyed, from *ūnus* = one and *oculus* = eye.

140

Latin compounds were formed not only by joining roots or stems but by adding to existing words suffixes of all sorts. Examples are the adjectival suffix *-ōso-* in the adjective *studiōsus* = studious, formed from the noun *studium* = zeal, or study; or the inceptive suffix *-sc-* in the verbs *discō* = I learn, *cognōscō* = I know, and many others. A common neuter suffix indicating means or instrument appears as either *-men* or *-mentum*, as in *agmen* = a means of leading, and hence a column (of soldiers or others), in which the root is *ag-* = lead; or in *frūmentum* = a means of enjoyment, and hence particularly grain supply, in which the root is *frū-* = make use of, or enjoy. The suffix *-tor* (feminine *-trix*) denotes agent, as in *uictor* = victor, from the root *uic-*, whose present *uincō* = I conquer shows an infix of *-n-*.

The formation of new words by suffixes was a process very similar to that of indicating moods, tenses, persons, or cases by the addition of suffixes called "endings." However, in the latter process the derivative verbal and noun forms remained closely attached to their basic words because of the recognizable and fixed patterns of declension or conjugation. Compounds in the strict sense often attained an alteration of form and an independence of significance quite removed from those of the prefixes, original stems, or suffixes that went into the formation of a given compound.

Whether or not Latin built up its vocabulary more readily by compounding simple words than does any other language would require elaborate statistical study, since compounding goes on continuously in all languages. Latin, however, because of its primitive isolation, had originally only a limited vocabulary as compared, say, with Greek. When it emerged as the language of the conquerors first of Italy and then of the Mediterranean, its inherent conservatism meant that the process of enriching its vocabulary to cope with more elaborate and varied concepts took the form of making compounds from its own roots, stems, prefixes, and suffixes rather than of creating wholly new words or of adopting terms from other tongues. Although borrowing from Greek was quite extensive, it was mostly for objects, practices, or concepts that the Romans took over from the Greeks, not for the new needs of vocabulary which their own expansion created for their language.

COMPOUNDS IN LATIN POETRY

The earliest Latin literature, which dates from the period of great expansion overseas during the second half of the third and the whole second century B.C., shows a marked fondness for elaborate compounds. This is notably true of the surviving comedies of Plautus (c. 251–184 B.C.) and of the extensive fragments from the epic and tragic works of his slightly younger contemporary Ennius (c. 239–169 B.C.). The great influence of Ennius made the use of compounds a permanent characteristic of poetic Latin, particularly in the epics of Lucretius (c. 94–55 B.C.) and of Vergil (70–19 B.C.).

For example, epic poets were fond of compounds in which the second parts were the verbal roots *fer-* and *ger-* = bear, or carry, as in *signifer, -era, -erum* = bearing signs, and hence, as a noun, a standard bearer, from *signum* = a sign and *fer-*; the rare adjective *glandifer, -era, -erum* = bearing acorns, from *glāns* (genitive *glandis*) = acorn and *fer-*; *armiger, -era, -erum* = bearing arms, from *arma* = arms and *ger-*; or *corniger, -era, -erum* = having horns, from *cornū* = horn and *ger-*.

Poets also employed compounds of two words, like *bellipotēns* = powerful in war, from *bellum* = war and *potēns* (an adjective of one termination) = powerful, or master of, whose root appears in the adjective *potis, -e* = master of, possessor of, and hence capable of, or possible. Two other examples are *montiuagus* = wandering on the mountains, from *mōns* (genitive *montis*) = mountain and the adjective *uagus, -a, -um* = wandering; and *bilinguis, -e* = two-tongued, or bilingual, which compounds a prefix *bi* = twice (with the same meaning as the adverb *bis*) and the stem of *lingua* = tongue, language.

In conclusion, the list of compounds of various types could be greatly extended. It testifies to the characteristic of Latin that what was presumably in origin a vocabulary limited to the needs of a small agricultural and pastoral community was adapted to the needs of an imperial state less by borrowing or by the introduction of new words than by the adaptation of existing words through the addition of prefixes and suffixes or through compounding.

XI

THE SYNTAX OF NOUNS

The word "syntax," from the Greek noun *suntaxis* = a putting together, or a putting in order, refers to that part of grammar which describes how words in their various morphological forms are assembled to express larger units of thought called "phrases," "clauses," or "sentences." The word "phrase" comes from the Greek noun *phrasis* = speech, or utterance, and hence something said. "Clause" comes from a late Latin noun *clausa*, which may be a feminine singular noun of the first declension taken from the neuter plural *clausa* of the passive perfect participle *clausus* of the verb *claudō* = I close, or I shut up, or off. If so, the feminine noun *clausa* would mean a group of words which, if isolated from other words, still reproduces a coherent thought. Or the feminine noun *clausa* may be a shortened form of the rhetorical term *clausula* = the end (of a work or a sentence). This in turn is a feminine diminutive noun from the same passive perfect participle *clausus*. The rhetorician Quintilian, writing at the close of the first century A.D., uses *clausula* in his textbook on oratory, the *Īnstitūtiō Ōrātōria* IX 4.67–75, to mean a series of words that are pronounced together without taking breath and which afford coherent sense without necessarily constituting a completed thought. In particular the term was used for the concluding words or phrase of sentences which in rhetorical Latin were supposed to follow certain metrical patterns. In Roman legal writers, a *clausula* is a particular proviso or condition within a general enactment. Perhaps from a combination of these two uses, *clausula* was defined by an early mediaeval grammarian called Audax as follows: *Clausula quid est? Compositiō uerbōrum plausibilī strūctūrā ad exitium termināta* = What is a *clausula?* A combining of words with a plausible (grammatical) structure (and) brought to an end, thus presumably expressing a complete thought. The word "sentence" comes from the noun *sententia* = significance, or meaning, and hence refers to a complete meaningful expression. It is often used for a pithy or wise apothegm.

In syntax, a phrase has the restricted meaning of a group of words related either by their forms (inflected cases or verb forms) or by certain words in the phrase, such as conjunctions or prepositions, so as to constitute a unit of sense but not to express a complete thought. A clause expresses a complete thought; that is, it normally has a subject and a verb, whether the verb has an object or merely denotes an action or state in relation to the subject. There may also be modifiers and prepositional phrases within the clause. The thought expressed in a clause may be subordinated to or made a part of a larger thought by some such word as a subordinating conjunction or a relative pronoun, adjective, or adverb. A clause may also be self-standing or independent but closely connected to another clause by a coordinating conjunction, so that the two or more successive clauses form parts of one general thought. When more than two clauses are strung together coordinately, the connecting conjunction "and" may be omitted; in modern texts its omission is indicated by a comma.

The line between a clause and a sentence is not well defined, but in general a sentence expresses a complete and independent thought. Either it may be simple, that is, itself a complete clause but not connected with any other clause; or it may be complex, that is, containing several subordinate or coordinate clauses. Roman rhetoricians, such as Quintilian in his *Inst. Ōr.* IX 4.124, use for "sentence" the Greek noun *periodos* (in Latin, *periodus*), literally meaning "a going around," from Greek *peri* = around and (*h*)*odos* = a road, but defined in rhetoric as a term meaning an utterance having in itself a beginning and end and a size easily taken in at a glance.

The term "period" is often used in English for a sentence, as well as regularly for the point placed at its end to indicate that the sense has come to completion, that is, to a full stop.

The Greeks and Romans did not punctuate very fully or very consistently. The point or period was used, but other punctuation was casual. Nevertheless, the names of the other usual modern marks, which were formalized during the Middle Ages, came, like "period," from Greek terms for smaller syntactical units. The Greek noun *komma,* from the verb *koptō* = I cut, means something cut off, and hence, in grammar, a cut-off or short clause or phrase, to be separated from the rest of the sentence by a slight pause, indicated in modern writing by the mark called a "comma." The Greek noun *kōlon* = limb, or member, came to refer in the study of the meters of verse to a metrical unit of several feet and in rhetoric to a clause within a sentence or period. Thus the punctuation marks colon and semicolon (a half, or lesser colon) serve to separate off more important divisions in a sentence than does the comma, but divisions that do not express so complete or full a thought as does a sentence punctuated at the end with a full stop or period.

Sentences may be put together into larger sequences of thought, as into a paragraph. This term derives from a Greek adjective *paragraphos* = written beside. It is an adjective of only two terminations; that is, the ending *-os* may be in agreement with either a masculine or feminine nominative singular noun, in this case with *grammē* = line, understood. Originally the *paragraphos grammē* was a line put in the margin of the text to mark a change of speaker in drama. Later *paragraphos* alone was used for a line marking off a major section of a prose text. Eventually it came to mean the section so marked off. In modern texts a paragraph is no longer indicated by a line but by setting its first word in from the left margin, or indenting it. Grammatically, however, the sentence, rather than the clause or colon, on the one hand, or the paragraph, on the other, is the largest unit of words that expresses a complete thought and in which the component words are put together in relationships expressed by their forms, such as endings and other changes, or by connecting words.

The syntax of a noun describes the uses of its various cases in a phrase, clause, or sentence. The syntax of pronouns and other words, phrases, or clauses serving as nouns may be regarded as the same as that of nouns. Adjectives have no syntax independent of the nouns, pronouns, or other words, phrases, or clauses serving as nouns that they modify, except when they themselves are used as nouns. Other words may serve as nouns, such as verbal nouns like the infinitive. In the sentence *amīcōs amāre bonum est* = to love (one's) friends is good (or a good thing) the infinitive phrase *amīcōs amāre* serves as a neuter nominative singular noun modified by the predicate adjective *bonum*. Frequently clauses, particularly those introduced by *ut* = that, or so that, serve as nouns and are called "substantive clauses," as in *mihi persuādet ut hoc faciam* = he persuades me to (literally that I should) do this, in which the substantive clause of purpose *ut hoc faciam* serves as the object of the main verb *persuādet*. In the passive form, *mihi persuādētur ut hoc faciam* = it is persuaded to me that I should do this, or I am persuaded to do this, the clause *ut hoc faciam* is in Latin the subject of the main passive verb *persuādētur*.

Each of the five or seven Latin cases denotes a different relationship of a noun to other words or to the whole idea being expressed. Although the range of connotations for the various cases is considerable, they all developed from a few relatively simple meanings, generally only one for each case.

NOMINATIVE

The nominative case, so called from the passive perfect participle *nōminātus* of the verb *nōminō* = I name, names the center of interest of the sentence, called the "subject." The term "subject" derives from the passive perfect participle *subiectus* of the verb *subiciō* = I throw under, because it indicates what the speaker puts at the base of his statement, the person or thing about whom or which he makes it. A nominative noun may serve as subject of the three kinds of statement, namely those in which the subject is the source of action (active voice, transitive or intransitive), those in which the subject is affected by the action (passive voice), and those in which the subject is said to be in some state or condition (statements of being or becoming). In a fourth type of statement, which is really a subdivision of the first (active), the subject acts upon himself (middle), but Latin has no independent forms for this voice.

In statements of being or becoming there may be a nominative form in the predicate, a term formed from the passive perfect participle *praedicātus* of the verb *praedicō* = I proclaim, which in turn is compounded from a form of *dīcō* = I say which has a short *-i-* in its stem. Thus the predicate is the statement proclaimed, or made, about the subject. In the sentences *Tarquinius rēx Rōmae fuit* = Tarquin was king of (or locative at) Rome and *Cicerō cōnsul creātus est* = Cicero was (or has been) elected consul, *Tarquinius* and *Cicero* are the subjects and the rest of the sentences are the predicates. The Latin word order places a predicate nominative, or a predicate adjective, before rather than after the verb, contrary to the English order; these are nevertheless parts of the predicate.

GENITIVE

The genitive, a term formed from the passive perfect participle *genitus* of the verb *gignō* = I bear, or I give birth to, takes its name from the concept of source or possession. But in fact the most general meaning of the genitive is to define and delimit the range of reference of another noun or verb; it is often described as the case indicating the area in which something else falls. Commonly it indicates possession, since what is possessed falls within the area of the owner's influence or control, as in *liber Marcī* = Marcus' book.

Also frequent is its use to denote the whole of which something or somebody is a part, as in *pars cīuitātis* = part of the state. This genitive is called "partitive," a term formed from the passive perfect participle *partītus* of the verb *partiō* (or deponent *partior*) = I share, or I divide. It therefore indicates that which is divided in relation to the noun on which it depends. It also came to be used with verbs expressing the concepts of filling, lacking, thirsting, desiring, and even remembering or forgetting, namely verbs whose action might make the subject participate in the concept expressed by the genitive noun. A common use of the partitive genitive is after neuter singular indefinite nouns, as in *nihil nouī* = nothing of new, instead of *nihil nouum* = nothing new; or *plūs honōris* = more of honor, instead of *plūs honor* = more honor.

The genitive is also employed to indicate a quality in which someone shares. The genitive of quality or description normally modifies a person rather than a thing and is used of inner or essential characteristics, as in *uir maximae uirtūtis* = a man of utmost courage, as against the ablative of quality or description, which denotes more external or incidental characteristics. However, the genitive of quality may be used to indicate measure, as in *mūrus decem pedum* = a wall of ten feet, that is, ten feet high; and in the adjectival phrases *eius modī* = of that sort, equivalent to *tālis* = such, and *cūius modī* = of what sort, equivalent to *quālis* = what sort, as in *eius modī rēs sunt ut magnā desperātiōne affectus sim* = things are of such a sort (namely so bad) that I am affected (overcome) by great despair. *Desperātiōne* is the ablative of means, and *affectus sim* is the first person singular passive perfect subjunctive in a result clause in primary sequence with the perfect used to denote a present state.

The genitive may also indicate the substance or material of which a thing consists, as in *talentum aurī* = a talent of gold. In this use, the genitive indicates the general substance of which some particular item forms a part, or is a portion. However, the material of which something consists is more commonly given by an ablative, usually with a preposition such as *de* or *ex* = out of, from. Thus the basic concept expressed by this ablative of material is one of source, that wherefrom something is derived or made.

Similarly the neuter singular of certain adjectives that indicate indefinite quantity may be used as a noun in the genitive to indicate price, though price is generally expressed by an ablative of means. For example, *est mihi tantī* means "it is to me of so much, or it is worth much to me." Occasionally a specific noun appears in the genitive of price, as in the second and third verses of the fifth poem of Catullus, a contemporary of Cicero: *rūmōrēsque senum seuēriōrum omnēs ūnius aestimēmus assis* = and let us value all the gossip of severe old men as (worth only) one ass. The ass was a small bronze coin of slight value. *Seuēriōrum* is the masculine genitive plural (agreeing with *senum*) of the comparative adjective in *-ior, -ius* used intensively and should be distinguished from the masculine genitive plural of the positive, *seuērōrum* without the *-i-*. And *aestimēmus* is first person plural of the active present subjunctive of a first conjugation verb used in an exhortation, namely a hortatory subjunctive.

The genitive often shows the subject or object of a feeling or action both of which may be regarded as basically possessive. Thus *amor patris* may mean either "a father's love (of his children)" or "(children's) love of a father." The context normally indicates in which direction the emotion moves. For example, it is almost certain that *amor patriae* means "love of (one's) country," whereas *odium Cicerōnis in Antōnium* means "Cicero's hatred for (literally toward) Antony," In the latter example a prepositional phrase is used in place of a second, objective genitive to distinguish the object of hatred from its source.

The genitive is used with many adjectives to show the object of reference, as in *iūris perītus* = skilled in law, or *plēnus fideī* (post-Augustan *-eī*) = full of good faith. This use was extended in poetry and imperial prose to many adjectives and is called a "genitive of specification," as in Horace (65–8 B.C.), *Odes* III 30.10, *pauper aquae* = poor in water. The usual earlier construction would be an ablative of specification, *pauper aquā* = poor in respect to water.

The genitive is often used with verbs to indicate not the person or thing directly affected by the action but the area within which the action falls. Such genitives after verbs may sometimes be classified as objective. *Meminī* = I remember and *oblīuīscor* = I forget take the accusative when they are used literally but the genitive when the meaning is "I am mindful, or forgetful, of someone or something." For instance, *auum meum meminī* = I remember my grandfather, but *hūmānae īnfīrmitātis meminī* = I am mindful of human infirmity. Compounds of *moneō* = I advise which mean "I remind," such as *admoneō,* take the accusative of the person reminded but the genitive for that of which one is reminded, except when this is a neuter pronoun, which goes in the accusative. For example, *mē officī meī admonet* = he reminds me of my duty, whereas *quod uōs lēx commonet* = (that of) which the law reminds you. Verbs of feeling take a genitive of the object of the feeling or, when used impersonally, of its cause; as *Cicerōnis misereor* = I pity Cicero, and *mē uītae taedet* = it tires me of life, or I am tired of life.

Genitives with other verbs are harder to classify. Verbs which mean "I accuse, condemn, or acquit" take a genitive of value or price to indicate the charge or penalty. For instance, *mē furtī arguit* = he accuses me of theft, or *eum pecūniae damnat* = he condemns him to a money (payment). Verbs signifying plenty usually take an ablative of means and those signifying want an ablative of separation, but both may be followed by a genitive, as in *auxilī egeō* = I need help. *Interest* = it is in the interest of and *rēfert* = it is to the advantage of, or it concerns, take a genitive of the person involved. These are not true impersonal verbs since the subject is that which concerns one or is to one's advantage, as *reī pūblicae interest Catilīnam morīrī* = it is to the advantage of the state that Catiline die, where the infinitive clause *Catilīnam morīrī* is subject of *interest*. Further examples of genitives with verbs may be found in any systematic Latin grammar.

Thus, although the uses of the genitive were in classical Latin much extended, particularly with adjectives and verbs, the case always retained something of the original concept of the larger sphere within which something less is included.

DATIVE

The term "dative" derives from the passive perfect participle *datus* of the Latin verb *dō* = I give. The term indicates that the case concerned was for the Romans primarily that of the indirect object, the person or thing to whom or to which something is given. More generally, the dative case indicates indirect implication in, or concern with, the action or state signified by the verb.

As the name suggests, a major use of the dative is to show the indirect object of the verbal action, that is, the person or thing toward which the object of the verb is directed by its action, as in *mihi librum dat* = he gives me a book. Often a dative of indirect object may be used with a verb connoting motion, as an alternative to an accusative of limit of motion (place to which), with or without a directional preposition. For example, *mihi litterās mīsit* = he sent a letter to me, that is, for my advantage or interest, whereas *litterās Rōmam mīsit,* or *litterās ad Pompēium mīsit* = he sent a letter to (in the direction of) Rome, or to Pompey. This use of the dative seems to be different from a rare and poetic use actually to indicate the place to which, as in Vergil (70–19 B.C.), *Aeneid* V 451, *it clāmor caelō* = a shout goes up to the sky. This dative may have originated in a poetic personification of the place to which and may therefore be a sort of dative of advantage. Indeed the general use of the dative after verbs of motion should probably be classified not as indirect object but as reference, that is, as indicating a person related indirectly, rather than directly, to the action of the verb in senses other than as indirect object.

Under the concept of reference fall many connotations of the dative. The dative of advantage or of disadvantage denotes the person for whose benefit or harm the action is directed, as in *laudat mihi frātrem* = he praises (my) brother for my sake, compared to the possessive adjective in *laudat frātrem meum* = he praises my brother. It would be incorrect to translate the first example as "he praises (my) brother to me," since "to praise" is not the sort of meaning to suggest an indirect object. In Latin *laudāre* would be construed with a preposition, either *apud* = in front of, followed by the accusative of a noun or pronoun, or *cōram* = in the presence of, followed by the ablative; that is, *laudat apud mē* (or *cōram mē*) *frātrem meum* = he praises before me (or in my presence) my brother. The accusative and ablative of the first and second singular personal pronouns have the same forms: *mē* and *tē*.

Closely allied to the dative of advantage or disadvantage is the so-called dative of possession, which is very common with the verb *sum* = I am, as in *liber est mihi* = there is a book to (or for) me, or I have a book (available). This differs in sense from *librum habeō* = I have (possess) a book, though it is often used as an equivalent. This dative of possession occurs with the dative of purpose after *sum* in a construction known as the "double dative," as in *hoc mihi cūrae est* = this is to me for a care, or I am worried about this. The dative of advantage or disadvantage may also be used instead of a possessive adjective when a part of the body is the direct object, as in *manum illī uulnerāuit* = he wounded the hand to him (that is, to his hurt), which brings the person indirectly concerned more to the fore than would a genitive, *manum ēius uulnerāuit* = he wounded his hand.

A dative of reference may be used after a verb meaning to take away instead of an ablative of separation with a preposition. For example, *hunc mihi terrōrem ēripe* really means "take this fear away as far as I am concerned," not "from me." Or it may be used with the gerundive, with the passive periphrastic (the gerundive plus forms of *sum* = I am), or in poetry with the passive perfect system in place of an ablative of agent with a preposition. For instance, *urbs nobīs capienda est* properly means "the city is to be captured as far as we are concerned," not "by us." Thus the terms applied to various uses of the dative of reference are really misnomers since these datives do not in fact connote possession, separation, or agency but always the person indirectly concerned in the action.

A faded variety of the dative of reference is sometimes called "ethical," an adjective formed from the Greek adjective *ēthikos* = moral, or concerning character. It was apparently so called because it indicates a certain emotional interest on the part of the person placed in the dative. For example, in Horace, *Epistles* I 3.15, *quid mihi Celsus agit* connotes "what is Celsus doing? I am interested." This expresses a more personal concern on Horace's part than would the possessive adjective, *quid meus Celsus agit?* = what is my (friend) Celsus doing?

The dative may also indicate the purpose or end of an action. This dative is commonly of an abstract noun and often joined with the dative of a noun or pronoun showing the person affected, that is, in the double dative construction, as in *suīs salūtī fuit* = he was for safety to his (men), or he saved his troops. The dative of more concrete nouns is used to show purpose in a few military expressions, such as *locum castrīs dēlēgit* = he chose a site for the camp, and freely in poetry, as in Vergil, *Aeneid* III 109, *optāuit locum regnō* = he selected a site for (his) kingdom. *Optō* may mean "I choose" as well as "I desire." The dative is similarly used with adjectives to denote that to which the quality signified by the

152

adjective is directed or the like, as in *castrīs idōneus locus* = a place suited for a camp.

The dative follows many verbs compounded with prepositions as a dative of indirect object. It is also used with a number of verbs which are transitive in English but intransitive in Latin so that they cannot have a direct object. These verbs are commonly given in grammars as those meaning "favor, help, please, trust and their opposites; believe, persuade, command, obey, serve, resist, envy, threaten, pardon, spare." However not all verbs with these meanings take the dative; some are transitive. For example, *subueniō* = I come (to help) takes the dative, but *iuuō* = I help takes the accusative; or *imperō* = I command takes the dative, but *iubeō* = I order takes the accusative.

These various connotations of the dative stem from the primary meaning of indirect concern with the action. All might properly be called "reference," though here they are roughly classified as indirect object, reference, and purpose.

ACCUSATIVE

The accusative derives its name from the passive perfect participle *accūsātus* of the Latin verb *accūsō* = I call to account, or I accuse. This verb in turn is compounded from the preposition *ad* = toward, or to, and a verbal root related to *causa* = a cause, or a (legal) process (or case). The Latin phrase *casus accūsātiuus* = accusative case was a mistranslation of the Greek *aitiatikē ptōsis*, in which the noun *ptōsis* = case and the adjective *aitiatikē* was mistakenly derived by the translator from a verb meaning "I accuse"; in fact it came from a noun *aitia* = cause and signified that the noun in the accusative was whatever the verb caused. The Roman translator may have thought of action primarily as legal and thus generalized the object of an accusation into the object of any action.

The words "object" and "objective" are indeed more general and suitable for this case, since they are formed from the passive perfect participle *obiectus* of the verb *obiciō* = I throw (or put) in front of. These terms indicate that the noun in this case is that which is put in front of or in the way of the action of the verb, as its recipient. Hence the accusative case is adverbial and indicates the goal or limit of the action that originates from the subject. English textbooks, more logically than American ones, place the accusative immediately after the nominative in examples, or paradigms, of declensions. In Latin, the accusative is most familiar as the case of the direct object of a verb, but it also has other uses.

The accusative may extend the concept inherent in the verb by making it explicit. For example, in *carmen canit* = he sings a song, the song is not so much the direct object of the act of singing as the content of the act itself. Such an accusative is called "cognate," meaning related to the verbal concept, or "inner," meaning internal to the verbal action. It is sometimes hard to determine whether an accusative is objective or cognate. For example, in *carmen canit*, the *carmen* may be regarded as cognate, but in *laudēs ac uirtūtēs ueterum canit* = he sings the praises and virtues of the ancients, the *laudēs ac uirtūtēs* are probably objects.

Certain classes of verbs take two accusatives. For example, in *Cicerōnem cōnsulem creāuērunt* = they elected Cicero consul, *cōnsulem* is not in apposition with *Cicerōnem* but is predicate to it. Verbs meaning "ask" or "teach" may take a double accusative, as in *puerōs linguam Latīnam docet* = he teaches the children the Latin language (literally tongue); or in Horace, *Odes* II 16.1, *ōtium dīuōs rogat* = he asks peace (from) the gods, or he asks the gods (for) peace. Often with verbs of asking, however, the source is in the ablative with a separative preposition, as in *pācem ā Rōmānīs petunt* = they seek peace from the Romans. Verbs compounded with prepositions may take a direct object and a second accusative, which originally followed the preposition but came to be regarded as independent, as in *Caesar mīlitēs flūmen trādūxit* = Caesar led (his) troops across the river.

The subject of an infinitive, unless the infinitive is used historically as an independent verb, is regularly in the accusative. This use perhaps originated from a construction in which the accusative and the infinitive stood in independent relations to the main verb, the first as object and the second as complementary, filling out the meaning of the verb. Thus *cōgō tē abīre* may initially have meant "I force you to a going away," inasmuch as the infinitive was originally the locative of a verbal noun used adverbially. Later the *tē* became closely associated with the *abīre* and the whole phrase was regarded as the object of *cōgō*. From this the accusative was generalized as the case for the subject for an infinitive, in whatever manner the whole infinitive clause was used.

The accusative seems to have had a second function besides that of being direct object, namely to indicate the limit, goal, or extent of motion in time or space. Classical Latin still used without a preposition the accusative of limit of motion, often called the "accusative of place to which," when the place concerned was a town, a small island (because small islands had only one town, of the same name as the island), or the nouns *domus* (genitive *-ūs*) = house, or home, and *rūs* (genitive *rūris*) = country (in contrast to city). Normally, however, a directional preposition—most frequently *ad* = toward, or to, or *in* = into, or to—was used before an accusative of limit of motion.

The same type of accusative appears in the use of the accusative of the supine with *eō* = I go, as in *mercātum it* = he goes to a marketing (not to market). Moreover, the accusative of extent of time or space, as in *annōs decem uīxit* = he lived ten years, may be an extension of the accusative of limit of motion or it may be an extension of the cognate accusative under the influence of such a phrase as *longam uītam uīxit* = he lived a long life. The accusative after prepositions appears to have developed as a means of making more precise the relation of the accusative of limit of motion to the verb. For example, *ad urbem uēnit* was clearer than *urbem uēnit* = he came to the city.

Latin developed a number of special uses of the accusative. One was the use adverbially of the neuter accusative singular of many adjectives and of all comparative adjectives. In classical Latin some special uses of the accusative had probably come to be regarded as adverbial. For instance, in the phrase *id temporis* = at that (of) time, the neuter accusative singular *id* is adverbial; the construction with the partitive genitive *temporis* was probably inherited in classical Latin from an earlier stage in the development of the language in which the accusative was one of specification. The construction resembles the use of a partitive genitive with neuter singular indefinite nouns instead of an adjective and noun. Another adverbial accusative is *uicem*, as in *meam uicem* = on my part (literally, turn); or *Marcī uicem* = on Marcus' part.

The accusative occurs regularly in exclamations, presumably because some verb is to be understood, as in *mē miserum* = unhappy me, *Ō fortūnātam rem pūblicam* = O fortunate state, or *prō deum fidem* = by the (good) faith of the gods. In this last, the *prō* is not the preposition but an exclamatory particle which also occurs with the nominative, and *deum* shows the original genitive masculine plural ending of the second declension, which in classical Latin was generally replaced by *-ōrum*.

Preliterary Latin may have used the cognate or inner accusative to indicate that in respect to which an action took place. In classical Latin this function was normally performed by the ablative of specification. However the neuter singular of pronouns continued to be used thus, in an adverbial fashion, as in *id misera maesta est* = (as respects) that, the unhappy girl is sorry; or in such a phrase as *nescio quid trīstis est* = he is sad about something or other, in which *nescio quid* = I do not know what, with the long *-ō* of *nesciō* shortened by iambic shortening, has come to mean "something or other." A certain type of clause introduced by *quod* stood to the main clause as an adverbial accusative of specification, as in *quod scrībis gaudeō* = (as to the fact) that you write, I am glad. Such *quod* clauses readily developed a causal connotation.

Common in classical Latin poetry is an accusative resembling one of specification but probably borrowed from the Greek and called "synecdochical," a term derived from the Greek noun *synekdochē*, applied to a rhetorical figure by which part of the whole is used for the whole, as in the English "fifty sail" for "fifty ships." The synecdochical accusative is somewhat different in concept. It indicates the part of the body affected by an action, as in *manūs nectuntur* = their hands are bound, or literally they are bound as to the hands. In Greek, this accusative is a regular construction corresponding to the Latin ablative of specification. The synecdochical accusative is probably distinct from the accusative used after a passive verb when this has a middle meaning, as in *ferrum cingitur* = he girds on (his) sword (literally, iron), whether the latter use is original to Latin or borrowed from Greek.

In sum, the various uses of the accusative, apart from those imitated from Greek, may be reduced to two primary connotations: that of the object of verbal action and that of the limit of motion. These in turn may originally have been identical, since the object of an action is, in a sense, its limit or end, so that in *mē amat* = he (or she) loves me, the *mē* is the place where the act of loving ends, somewhat as in *Rōmam it* = he goes to Rome, *Rōmam* is the end of the act of going.

ABLATIVE

Of all the Latin cases, the ablative affords the greatest variety of uses. It absorbed in Latin the functions of three originally distinct cases. The ablative proper denotes separation, and its name derives from the passive perfect participle *ablātus*, which is used as that of the verb *auferō* = I take away. The form *lātus, -a, -um* = lifted up, or carried, comes from a root *tul-*, which is related to *tollō* = I lift, or bear. The root *tul-* was reduced to zero ablaut to yield *tl-*. Since the Romans found *tl* difficult to pronounce, the *t-* was dropped. To the *l-* was added a long *-ā-* and the ending for the passive perfect participle *-tus, -a, -um*. This process produced *lātus*, which was used as the passive perfect participle of both *tollo* and *ferō*. Besides its separative connotation, the ablative has absorbed two other originally distinct instrumental and locative cases, though a few distinct locative forms survive in Latin.

The ablative of separation may be used alone, particularly with verbs in which the basic meaning is strongly separative or which are compounded with a separative proposition, as in *oculīs sē prīuāuit* = he deprived himself of (literally from) eyes, or *cōnsulātū abiit* = he left the consulship. With compound verbs an ablative of separation is often used without a separative preposition such as *ā (ab)* = from, *dē* = down from, or *ē (ex)* = out from when the meaning is figurative, but a preposition is regularly used when the separation is literal. Thus the separation is figurative in *uītā excessit* = he went out from life, or he died, but literal in *ex urbe excessit* = he went out from the city. The same types of words that are used without a directional preposition in the accusative of place to which are also used without a separative preposition in the ablative of place from which. These are names of towns and small islands, and *domus* and *rūs*. Adjectives denoting "freedom from or want of" are followed by an ablative of separation, as in *līberīs orbus* = bereft of children.

There are several extensions of the ablative of separation. The ablative may indicate source, as in *Ioue nātus* = born from Jupiter; or material, for which, however, a separative preposition is common, as in *ex aere cōnstat* = it consists (or is made) of (literally from) bronze; or cause, with or without a preposition, as in *irā ardet* = he burns with (because of) anger, or *certīs dē causīs* = for valid reasons. The ablative is used after a comparative (of comparison), as in *Cicerōne ēloquentior* = more eloquent than Cicero, where the concept is that the comparative degree removes the quality from, or further than, that with which something is compared. The ablative may show an agent, always with the preposition *ā* (*ab*), as in *urbs ā mīlitibus capta est* = the city was (or has been) taken by the soldiers.

With respect to the ablative of comparison, an alternative construction is to use *quam* = than followed by the other member of the comparison in the same case as is the first member, as in *illa studiōsior est quam ille* = she is more studious than he. With respect to the ablative of the agent, three points are significant. Though the dative of reference used with the gerundive is often called the "dative of agent," in fact it gives a very different connotation from that of the agent as the source of the action, which is expressed by the ablative of agent. The ablative of agent is always used of a person or a personified object; things as instruments are put in the ablative of means or instrument without a preposition. In Latin of the late Republic and Empire, the agent came often to be regarded as a vehicle or instrument of the action, rather than as its source, so that *per* and the accusative could be used, as in *per explōrātōres Caesar certior factus est* = Caesar was informed by (literally through the instrumentality of) scouts, instead of *ab explōrātōribus*.

The ablative of means or instrument denotes that whereby the action is performed, which is always a thing, never a person. It is regularly used with verbs, as in *certantēs pugnīs* = fighting with (their) fists, and may be used with adjectives whose meaning is related to verbs, as in *uīta plēna uoluptātibus* = a life filled with pleasures. Five deponent verbs, basically middle in meaning, are followed by an ablative of means in Latin, whereas in English they are transitive and take a direct object, namely *ūtor* = I use, *fruor* = I enjoy, *fungor* = I perform, *potior* = I possess, and *uescor* = I eat (or feed on). Of these, *potior* may also take a genitive, as in *potīrī rērum* = to be master of affairs, or commonly of the state.

From the ablative of means developed a number of related ablatival constructions. The ablative of price closely resembles means, as in *agrum uendidit sex dēnāriīs* = he sold the field for six denarii. A denarius was a silver coin about the size of a United States ten-cent piece but in Roman times of much greater purchasing power. Price may also be indicated by the neuter singular genitive, used as a noun, of certain adjectives that signify indefinite quantity, as in *ille tibi tantī fuit?* = was he of so much (value) to you?

Two other constructions derived from the ablative of means are preceded and governed by the preposition *cum* = with. The first is the ablative of accompaniment, as in *cum mīlitibus uēnit* = he came with soldiers (or the soldiers), or in *pāx uōbīscum* = peace (be) with you. In the latter the *cum* becomes a postpositive enclitic attached to the personal pronoun *uōbīs*. The second is the ablative of manner, as in *cum celeritāte uēnit* = he came with speed. When the ablative noun in this construction is modified by an adjective, the *cum* occurs between them, as in *magnā cum celeritāte uēnit* = he came with great speed. The context must serve to determine which of the two connotations, of accompaniment or of manner, is appropriate to a given phrase containing *cum* and an ablative.

The ablative of degree of difference, also a development of the ablative of means, is employed after comparative adjectives, adverbs, or other words implying a comparison to show by how much more or less somebody or something differs from somebody or something else, stated or implied, as in Vergil, *Eclogues* IV 1, *paulō maiōra canāmus* = let us sing things greater by a little, or somewhat greater, with the implied comparison "than we have been singing." The ablative of degree of difference is common in such phrases as *multīs ante annīs* = before by many years, or many years earlier; *ante* is here the adverb, not the preposition. The ablative of degree of difference should be distinguished by the context from the ablative of comparison, which is a form of the ablative of separation. For example, in the sentence *Cicerō ēloquentior Caesare erat* = Cicero was more eloquent than Caesar, the ablative *Caesare* is of comparison, whereas in *Cicerō multō ēloquentior erat* = Cicero was more eloquent by much, or much more eloquent, the ablative *multō* shows degree of difference. The two constructions may be combined, as in *Cicerō multō ēloquentior Caesare erat* = Cicero was much more eloquent than Caesar.

From the ablative of means developed two further constructions, the ablatives of description or quality and of specification. The ablative of description indicates an external or adventitious characteristic or quality of somebody or something, as in *mulier eximiā pulchritūdine* = a woman of exceptional beauty. Inner or essential qualities are expressed by the genitive of quality or description, as in *mulier magnae sapientiae* = a woman of great wisdom. The ablative of specification closely resembles that of description, but it usually occurs with an adjective modifying that to which the quality is attributed or with a verb of which the subject has the quality. Thus in *mulier eximiā pulchritūdine* = a woman exceptional for (or in respect to) beauty, the *eximiā* is feminine nominative singular agreeing with *mulier*, whereas in the preceding illustration of the ablative of description, *eximiā* is feminine ablative singular in agreement with *pulchritūdine*. The distinction between these two ablatival constructions is easier when that of which the quality is predicated differs in gender from the quality, since the endings of the adjectives then differ according to their agreement in gender, as in *homō eximiā altitūdine* = a man of exceptional height, as against *homō eximius altitūdine* = a man exceptional for (his) height.

The ablative of specification with a verb is illustrated by *totidem annīs mihi aetāte praestabāt* = he excelled me in (respect to) age by just as many years. In this sentence, *totidem* is an indeclinable adjective modifying *annīs*, and it is compounded from *tot* = as many plus a connecting short *-i-* and a demonstrative suffix *-dem*. *Annīs* is an ablative of degree of difference with the comparative concept in *praestābat* = I stand in front of, or I excel; *mihi* is a dative of reference used after *praestābat* as an intransitive verb, though *praestō* may also be transitive and followed by a direct object in the accusative; and *aetāte* is the ablative of specification showing wherein one person excelled the other.

The common Latin construction called the "ablative absolute" is of uncertain and perhaps mixed origin. It seems to be a special type of ablative of accompaniment or attendant circumstance, perhaps with some influence of the locative ablative. In this construction, a noun or pronoun with a participle in agreement stands independently of any syntactical connection with the rest of the sentence, and hence is absolute. Often two nouns or a noun and an adjective thus stand independently, in which case the nonexistent present active participle of *sum* = I am is to be supplied mentally, though presumably it was never required syntactically. The relation of the thought that the ablative absolute expresses to the rest of the sentence varies greatly: circumstance, time, cause, concession, or condition. The precise connotation must generally be supplied from the context of thought. For instance, *litterīs acceptīs, Caesar nuntium mīsit* may mean "when, or after, the letters were received, that is, after he had received the letters, Caesar sent a messenger"; equally it may connote "because the letters had been received," or even "although the letters had been received." Two nouns in the ablative absolute are regularly used to show who was in office when something happened, as in *Cicerōne cōnsule* = when Cicero was consul, or *Caesare imperātōre* = under Caesar as general.

Occasionally in imperial Latin a clause takes the place of the noun in an ablative absolute, as in *incertō quid peterent* = since it was uncertain what they were asking (or should ask). English occasionally uses a similar absolute construction, such as "this being so." However the Latin ablative absolute should normally be rendered by an appropriate subordinate clause in English. Occasionally the passive perfect participle can be rendered as an active participle in agreement with the subject, as in *hostēs, intermissō spatiō, impetum fēcērunt* = the enemy, pausing for a while (literally when an interval had been interposed), made an attack.

The third main type of ablative, the locative, is most common as the ablatives of place where and of time when. The ablative of place where requires the preposition *in* to govern the ablative, except when the place is the name of a town or small island, or *domus* and *rūs*. These are the same types of words that do not require a preposition in the constructions accusative of place to which and ablative of separation or place from which. Time when is expressed by an ablative without a preposition, as in *illō diē* = on that day. An ablative alone may also indicate time within which, and this use should be carefully distinguished from the accusative of extent of time or time how long. Thus *diēbus tribus uentūrī sunt* = they are about to come within three days may be contrasted with *diēs trēs prōgressī sunt* = they proceeded for three days. By the first statement, some point of time within the total is indicated; by the second, the whole duration. There is no ablative of space within which corresponding to that of time within which, as place where (usually with *in*) corresponds to time when (ablative alone).

A locative ablative is used with three adjectives that have verbal overtones: *contentus, -a, -um* = content (with); *frētus, -a, -um* = supported (on, or by); and *laetus, -a, um* = happy (with). Two further adjectives, *dignus, -a, -um* = worthy (of) and *indignus, -a, -um* = unworthy (of) are also construed with an ablative but after them the ablative is probably one of specification.

In sum, the many uses of the ablative in classical Latin developed from its own original separative connotation and from the connotations of the two previously different cases that it absorbed: the instrumental and the locative. Unlike the constructions of the genitive and dative, and to a larger extent than those of the accusative, the ablatival constructions tended to substitute or develop prepositional phrases in place of the simple case, for example, for source and agency, for accompaniment and manner, and for place where. And alone among Latin cases—unless the vocative and the accusative of exclamation be considered as such—the ablative developed an absolute construction, which became a common substitute for a wide range of subordinate clauses.

VOCATIVE

The vocative indicates its function by its name, derived from the passive perfect participle *uocātus* of the Latin verb *uocō* = I call. It is the case of address and has no syntactical relation to the rest of the sentence save insofar as it may be regarded as being in apposition to the subject, as in *Marce, uenī* = Marcus, come.

Except in the singular vocative masculine of the second declension, which ends either in short *-e*, like *Marce*, or in long *-ī* for nouns in *-ius*, as in *Claudī*, the vocative is in form the same as the nominative. Hence, when the nominative and accusative have the same form, it may be difficult to decide whether an exclamatory form is vocative or accusative of exclamation. For example, when Cicero exclaimed early in his first speech against Catiline, *Ō tempora, Ō mōrēs*, was he apostrophizing the times and customs with a vocative, or exclaiming against them with an accusative? Probably the latter.

LOCATIVE

The term "locative" is formed from the passive perfect participle *locātus* of the verb *locō* = I place, which in turn contains the root of the noun *locus* = a place. The locative was the original case to indicate place where. Latin preserved separate endings for it only in the singular of feminine nouns of the first declension and also in the singular of masculine nouns of the second declension. The endings are in the first declension *-ae* and in the second declension long *-ī*. They occur principally on the names of cities, as on *Rōmae* = at Rome and *Corinthī* = at Corinth. The fourth declension feminine noun *domus* also has a locative ending in long *-ī*, namely *domī*. This noun has acquired several endings of the second declension masculines.

In the singular of nouns of the third declension, a long *-ī* may appear on an ablative used locatively even though the normal ending of the ablative is short *-e*. The locative of *rūs* = country is *rūrī* = in the country, although the ablative is regularly *rūre*. Both *Carthāginī* and *Carthāgine* are found in the meaning "at Carthage," although the latter is the regular ablative. Locative uses of the ablative are preserved in such idiomatic phrases as *terrā marīque* = on land and sea, without the preposition *in*, and often also without *in* when an ablative of place where is modified by an adjective, for example, *mediā urbe* = in the middle (of the) city. Many locative

163

forms survived as adverbs, such as *ibī* (or *ibī*) = there and *humī* = on the ground.

Probably the suffixes *-re* of the present and *-se* of the active perfect infinitives represent what was originally a locative or dative ending *-si*. The final *-i* weakened to *-e*. Since in the active present infinitive the *-s-* came between the final vowel of the stem and the final *-e* of the termination, it became *-r-*. Since the active perfect stem originally ended in *-s-*, the *-se* survived. Probably also the final long *-ī* of the passive present infinitive was a dative ending which was added either to the *-r-* of the active present infinitive in the first, second, and fourth conjugations or directly to the consonant stem in the third. If all the noncompound infinitives had in origin dative endings added to the stem of the verb serving as a verbal noun, they presumably indicated purpose. The infinitives of, for example, the first conjugation stem *amā-* = love formed the active present infinitive *amā-re* = to love, the active perfect infinitive *amā-uis-se*, often contracted to *amās-se* = to have loved, and the passive present infinitive *amā-r-ī* = to be loved. The corresponding infinitives of the second conjugation stem *monē-* = advise are *monē-re*, *mon-uis-se*, and *monē-r-ī*. Those of the third conjugation stem *reg-* = rule are *rege-re*, *rex-is-se*, and *reg-ī*. Those of the fourth conjugation stem *audī-* = hear resemble those of the first, *audī-re*, *audī-uis-se*, often contracted to *audīs-se,* and *audī-r-ī*.

In general, Latin never wholly lost the locative case, which it had inherited from Indo-European.

In conclusion, the various uses of each case of the Latin noun may seem confusing and arbitrary to anyone not familiar with an inflected language. They developed, however, from a single original relationship as expressed by each case, or at most from a few related relationships. The need to express a wider range of relationships did not produce new cases. Indeed, some earlier cases were absorbed by others, as the vocative by the nominative or the instrumental and locative by the ablative. Latin met the challenge of expressing more varied relationships by extending the implications of the genitive and dative, and either by extending the implications of the accusative and ablative or by using prepositions with them.

Granted that even the prepositions not of adverbial origin probably originally had adverbial implications, prepositional phrases may have grown out of the use of prepositions as adverbs to clarify and make precise a verb-object relationship. Such a development would account for the frequency with which prepositions combine with verbs. The noun in the accusative or ablative that originally indicated the limit, means, source, or place of action for such a verb came to be regarded as governed by the preposition. The prepositional phrases thus created increasingly took over the functions of the simple cases, as in the use of *in* followed by an ablative instead of a simple locative ablative. Similarly, *per* with the accusative became much more frequent, especially in imperial Latin, to denote instrumentality and even agency. In the Romance languages, the various forms taken by *per* came to be the only means of denoting instrumentality or agency, since cases almost wholly vanished.

In short, by the time that classical Latin had taken shape, many of the earlier case constructions for nouns survived only as residues from preceding linguistic stages of development, and some of those that can be determined to have existed in earlier stages had in the classical period already become extinct or restricted to special, generally adverbial uses. At the same time, the early and presumably simple constructions of the cases that continued to be vital developed an ever-widening variety of connotations engendered from the original implications of the cases. Simultaneously there was a growing employment of prepositional phrases instead of case constructions.

XII

THE SYNTAX OF VERBS

The syntax of the finite forms of the Latin verb is even more varied and complex than that of the noun. Of the nonfinite forms, only the infinitive affords syntactical richness; the other nonfinite forms are reasonably simple with respect to the constructions in which they appear. As regards the finite forms, voice has little syntactical use. Though in general Latin had lost the middle voice which Greek preserved, the passive voice may occasionally have a middle meaning, that is, may indicate that the subject acts upon himself, whether as an inheritance from an earlier linguistic stage of the language or under Greek influence.

Certain verbs appear almost wholly in the passive voice, even though their meanings are active, both transitive and intransitive. Such verbs are called "deponents," from the active present participle *dēpōnēns* of *dēpōnō* = I lay aside, because they have laid aside, or dispensed with the active voice. For example, the principal parts of a deponent of the first conjugation are *cōnor* = I try, *cōnārī* = to try, and *cōnātus sum* = I tried, or I have tried. Deponent verbs do have a few active forms, namely the present and future participles, two verbal nouns, the supine and the gerund, and the verbal adjective called the "gerundive." For *cōnor* these are *cōnāns*; *cōnātūrus, -a, -um*; *cōnātum*; *cōnandī*; and *cōnandus, -a, -um*. Moreover the passive perfect participles of deponents may be active or passive in meaning. For example, *cōnātus* means "having tried," as in the compound perfect *cōnātus sum*, and also "having been tried."

A few verbs are active in the present system but compound passive in the perfect and are therefore called "semideponents." The four most commonly used are *audeō* = I dare, *fīdō* = I trust, *gaudeō* = I rejoice, and *soleō* = I am accustomed. As an example, the principal parts of the first of these are *audeō*, *audēre*, and *ausus sum*. An impersonal third person singular passive of a semideponent may be used, as in the present indicative *gaudētur* = there is rejoicing.

The syntax of the verb is mainly concerned with the many constructions in which appear the moods and tenses, and in compound sentences with the interrelation of moods or tenses. Sentences may be simple, that is, have no subordinate clauses. In such sentences, the moods and tenses are determined merely by the tone of meaning that the speaker wishes to convey. The complexity of the syntax of the Latin verb therefore appears chiefly in compound sentences, in which a main statement is enlarged and qualified by subordinate clauses, and the mood and tense of the subordinate verb are determined by their relation to the mood and tense of the verb of the main statement.

INDEPENDENT INDICATIVE

In the indicative mood, the tenses, whether used independently or subordinately, usually have the absolute temporal significance that Latin developed from the Indo-European connotation of aspect. The Latin present had a number of connotations that may be distinguished in English. Thus *faciō* may denote a simple present action, "I make," a continuing one, "I am making"; a general truth, as in English "I make chairs"; immediate futurity, "I am going to make"; or even in action attempted but not completed, a use called "conative" from *cōnor* = I try, as in *fertur in hostēs* = he (tries to) rush (literally he is borne) among the enemy. In vivid narrative, the present is frequently used for the perfect and is then called "historical." As in French, the present with such

167

phrases as *iam diū* or *iam dūdum* = now for (a) long (time) in-dicates an action begun in the past but continuing in the present, as in *tē iam dūdum hortor* = I have been (literally am) urging you for (a) long (time), in which the verb *hortor* is a deponent.

The imperfect indicative denotes continuing or incompleted action in past time and has the varieties of connotation of the present. It may express customary or general action, as *uīuēbat* = he was living. It may show repeated or habitual action, as in *dīcēbat* = he used to say, or he kept saying. It may show that an action begun earlier is continuing at the time of utterance, in which case it is accompanied by some such adverbial phrase as *iam diū* = now for a long time, as in *iam diū tē exspectābat* = he has been expect-ing you for a long time, with the implication that he still is. With a negative the imperfect indicative may express the impossibility of an action, as in *nec eōs aspiciēbat* = nor could (literally did) he see them. In a somewhat similar connotation of unreality, the im-perfect indicative may be used instead of an imperfect subjunctive in the conclusion of a condition that expresses a contrary-to-fact hypothesis. In this use the imperfect presents the hypothetical but unreal action as having been on the point of occurring had not something else, given in the "if" clause, prevented it. For example, *si licēret ueniēbam* = if it were permitted I would come, that is, I was on the point of coming when I learned that it would not be permitted. The normal conclusion would be *uenīrem*. The plu-perfect indicative is similarly used in the conclusion of conditions expressing a past contrary-to-fact thought.

The imperfect indicative is used in Latin where English would use the present, to express something that the speaker has now realized but which was true before, as in *Ō, tū quoque aderās* = O, you also are (literally were) here. It is also used in letter-writing for something which, though contemporary for the writer, will be past for the reader on receipt of the letter, as in *haec cum scrībēbam, eram sōlus* = when I write (literally was writing) this, I am (literally was) alone. Similarly, the pluperfect is used in letters for something which the writer regards as in past time with respect to himself and which the recipient of the letter will therefore regard as doubly past since for him the writing of the letter will be in past time. For instance, the writer of a letter might wish to say that he had replied already to something on the day preceding that on which he was writing. He would therefore write *rēscrīpseram prīdiē* = I had replied yesterday, because he would envisage his action from the point of view of the recipient of his letter. Occasionally also in letters the perfect may be used where English uses the present, that is for an action which, though present to the writer, will be past to the recipient. For instance, to express "I am writing a letter," a writer would say in Latin *litterās dedī*, which means literally "I gave a letter." These uses of the imperfect, perfect, and pluperfect indicative in letters are called "epistolary" from *epistula* = letter, which is more literary than *litterae*.

The future indicative indicates an action or state in the future. As in English, it may have an almost imperative force, as in *faciēs ut sciam* = you will let me know (literally you will make it that I know), or do let me know. In subordinate clauses that use the indicative, Latin is often more literal in the use of the future than is English, as in *cum aderit, uidēbit* = when he comes (literally will be here), he will see.

The Latin perfect indicates both simple past time (aorist) and completed action in past time (true perfect). It is the common past tense, as compared to the imperfect. The perfect of completed action often connotes that the past action has led to a present state. Plutarch, who wrote a life of Cicero in the late first or early second century A.D., says in chapter 22.2 that when Cicero had had certain associates in Catiline's conspiracy put to death, he announced this to the people by saying "they lived." Plutarch uses a Greek aorist, which must represent the Latin perfect *uīxērunt* = they have lived. This perfect of the completed action of living connotes the present state, that of death. Thus Cicero avoided either the ill omen of saying "they are dead," or the political unpopularity of saying "they have been executed." A few verbs exist only in the perfect since their completed action leads to a present state. Such defective verbs are regularly *coepī* = I have come to begin, or I begin; *meminī* = I have come to remember, or I remember; *ōdī* = I have come to hate, or I hate; and frequently *nōuī* = I have come to know, or I know. Instead of *nōuī* as denoting a present state, *nōscō* = I begin to know is common for the present. In verbs like *nōscō* an ending -*sc*- added to the root marks them as indicating that the action begins. Such compounds are called "inceptives" from the passive perfect participle *inceptus* of *incipiō* = I begin.

The pluperfect and future perfect indicative relate in time to the perfect, as do the imperfect and future to the present, and, like them, are used in Latin with more precision than is often true in English. For example, in *cum uēnerit ipse, laetābimur* = when he himself comes (literally shall have come), we will rejoice, *uēnerit* is the third person singular of the active future perfect indicative of the verb *ueniō* = I come, and *laetābimur* is the first person plural of the passive (in form) future indicative of the deponent verb *laetor* = I rejoice. Thus the Latin clearly dates the future coming as antecedent to the future rejoicing. Similarly, in *hīc erat locus quem castrīs dēlēgerat* = this was the place which he chose (literally had chosen) for a camp, *erat* is the third person singular of the active imperfect indicative of the verb *sum* = I am, and *dēlēgerat* is the third person singular active pluperfect indicative of the verb *dēligō* = I choose, so that the past choosing is made antecedent to the past statement about the place.

INDEPENDENT SUBJUNCTIVE

The syntax of the subjunctive is likely to seem difficult for those who speak English, which has almost entirely lost this mood as far as morphology goes. The connotations of the subjunctive figure in English and in other languages by being indicated in various ways, as by the context, the tone of voice, adverbial modifiers, or other devices.

The Latin subjunctive combined in itself the connotations of will, of wish, of likelihood or expectation, and of contingency. The subjunctive denoting will is often called "volitive," from the verb *uolō* = I wish, or "voluntative," from the noun *uoluntās* = wish. The subjunctive of wish is often given the name of the Greek mood of wish, "optative," from the passive perfect participle *optātus* of the verb *optō* = I desire, or wish. The subjunctive of likelihood may be called "prospective," from the passive perfect participle *prōspectus* of the verb *prōspiciō* = I look forward. The subjunctive of contingency may be called "potential," from the active present participle *potēns* (used as an adjective) of a verb that also survived in the perfect *potuī* and which means "to be in control of," or "to be able," and hence "to be possible."

The distinction between will and wish or between prospective futurity and potentiality is often not easy to draw. These distinctions of later Latin grammarians may well be more refined than was the feeling of the early speakers of Latin, and even of those of the classical period, for whom the tone of the mood would have been given more by the context than by any precise grammatical consciousness. However, even though many uses of the subjunctive cannot surely be classified specifically under one of these four connotations, the distinction into types is useful.

The volitive or voluntative subjunctive is common for exhortations, commands, advice, and the like, particularly in the first and third persons, for which there was no present imperative, as in *fiat iūstitia* = let justice be done, or *eāmus* = let us go. This use of the subjunctive is called "hortatory," from the passive perfect participle *hortātus* of the deponent verb *hortor* = I exhort. The first person plural of the hortatory subjunctive is much commoner than the first person singular because one seldom exhorts oneself but frequently a group of which one is a member. In early Latin the second person singular of the hortatory subjunctive was usual as a polite positive command, instead of the more abrupt imperative. But the second person plural was not common at any period. For example, *faciās, amābō* is common in Roman comedy to mean "do it, please," rather than the direct imperative *fac*. *Amābō* literally means "I will love" and is placed after *faciās* without any connective. Such an unconnected sequence of two words or phrases is called "asyndeton" from a Greek word meaning "not tied together." In this case the statement might be rendered "may you do (this and) I will love (you)." In the plural, *ueniātis* is seldom used at any time instead of *uenīte* for "come." The refrain of a familiar Christmas carol illustrates the combined use of an active present second person plural imperative and an active present first person plural hortatory subjunctive: *uenīte, adorēmus* = "(O) come, let us adore (him)."

Negative commands are regularly expressed by *nē* with a hortatory subjunctive rather than by a present imperative, as in *nē eīs dīcās* = do not tell them. As an alternative, *nolī* or *nolīte*, the second person singular and plural of the active present imperative of *nolō* = I do not wish, may be used with an infinitive, as in *nolīte Cicerōnem cōnsulem creāre* = do not elect Cicero consul.

A variety of volitive subjunctive is the concessive or permissive, as in the first half of *ruat caelum*; *fiat iūstitia*. The literal meaning of this phrase is "let the sky fall; let justice be done"; that is, it contains two volitive subjunctives without a connective, or in asyndeton. But the first subjunctive, originally coordinate, acquired a concessive connotation, so that the sentence may be translated, with subordination of *ruat caelum*, "although the sky fall, let justice be done."

A concessive clause introduced by *licet* = it is permitted developed similarly. In its full verbal force, *licet* is ordinarily construed with a dative of indirect object and an infinitive as subject, as in *licet mihi īre* = to go is permitted to me, or I may go. But *licet* was often used almost parenthetically with a volitive subjunctive, as in *licet*; *ruat caelum* = it is permitted; let the sky fall. This usage is not called asyndeton, since no conjunction is omitted, but "parataxis," from a Greek noun meaning "putting side by side, or parallel." From this coordinate relationship, either *licet* came to be regarded as a main verb on which the subjunctive *ruat* depended, and indeed an *ut* = that was often introduced to show the subordination of the subjunctive; or more often *licet* was regarded as itself a subordinating conjunction meaning "although" and governing the subjunctive. Thus *licet ruat caelum, fiat iūstitia* means, as does the sentence without *licet*, "although the sky fall, let justice be done."

The subjunctive of wish or optative subjunctive occasionally occurs simply, as in *dī tē ament* = may the gods love you. But it is usually introduced by *ut* or *utinam* = (would) that, and in early Latin also by a relative adverb *quī*, an old *i*-stem ablative of the relative pronoun *quī* = who (instead of the usual neuter ablative *quō*). This *quī* came to mean "how" and hence to intensify the wish, as in *quī dī eum perdant* = (how) may the gods ruin him. In wishes, the present subjunctive expresses a simple possible wish; the imperfect expresses one contrary to fact (that is, probably impossible or at least unfulfilled) in present time; and the pluperfect expresses one contrary to fact in past time. The perfect subjunctive is rare in wishes. Wishes may also colloquially be expressed by the potential subjunctive of *uolō* = I wish, as in *uelim* (present) or *uellem* (imperfect), followed by either an objective infinitive or a parallel or paratactic optative subjunctive, as in *uelim, tibi persuādeās* = I would wish, may you persuade yourself, that is, I would like you to believe. The negative in wishes is *nē*, as in *nē pereāmus* = may we not perish.

It might be expected that the use of the subjunctive to express deliberation or doubt arose from the potential connotation, as in *quid agam?* = what am I to do? or what should I do? But it seems more probable that this subjunctive, which often expresses indignation or suggests the answer "no," was in origin volitive; that is, the preceding example originally meant "what may I do?" The negative is *nōn*, as in *cūr nōn eat* = why should he not go?

The prospective subjunctive of uncertain futurity and the potential subjunctive are so close in connotation that it has been doubted whether any true prospective subjunctives survived in classical Latin. Thus *maneam, opīnor* combines in parataxis a subjunctive and an indicative and might mean "I may wait, I think" in either a prospective or a dubitative sense, or might even have a volitive sense of "I want to wait, I think."

The potential subjunctive is very common in Latin to give a tone of contingency, possibility, or conceivability. The present and perfect both refer to the immediate future; the imperfect to the past; and the pluperfect to what might have happened. The negative is either *nōn* or *haud* = not. For example, *haud sciam an* = I would not know whether, or I should think that; *crēderēs victōs* = you would have believed them beaten; or *aliquis dīcat* = somebody may say.

In general, the independent uses of the subjunctive imply will, wish, possibility, contingency, or uncertainty. They frequently developed from simple subjunctives into subjunctives either accompanied by introductory particles or dependent on verbal forms with which they originally stood on an equal footing, in parataxis.

DEPENDENT INDICATIVE AND CLAUSES
WITH DEPENDENT INDICATIVE OR DEPENDENT
SUBJUNCTIVE

The criterion for use of the indicative in subordinate clauses, as in independent clauses, was in origin one of actuality, but here in relation to the action in the main clause rather than absolutely. Thus it is not correct always to regard the use of the indicative in subordinate clauses as giving the action as a matter of fact and the use of the subjunctive as indicating that the action is uncertain or potential; subordinate clauses in the subjunctive are often fully factual. But it is safe to regard subordinate clauses in the indicative as always factual. The subordinate uses of the subjunctive bulk so large in Latin grammar that the uses of the indicative in subordinate clauses tend to be taken for granted. In analyzing the syntax of a Latin sentence, any subordinate indicative which it contains merits as full an explanation as is given for any subordinate subjunctive.

Many subordinating conjunctions or relative pronouns and adjectives may introduce a subordinate clause in which the verb is either indicative or subjunctive according to whether the speaker desires simply to add some factual statement or to indicate some sort of uncertainty, relativity, or conditionality in the subordinate clause. For instance, among temporal subordinating conjunctions, *postquam* = after regularly takes an indicative verb because if one action takes place after another, clearly the first is a matter of fact. Among the conjunctions meaning "when," *ut* (in this meaning) takes the indicative, but *cum* takes the indicative or subjunctive depending on whether the temporal clause gives a factual point of time or a general, almost conditional circumstance. For example, in *cum tacent, probant* = when they are silent, they approve (or show approval), the *cum* clause simply indicates a coincidence of time between the silence and the approval. In *cum Athēnis essem, Zēnōnem frequenter audiēbam* = when (or whenever) I was at Athens, I frequently heard (or used to hear) Zeno, the *cum* clause gives a general circumstance or condition of the hearing. The subjunctive with temporal *cum* is always imperfect or pluperfect.

Similarly after *antequam* and *priusquam* = before, the indicative connotes that an event before which another takes, will take, or took place also itself in fact occurred, while the subjunctive shows that the second event is anticipated as a possible occurrence, often dependent on the occurrence of the earlier event. For example, Cicero says, in *Prō Mūrēnā* 1.2, *antequam prō Mūrēnā dīcere īnstituō, prō mē ipsō pauca dīcam* = before I begin to speak on behalf of Murena, I will say (or let me say) a few (words) on behalf of myself. Here, although the *antequam* clause looks to the future, the simple active present indicative is used to show that the subject is in fact going to speak for Murena. In the main clause, *dīcam* may be active first person singular of either the future indicative or the present subjunctive; in either case it is prospective, of action about to occur. In *is, antequam in Pontum ueniat, litterās ad Pompēium mittet* = he, before he arrives in Pontus, will send letters to Pompey, the arrival in Pontus, expressed by the third person singular of an active present subjunctive, is indicated as not merely prior to but to some extent dependent on, or conditioned by, the sending of letters.

In relative clauses, the indicative is very common to show that the clause merely specifies who or what its antecedent is. The equally frequent subjunctive makes the relative clause characterize the antecedent as the sort of person or thing who in general has, or who might possibly have, the quality given in the clause. For example, in *uir quem uideō Marcus est* = the man whom I see is Marcus, the relative clause simply defines what man is being discussed. But in *uirī quī pācem ament sapientēs sunt* = (the sort of) men who love peace are wise, the relative clause defines, or gives a general characteristic of, the sort of men who are wise. The latter type of relative clause is called a "relative clause of characteristic."

A special form of relative clause with the indicative is introduced by the neuter singular accusative relative pronoun *quod* = which. The *quod* in such a clause was originally an internal or cognate accusative with the verb in the relative clause, and the clause itself was used as a noun in the whole sentence. *Quod* in these clauses may be rendered "as far as," "as to the fact that," or simply "the fact that." For example, in *quod ad mē attinet, nihil bene fēcistī* = as far as I am concerned (literally as to what pertains to me), you did nothing well, and in *quod Cicero uerba fecit, ita censeō* = as to (that) which Cicero said (literally made words), I vote (literally think) as follows, the clause is a sort of adverbial accusative of specification. In *quidnam hoc est negōtī quod filia mē expetit?* = what trouble is this (literally what is this of trouble) that my daughter seeks me? the *quod* clause is in apposition with the *hoc negōtī*, a neuter pronoun with the partitive genitive.

The relative clauses introduced by *quod* that may be regarded as standing to the main clause like an adverbial accusative of specification easily came to have a causal connotation. For example, such a sentence as *quod mihi grātulāris uehementer laetor* passed from the meaning "(as to the fact) that you congratulate me, I rejoice exceedingly" to the meaning "because you congratulate . . ." Such clauses, called "*quod* causal clauses," take the indicative when the speaker asserts the reason as a fact, but the subjunctive when he suggests it not on his own authority but as the reason presumably in the mind of the person or thing about whom he is talking. For example, in *quod eum accūsās, ego tibi non succēnseō* = because you accuse him, I am not angry at you, the *quod* clause gives the speaker's own reason for not being angry; whereas in *quod Africānus fuerit abstinēns, Paenatius eum laudat* = because Africanus was abstinent, Panaetius praises him, the *fuerit* is third person singular active perfect subjunctive because the reason is given as that of Panaetius, not of the writer.

Quia, a neuter plural relative pronoun, also came to connote "because" and to take either the indicative or the subjunctive, like the commoner *quod*. *Quoniam*, originally *quom* (*cum*) plus *iam* = now that, acquired the connotation of "since." Because from its original meaning *quoniam* indicates something that really is so, it regularly takes the indicative. So also does *quandō* when it is causal in connotation rather than temporal, that is, to be rendered "since" rather than "when."

The use of mood with the temporal conjunctions *dum* = while, *dōnec* = while, or until, and *quoad* = until depends on the use of the indicative to denote fact and of the subjunctive to show uncertainty or futurity. In consequence, with all save *dum* the indicative normally occurs only in the past tenses, since if the clause is present in time, it suggests uncertainty or futurity. For example, in the present, *expectās fortasse dum dīcat* = you are waiting perhaps for him to speak; and in the past, *dōnec rediit silentium fuit* = until he returned there was silence. But when these three conjunctions mean "as long as," they take the indicative for either present or past time, as in *dum anima est, spes esse dīcitur* = as long as there is soul (or life), there is said to be hope; and *quoad potuit, fortissimē restitit* = as long as he could, he resisted bravely.

Dum = while regularly takes the present indicative when the action of the subordinate clause is conceived of as coextensive with or inclusive of that of the main clause, even when the action is in past or implied future time, as in *hoc dum narrat, forte audiuī* = while he was (literally is) telling this, I by chance (over)heard; and *ego in Arcānō opperior, dum ista cognōscō* = I (will) wait in Arcanum (a villa near Arca) until I learn (literally come to know) those (matters). This use of the present indicative after *dum* = while, or until, for contemporaneous action either in present, past, or implied future time is perhaps a survival of the original aspect or character of the present as indicating that something happened along with something else, no matter when.

In the same way, conditions in Latin have the indicative in both parts, in the clause introduced by *sī* = if and in the conclusion, if both state simple facts and even when the "if" clause is hypothetical. Such simple conditions may be present, past, future, or mixed in time. Examples of simple conditions are, in the present, *sī id facis, bene est* = if you do it, it is well; in the past, *sī hīc erās, eum uīdistī* = if you were here, you saw him; in the future, *grātiās tibi agam sī litterās mihi mittēs* = I will give you thanks if you send one a letter; and mixed, *ībō, sī mē iubēs* = I will go, if you tell me to; or *sī uērum dīxit, nunc in Asiā est* = if he spoke the truth, he is now in Asia.

When the condition indicates possibility or unreality, the subjunctive is used. Conditions of possibility are called "future less vivid"; a future more vivid would be a simple future condition. Future less vivid conditions ordinarily have the present subjunctive in both clauses, rarely the perfect. Examples are *tū sī hīc sīs, aliter sentiās* = if you should be here, you would feel differently; and *nēquīquam Capitōlium seruāuerim, sī cīuem in uincula dūcī uideam*

= I would have saved the Capitol in vain, if I should see a citizen led to prison (literally chains), in which the main clause is active perfect subjunctive to show time previous to the "if" clause in the present active subjunctive.

Unreal conditions are generally called "contrary to fact." They have for present time the imperfect subjunctive in both clauses and for past time the pluperfect. Examples are *pācem nōn peterem nisi ūtilem crēderem* = I would not seek peace unless I thought (peace) useful, that is, the not seeking peace is contrary to the implied fact that he is seeking peace; and *sī Metellī fideī diffīsus essem, iūdicem eum nōn retinuissem* = if I had distrusted Metellus' (good) faith, I would not have retained him (as) judge, that is, a past distrust would be contrary to the fact that he did keep him as judge. A contrary-to-fact or unreal condition may be mixed in time. That is, the imperfect subjunctive may appear in one clause to signify present unreality, and the pluperfect subjunctive may appear in the other clause to signify past unreality. Examples are *sī tū ibi fuissēs, ego nunc contentus essem* = if you had been there, I would now be content, that is, you were not there and I am not content; and *sī id putāret, ā magistrō pessimē ēducātus esset* = if he were to think that, he would have been badly taught by his master (or teacher).

Occasionally the event that did not occur is imagined as so close to realization that the imperfect indicative is used instead of the imperfect subjunctive. The historian Tacitus, who wrote in the early second century A.D., describes in his *Annales* XI how the empress Messalina sought to avert the wrath of her husband Claudius, caused by her flagrant infidelity. In 34.3 Tacitus says *urbem ingredientī offerēbantur commūnēs līberī, nisi Narcissus āmouērī eōs iussisset* = to him (Claudius) (as he was) entering the city, their common children were (on the point of) being offered (or would have been presented), unless (or had it not been that) Narcissus (an imperial freedman) had ordered them to be removed. The awkwardness of this translation illustrates the difficulty of rendering accurately into English such a vivid, but unreal, imperfect indicative.

In conditions, the "if" clause is frequently called the "protasis," from a Greek noun meaning basically "a putting forward, or a proposition," which grammarians applied to the hypothetical part of the condition. The conclusion is called the "apodosis," also from a Greek noun meaning "a giving back," that is, in grammar a clause answering to the protasis. The division of conditional clauses into present, future more vivid, future less vivid, and contrary to fact was borrowed from Greek grammar and is not fully applicable to Latin. Latin has only three types: simple or factual, potential or uncertain, and contrary to fact or unreal. The first takes the indicative in any tense; the second usually has the present or prospective subjunctive in both parts, though the perfect subjunctive may appear in the protasis; and the third takes the imperfect subjunctive for present and the pluperfect subjunctive for past, both denoting unreality, in protasis and apodosis.

Only occasionally does Latin differentiate from particular conditions those that derive general conclusions from general hypotheses and are therefore called "general." For example, the English statement "if only the rich were the clever, the world would be better than ever we possibly thought that it could be" is a general present contrary-to-fact condition. It would be expressed in Latin with the imperfect subjunctive in both clauses, just as would also a particular present contrary-to-fact condition.

In general, the difficulty in grasping the differences between the use of the indicative and of the subjunctive in subordinate clauses, particularly with conjunctions or relative words that may take either, is reduced if attention is paid to the actuality or the uncertainty which the clause connotes.

DEPENDENT SUBJUNCTIVE

The dependent uses of the subjunctive become very involved, particularly when they are introduced by subordinating conjunctions or by relative and interrogative pronouns and adjectives that may also take the indicative. It is also often hard for a speaker of English to grasp the difference between constructions taking a subordinate subjunctive (or even a subordinate indicative) and those taking an infinitive, for example, to understand the difference in concept between indirect question and indirect discourse, or between verbs that take a substantive clause of purpose or an objective infinitive.

Hence systematic Latin grammars ordinarily classify subordination under types of clauses or under the subordinating words instead of giving a detailed analysis of the origins of such constructions in the various connotations of the subjunctive.

It has been argued that all dependent uses of the subjunctive in Latin were originally independent and construed paratactically with the verb to which they were later subordinated. Two examples of parataxis are *licet, ruat* = it is permitted, may it fall, or although it may fall; and *maneam, opīnor* = I may remain, I think, or I think that I will remain.

In Roman comedy, the imperatives of such verbs as *sinō* = I permit, *faciō* = I do, and *caueō* = I beware namely *sine, fac*, and *caue* (often in speech pronounced *cau'* with loss of the final long *-ē*), as well as the first person singular active of the present volitive subjunctive of *uolō* = I wish, namely *uelim*, are frequently construed with a parallel or paratactic subjunctive, as well as with a subordinate subjunctive introduced by *ut* or *nē*, that is, with a substantive clause of purpose. For example, in *haec cūrāta sint fac sīs* = see to it, please, that these (matters) be cared for, the passive perfect subjunctive indicates that the speaker desires such quick action that the matters practically have already been attended to. *Sīs* is a contraction of *sī uīs* = if you wish, or please, not the second person singular of the present subjunctive of *sum* = I am, which has the same spelling. However, in *fac mē ut sciam* = make me that I know, that is, inform me, the *ut* = that is expressed to subordinate the *sciām* to the *fac* but the meaning is the same as in the preceding example. An example of the omission of *ut* after *caue* is *caue putēs hominēs magis umquam esse mīrātōs* = beware (lest) you think (or be careful not to think) that men ever wondered more at anything. In this sentence *esse mīrātōs* is the perfect infinitive, passive in form but active in meaning, of *mīror* = I wonder, a transitive deponent verb. The passive perfect participle *mīrātōs* is masculine accusative plural in agreement with the subject of the infinitive, *hominēs*. *Ut* is similarly omitted in *nōllem dīxissem* = I would wish that I had not said (it). The imperfect and pluperfect subjunctives give a contrary-to-fact connotation. *Nōllem* is shortened from *nōn uellem*; regularly the negative in Latin is put with a main verb rather than, as in English, with the subordinate verb.

The fact that subordination is common in all Indo-European languages indicates that it had already developed in the parent tongue. The subordinate uses of the subjunctive in Latin can by and large be related to the three independent connotations, namely the volitive or voluntative, the optative or wish, and the potential; the prospective connotation had almost, if not entirely, vanished in Latin. It is therefore difficult to determine whether the Latin subordinate constructions of the subjunctive developed from the independent ones or whether subordinate constructions inherited from Indo-European gave rise to the independent uses. Perhaps the process worked in both directions to produce an assimilation of independent and dependent uses.

Clauses taking the subordinate or dependent subjunctive express in general the following concepts: a future (uncertain) or contrary-to-fact (unreal) condition, indirect question, characteristic (with relative words), time, concession, proviso, cause, general statement, purpose, and result. Such subordinate clauses may perform the functions of nouns, adjectives, or adverbs.

A common use of a subordinate clause with its verb in the subjunctive as a noun is to express an indirect question, that is, a question dependent on a main verb, chiefly as object but also as subject or in apposition with a noun or pronoun construed with the main verb. Examples of an indirect question as object of a verb meaning "to ask," "to say," or the like are *rogat mē quid sentiam* = he asks me what I feel and *quid sentiam expōnam* = I will expound what I feel. In the first example, the verb *rogat* takes a double accusative, of the person and of the question asked. An example of an indirect question as subject of a verb is *doleam necne doleam nihil interest* = whether or not I grieve does not matter. Here *nihil* is used adverbially, for intensive *nōn*. Here also Latin uses a single interrogative conjunction *necne* between the alternative indirect questions. Often Latin, like English, expresses both conjunctions, as in the next example of an indirect question in apposition, *hoc dubium est utrum eam an remaneam* = this is dubious (namely) whether I should go or remain. The double indirect question is in apposition with *hoc*, which is subject of *est* and modified by the predicate adjective *dubium*.

Latin, unlike English, uses different constructions for indirect questions and for indirect statements or discourse. In English both are expressed by subordinate clauses. English indirect questions are introduced by an interrogative word, and indirect statements by a conjunction, which is often omitted in colloquial style. For example, the indirect question in "I ask whether he is coming" does not differ in syntax from the indirect statement in "I say that he is coming." The difference is only of the interrogative conjunction "whether" and the subordinating conjunction "that." In Latin, indirect questions are subordinate noun clauses introduced by interrogative words, while indirect statements are construed as subordinate infinitive clauses with their subjects in the accusative. The preceding English examples would read in Latin *rogō ueniatne* and *dīcō eum uenīre*. In the indirect question *-ne* is an enclitic interrogative conjunction, that is, one which follows and is attached to the first word of the subordinate clause. In the indirect statement the subject *eum* is expressed as a weak demonstrative pronoun in the masculine singular accusative. Latin has no simple pronoun of the third person to correspond to those of the first and second persons.

Another instance of the use of a subordinate clause as a noun is the so-called substantive clause of purpose or result, which though normally adverbial, may serve as the subject or object of a verb, as in *licet tibi ut eās* = it is permitted to you that you may go (subject clause of purpose), or *mihi persuādēs ut eam* = you persuade (to) me that I should go (object clause of purpose).

Relative clauses often seem to serve as subjects or objects, but in such cases an omitted antecedent must be supplied from the context, as in *quī aquilam ferēbat occīsus est*, where some such antecedent as *mīles* must be understood as the subject of *occīsus est*, to mean "(the soldier) who carried the (legionary) eagle (standard) was slain"; or in *quī cognōscerent mīsit*, where some such antecedent as *uirōs* must be understood as the object of *mīsit*, to mean "he sent (men) who should learn, or to learn."

Relative clauses are the principal type of subordinate clause used adjectivally. With a verb in the subjunctive, they may express purpose, as in the second of the preceding examples, or result, as in *tālis est quī nēminī noceat* = he is such as would harm no one, where the verb of harming takes a dative. Relative clauses often have a conditional connotation and take the three constructions possible in conditions. Such conditional relative clauses are usually general in tone. Thus in *quisquis hūc uēnerit uāpulābit*, if the first verb *uēnerit* is third person singular of the active perfect subjunctive, the relative clause is general and means "whoever may come here will get a beating," that is, "if anyone has come (or may have come) here, he will get a beating." But *uēnerit* may be active future perfect indicative, giving the meaning "if any one shall have come here . . ." In any case, the conditional relative clause here serves as subject of the third person singular of the intransitive active future indicative verb *uāpulābit*.

Relative clauses may also have a causal or concessive meaning and, like other such clauses, take the subjunctive, as in *ille simplex est quī nōs nihil cēlet* = he is guileless who (or because he) conceals nothing from us. In this example the verb *cēlāre* = to conceal, here in the third person singular of the active present subjunctive, takes a double accusative. If this sentence read *quī nōs nihil cēlet simplex est*, it would be a simple general relative clause meaning "who(ever) conceals nothing from us is guileless."

Most of the foregoing adjectival relative clauses with the subjunctive may, when they modify a noun, be included under the general heading of characteristic. Simple adjectival relative clauses with the indicative identify and define given persons or things; that is, they make factual statements about them. Adjectival relative clauses with the subjunctive generalize about the nouns that they modify or give them some sort of characteristic; that is, the relative clause does not say that somebody or something is so-and-so but defines its antecedent as the sort of person(s) or thing(s) to be or do so-and-so.

Probably the most common subordinate or dependent clauses with the subjunctive are those used adverbially. Their meanings may be conditional, concessive, provisional, causal, temporal, purposive (final, denoting the end of the main action), and resultant (consecutive, denoting the consequence of the main action). The syntax of subordinate clauses introduced by *quīn* = but that, *quōminus* = that . . . not (literally by which the less), *nē* = that not, *an* = whether, or *an nōn* = whether not after verbs meaning to doubt, hinder, oppose, or the like requires a more detailed explanation to be found in any systematic grammar.

Many adverbial temporal clauses are introduced by conjunctions that originated as temporal adverbs, such as *cum* and *quandō* = when. The conjunction *cum*, originally *quom*, is distinct from the preposition *cum* = with; the conjunction comes from the relative and interrogative root *qu-*. As a subordinating conjunction, it may be temporal, meaning "when," causal, meaning "since" or "because," or concessive, meaning "although." *Quandō* may also mean "since." Two other common temporal conjunctions are *ubi* and *ut* = when, both of which are likewise relative in origin, though they have lost the root *qu-*. *Ubi* may also mean "where," and *ut* may also mean "as" or "that." Adverbial temporal clauses generally take the indicative, present or perfect, when they simply denote the time at which the main event occurred, and the subjunctive, ordinarily imperfect or pluperfect, when they are general, that is, when they mean "whenever" or when the action of the temporal clauses in some way influences or conditions the action of the main clause. Thus, in *Pompēius, ut equitātum suum pulsum uīdit, aciē excessit* = Pompey, when he saw that his cavalry (had been) repulsed, withdrew from the battle line, the temporal *ut* clause simply gives the time of his withdrawal. Had the temporal clause read *cum . . . uidēret* (or perhaps *uīdisset* to show time prior to his withdrawal), it might be taken as either temporal or causal, meaning either "when" or "because."

The conjunction *ut* is not only used temporally, to mean "when," or comparatively, to mean "as," but most commonly occurs with the meaning "that" in clauses which give either the purpose or the result of the action of a main verb, that is, in clauses also called either "final," because they give the end or purpose of the main action, or "consecutive," because the result follows from the main action. The use of *ut*, with the negative *nē* = that not, to introduce purpose clauses developed from its indefinite character, so that the subjunctive subordinated by it connoted supposition, possibility, and hence intention. An example of a purpose clause is *esse oportet ut uīuās, nōn uīuere ut edās* = (you) ought to eat to live, not live to eat. In this sentence *esse* is the active present infinitive and *edās* the active present subjunctive second person singular of *edō* = I eat. The former is not the infinitive *esse* of *sum* = I am, despite the similarity of spelling. Another example of a purpose clause is *dēcrēuit senātus ut cōnsul uidēret nē quid rēspūblica dētrīmentī caperet* = the senate decreed that the consul should see (to it) that the state received no harm (literally not anything of harm). Here there is a positive purpose clause subordinate to the main clause to give the purpose of the senate's decree and within this a negative purpose clause dependent on it to give the purpose of the action enjoined upon the consul. In *quid dētrīmentī* the *quid* is the neuter accusative of *quis* used as an indefinite pronoun in place of *aliquid* = anything. The pronoun is used with a genitive instead of an indefinite adjective modifying a noun, *aliquod detrimentum*. After the subordinating conjunctions *sī* = if, *nisi* = if not, or unless, *num* = whether, introducing a direct or indirect question, and *nē* = that not, *quis, quid* is used as an indefinite pronoun in place of *aliquis, aliquid*. This last example gives the formula of what in the later Republic was called the *senātūs cōnsultum ultimum* = the final (or emergency) decree of the senate which authorized a consul or the consuls to use force to protect the state, usually from internal conspiracy or revolt.

Since a result clause expresses something that actually occurs, the use of the subjunctive is less obvious. In such clauses the subjunctive expresses a connection from cause (the main clause) to effect (the *ut* clause). The negative is *ut nōn* = that not. And the result clause is often preceded in the main clause by a demonstrative adjective such as *is, ea, id* = that, or an adverb such as *sīc* or *ita* = so. Examples are *nōn is sum ut mē periculum dēterreat* = I am not the sort (or person) that danger terrifies me, or would terrify me; and *ita laudō eum ut nōn pertimescam* = I so praise him that I am not afraid. Relative clauses of characteristic often have a connotation of either purpose or result. An example of a relative clause of purpose is *ea quī cōnficeret Trebonium legātum relīquit* = he left the legate Trebonius who should complete (or to complete) these (operations). An example of a relative clause of result is *sōlus es, Caesar, cūius in uictōriā occiderit nēmō nisi armātus* = you, Caesar, are the only one in whose victory no one fell except (if) bearing arms (against you).

In sum, it is often difficult to tell whether a given clause introduced by *ut* = that is used as a noun, substantively, or as an adverb. For instance, in the two sentences *hoc facit ut eam* = he does this so that I may (or should) go and *mihi persuādet ut eam* = he persuades me to go (literally that I should go), both *ut* clauses give the purpose of the main action, but in the first sentence the verb *facit* has the direct object *mē* so that the *ut* clause is adverbial, whereas in the second sentence the verb *persuādet* = persuade takes a dative of the person persuaded and an accusative object (the *ut* clause) of what is persuaded so that the clause is substantive. However, it is harder to differentiate between the use of the *ut* clause in *hoc facit ut eam* and in *mē rogat ut eam* = he asks me to go (literally that I should go). In the second case, the verb *rogāre* = to ask takes a double accusative, of the person and of the thing asked, so that the *ut* clause is substantive. Thus students must give some thought to the syntactical function of subordinate clauses, whether their verbs are indicative or subjunctive, in order to determine whether they are used as nouns (substantives), as adjectives, or as adverbs.

SEQUENCE OF TENSES

Perhaps the most confusing feature of subordinate or dependent subjunctives is the so-called sequence of tenses. This relationship arose from two developments in Latin. The first, which may reflect the Indo-European division of verbal action into contemporary and simple or aoristic aspects, was that of regarding tenses present or future in connotation as primary. Primary tenses in the indicative were the present, the future, the perfect when it denoted a present state resulting from completed action, and the future perfect; those in the subjunctive were the present and perfect; and those in the imperative were both present and future. Past tenses were regarded as secondary, namely in the indicative the imperfect, perfect of simple past time (aorist), and pluperfect; and in the subjunctive the imperfect and pluperfect. The infinitive functioned as a secondary tense when used historically as a main verb instead of a past finite form.

The second development was that the temporal reference of tenses of subordinate subjunctives shifted from the time of the speaker to the time of the action on which the subjunctive was

186

dependent. That is, the tenses of subordinate subjunctives became relative to the time of the main verb, not absolute.

Because of the first development, a primary tense of the indicative in a main clause is followed by a primary tense of the subjunctive (present or perfect) in a dependent clause, and a secondary tense of the indicative is followed by a secondary tense of the subjunctive (imperfect or pluperfect). In consequence of the second development, a subordinate present subjunctive dependent on a main primary tense of the indicative indicates time contemporary with that of the main verb, while a subordinate perfect subjunctive indicates time anterior to that of the main verb. Similarly, in secondary sequence, a subordinate imperfect subjunctive indicates time contemporary with that of the main verb, while a subordinate pluperfect subjunctive indicates time anterior to that of the main verb. However, this practice never became rigidly fixed. Variations are not uncommon when they serve to make the sense clear, when they give emphasis or variety, or when they are simply the result of careless writing.

IMPERATIVE

The imperative mood occurs only in direct discourse and, in its most used tense, the present, only in the second person singular or plural. The so-called future imperative, which has both second and third persons, is really a tense of legal or religious injunction, which may either be addressed to persons or be applied to actions enjoined by law or ritual. All imperatives have an overtone of futurity. When the futurity of a future imperative is emphasized, it is usually accompanied by a temporal adverb, as in *crās petitō*; *dabitur* = ask tomorrow; it will be given. *Petitō* is the second person singular of the active future imperative, here used of actual future time. The two verbs are in asyndeton, that is, not connected by some conjunction such as *et* = and.

Various circumlocutions are employed to avoid the directness of an imperative, such as the hortatory subjunction. This is necessary for commands in the present tense which are in the first and third persons singular and plural and is not uncommon for the second person singular. Or use is made of such an introductory phrase as *cūrā ut* = take care that, *fac* or *fac ut* = see to it that, or *uelim* = I would (that), all with the subjunctive and, when there is no *ut* = that, in parataxis. While negative commands may have the imperative with the negative adverb *nē* = not, more common are the polite circumlocutions of *nōlī* = do not wish followed by an infinitive, *cauē* = beware (lest) followed by a present subjunctive in parataxis, that is, without a subordinating conjunction, or *nē* followed by a hortatory perfect subjunctive. Examples of the various forms of command are *uīue ualēque* = live and be well (a formula of farewell); *ueniāmus* = let us come; *gaudeās* = may you rejoice (in place of *gaudē*); *cūrā ut Rōmae sīs* = take care that you be in Rome (or to be in Rome); in which *Rōmae* is locative; *id mihi uelim mittās* = I wish (that) you would send it to me, with parataxis of the subjunctives; *nē īte* = do not go; *nōlī putāre* = do not think; *cauē festīnēs* = do not make haste; *nē illī quidem dīxeris* = do not tell even him.

INFINITIVE

Of the three verbal nouns, the infinitive is used most frequently and in the widest variety of constructions. Since it simply names the action, it should properly have no independent verbal use. However, it came to be employed in place of a finite verb in past time, generally imperfect, to make action vivid by stating it absolutely, without the qualification of tense or personal endings. Though this independent infinitive is called "historical," it is more properly named "descriptive" or "narrative," since it emphasizes the movement of action rather than simply stating a fact. The subject of a historical infinitive is in the nominative—the only infinitival construction in which this is so. The historical infinitive is particularly favored by writers like Sallust and Tacitus, who sought vivid, direct, and elliptical expressions; it may be regarded as part of the generally anti-Ciceronian style of these writers.

The other uses of the infinitive are all dependent, consonant with its character as a verbal noun. Its subject is then in the accusative. Commonly the infinitive is closely attached to such verbs as *possum*

= I can or *uolō* = I wish, and its action proceeds from the same
subject as does that of the verb whose meaning it complements or
fills out. The term "complementary" should be distinguished from
"complimentary." The former derives directly from the Latin verb
compleō = I fill out; the latter comes from by-forms of its infinitive
complēre, which were developed in the Romance languages, namely
the Italian *compire* and the Catalan *complire*. Italian adopted *com-
plimento*, a noun derived from the second form, to mean "the
fulfillment of an obligation of courtesy"; hence comes the English
noun "compliment," meaning "a polite or flattering remark." The
complementary or fulfilling infinitive is also called "prolative,"
from the passive perfect participle *prōlātus*, used with the Latin
verb *prōferō* = I carry forward, since it carries out the meaning of
the verb. However, "complementary" is the term commonly used in
American grammars.

A complementary infinitive has no subject, because it fulfills the
action of the subject of the main verb. In consequence, predicate
nouns or adjectives are in the nominative, in agreement with the
main subject, as in *uolō bonus esse* = I wish to be good, or *nequeō
cōnsul creārī* = I cannot be elected consul. With some verbs both
the complementary and the object infinitive are possible. Thus in
uult īre = he wishes to go, the complementary infinitive *īre* might
for emphasis be replaced by an object infinitive with a reflexive
pronoun as subject, as in *uult sē īre* = he wishes himself to go. The
latter corresponds in construction to *uult mīlitem īre* = he wishes
the soldier to go. In the second example, however, the subject of
the object infinitive is different from the subject of the main verb.
The complementary infinitive should be carefully distinguished
from the object infinitive.

As a noun, the infinitive may be used as the subject of a verb,
usually of *sum* = I am or of similar verbs, or in apposition with
the subject, or as a predicate nominative. An example of the infinitive as subject is *uīuere bonum est* = to live is good (or a good
thing); of the infinitive in apposition is *hōc, uīuere, est summum
bonum* = this, (namely) to live, is the highest good; and of the
infinitive as predicate nominative is *officium est patriam seruāre* =
(one's) duty is to save (one's) country. The subject infinitive is
also common with verbs which in English are regarded as imper-

sonal, as in *uīuere mē paenitet* = to live makes me regret, or in English, I regret living. An extension of the subject infinitive is the use of an infinitive with its subject in the accusative as the subject of a passive verb meaning "to be said," which is generally in a compound tense, as in *omnēs mortuōs esse dictum est* = it was said that all were dead. The tense of the infinitive is relative to that of the main verb, not to the present time. Thus in the example, the infinitive *esse* is present because the people were dead at the past time of the speaking and the participle *mortuōs* is used as a predicate adjective rather than as a component of a compound passive perfect infinitive. This construction of an indirect statement as subject of a compound passive verb of saying should be distinguished from the construction common with passive present verbs of saying in which the subject of the infinitive becomes nominative as subject of the verb of saying and the infinitive remains in the predicate, with modifiers of the subject in the nominative, as in *omnēs dīcuntur mortuī esse* = all are said to be dead.

The infinitive may also be used as the direct object of a verb, as in *beātē uīuere in uoluptāte pōnitis* = you base to live happily (or the happy life) on pleasure.

The subject and object infinitive may themselves have subjects or objects as well as adverbial modifiers. The object is in the accusative after the transitive force of the verbal noun. The development of the accusative as the case of the subject of all infinitives that have a subject, except of the historical infinitive, was more complicated. The construction apparently began with the use of the infinitive as a sort of double accusative after a verb that already had a personal object, as in *cōgit tē abīre*, where both the person and the going away are each an object of the forcing, and hence the sentence means either "he forces you (into) going away" or "he forces going away (on) you." The obvious English translation "he forces you to go away" does not contain a double infinitive, since the phrase "to go," combining a preposition and the simple verb, may be equivalent to the Latin infinitive but may also fulfill the function of an adverbial clause, which is here "that you should go." In the Latin construction, the personal object (here *tē*) became disassociated from the main verb (here *cōgit*) so that it could be regarded as a subject of the infinitive (here *abire*). From this, the use of the accusative case for subjects of any sort of infinitive except the historical became general.

Often only the context shows which of two accusatives with an infinitive is its subject and which its object. Well known is the supposed reply of the oracle of Delphi to Pyrrhus, when he was planning to invade Italy in the third century B.C.: *āiō tē, Aeacidā, Rōmānōs uincere posse*, which Pyrrhus took to mean "I state, O descendant of Aeacus, that you can conquer the Romans," but which turned out to prophesy the opposite. When the subject of the infinitive is the same as that of the main verb, it may be omitted, except in indirect discourse, and any predicate adjective modifying the subject of the infinitive or predicate noun in agreement with it then becomes nominative, in agreement with the subject of the main verb, as in *omnēs uolunt beātī esse* = all wish to be happy, or everybody wants to be happy.

The use of the infinitive in indirect discourse or indirect statement apparently arose from the use of the accusative subject with an object infinitive. That is, both the person and the action were regarded as objects of the verb of saying, thinking, seeing, or the like. Thus in the sentence *uideō Caesarem uenīre* = I see Caesar coming (literally to come), the main verb *uideō* covered initially both Caesar and the act of coming. The composite phrase that resulted, combining an accusative noun and an infinitive, bears a close resemblance to the object infinitive with a subject accusative, and they are sometimes hard to distinguish. For example, *iubeō* = I order and *uetō* = I forbid take an object infinitive with accusative subject, as in *iussit Antōnium abīre* = he ordered Antony to depart. To the speaker of English, this appears to differ little from *dīxit Antōnium abīre* = he said that Antony was departing, which is indirect discourse. Yet indirect discourse has one feature that distinguishes this construction from the object infinitive. In indirect discourse, the accusative subject is regularly expressed, even though it may be the same as the subject of the main verb; in that case a reflexive pronoun is used, as in *dīcit sē esse ōrātōrem* = he says that he (himself) is an orator.

The tenses of the infinitive in indirect discourse are present, perfect, or future in relation to the time of the main verb, not to the actual time of utterance. That is, in the preceding example *dīxit Antōnium abīre*, the active present infinitive *abīre* shows that Antony was going away when somebody said that he was, whereas the active perfect infinitive *abīsse* would show that he already had departed, and the active future infinitive *abitūrum esse* would show that he was about to depart or going to do so at some future time.

Subordinate clauses in indirect discourse that are part of the quoted utterance go into the subjunctive and take the tense appropriate to the tense of the main verb of saying, not to that of the infinitive, in accordance with the rules for sequence of tenses. A subordinate clause that represents the speaker's own opinion, however, remains in the indicative. Thus in *dīxit Antōnium, quī Caesarī amīcus esset, abīre* = he said that Antony, who (or because he) was a friend to Caesar, was going away, the subjunctive shows that the relative clause gives Antony's reason for going, whereas if the verb were *erat*, this would show that the subject of the main verb (the speaker) simply himself identified Antony as a friend to Caesar.

When the verb of saying is passive, the more usual construction is for the subject of the indirect discourse to serve as the nominative subject of the passive verb of saying and the infinitive to remain in the predicate. In this case modifiers of the subject are in the nominative, as is *caecus* in *Homērus dīcitur caecus fuisse* = Homer is said to have been blind. However, the whole indirect discourse may become subject, particularly with the compound passive perfect tenses, in which case the subject and its modifiers remain in the accusative, as in *traditum est Homērum caecum fuisse* = it is (or has been) said that Homer was blind. Here the English idiom makes the main verb impersonal, but in Latin the infinitive phrase is subject.

In exclamations, an infinitive with a subject in the accusative may apparently stand independently, but in such utterances there is the suppression of a verb of saying or the like, as in Juno's exclamation in Vergil, *Aeneid* I 37, *mēne inceptō desistere uictam* = I desist, defeated, from my undertaking, which represents some such thought as "do you think that I would desist?"

The Latin infinitive did not ordinarily indicate purpose, as does the English infinitival phrase. However, in early Latin the infinitive may express purpose, usually after verbs of motion. This usage may have originally been that of the infinitive as a noun in the dative of the end aimed at by the main action. Cato the Elder, who was a distinguished Roman of the late third and early second centuries B.C., has left a book on farm management, or agriculture, the *Dē Agrī Cultūrā*. In chapter 89 he gives advice on fattening hens or geese, in the course of which he remarks *meridiē bibere datō* = at midday give (them something) to drink. In this sentence the present active infinitive *bibere* appears to be a dative which expresses the purpose of the giving enjoined by the active future imperative second person singular *datō*. This construction would then be extended to verbs of motion to show the end toward which they are directed, as in *uēnerat aurum petere* = he had come to seek gold (or money). However, if the purpose toward which a verb of motion points is a simple verbal action, the form used is normally the supine. Purpose is regularly expressed by one of two constructions: a prepositional phrase in which *ad* is followed by either a gerund or a noun modified by a gerundive; or alternatively a clause introduced by *ut* and with its verb in the subjunctive. An often cited warning against using the infinitive of purpose is the usual form of the motto of the Society of the Cincinnati, *omnia relinquit seruāre rem pūblicam* = he leaves all to save the state. That at the time of the founding of the society after the American Revolution somebody was disturbed by this is suggseted by the form used on the society's medal, *omnia relinquit; seruat rem pūblicam*, which places two present indicatives in asyndeton, to mean "he leaves all; he saves the state."

The infinitive may be used in Latin after perfect passive participles employed as adjectives when they are participles of verbs that themselves take an infinitive, as in *mīles parātus pūgnāre* = a soldier prepared to fight. More commonly, however, such passive perfect participles take a gerund or gerundive construction, in the genitive, in the dative, or in the accusative with *ad*; as in *insuētus nāuigandi* = unused to making sea voyages, *alendīs līberīs suētus* = accustomed to supporting children, and *insuētus ad onera portanda* = unused to bearing burdens. Imitating a Greek practice, the Roman poets extended the use of the infinitive to many adjectives, as in Vergil, *Eclogue* V 54, *cantārī dīgnus* = worthy to be sung, or hymned.

The many uses of the Latin infinitive can be dealt with only summarily in this book and should be studied in more detail in a systematic Latin grammar. In particular the use in indirect discourse of the tenses of the infinitive and of the subjunctive in subordinate clauses merits attention. Latin writers feel free to make exceptions to the regular constructions when they find that the expression of their thought requires departures from usual practice.

GERUND

The gerund is a neuter verbal noun with active force. It supplies the oblique cases of the infinitive when the verbal concept limits or defines another noun, as in *cōnsilium pūgnandī* = a plan of (or for) fighting; or after adjectives and some verbs that govern a dative, as in *mīles idōneus pūgnandō* = a soldier suitable for fighting; or as ablative of manner, means, cause, and so forth, as in *multa pollicendō persuādet* = he persuades by promising much (or by large promises). Though the infinitive may be used when the verbal concept is a simple object of another verb, the accusative of the gerund or an accusative noun modified by a gerundive must be used after certain prepositions, in particular after *ad* to express purpose, as in *mē uocās ad scrībendum* = you summon me to write. Similarly a gerund or a noun modified by a gerundive in the genitive, the dative, or the accusative with *ad* is more common than the infinitive after adjectives. For example, *uir parātus ad labōrandum* is preferable to *uir parātus labōrāre* to mean "a man prepared to work."

The gerund does not have a subject, or adjectival or adverbial modifiers. It may take an object, particularly a neuter pronoun, as in *artem uēra ac falsa diiūdicandī* = the art of distinguishing true and (or from) false. Usually, however, when the verbal idea has an object, the alternative construction is used, that of putting the noun (the object) into the case required were the gerund to be used and modifying it by the passive verbal adjective, the gerundive. For instance, *cōnsilium urbem capiendī* = a plan of (or for) taking the city is rare, as against *cōnsilium urbis capiendae* literally = a plan of the city to be taken. If the gerund is from a verb that takes the dative, the gerund is also used with the dative, as in *ueniunt ad mihi parendum* = they come to obey me; *ad mē parendum* (gerundive) would be incorrect.

SUPINE

The supine as a verbal noun exists only in the accusative and ablative. The accusative is used after verbs of motion to express the end of motion, or purpose, and may take an object, as in *admonitum uēnimus tē* = we have come to advise you. Here the supine is sufficiently verbal to take as object *tē*. A special development of this construction is represented by the passive future infinitive, as in *amātum īrī* literally = to be gone toward a loving, hence to be going to be loved. The ablative is used as an ablative of specification after certain adjectives, as in *rēs uīsū foeda* = a matter disgusting to behold, as well as after the noun *opus* = need, and the words *fās* and *nefās* which, though nouns meaning "(divine) law" and "(divine) unlawfulness," are generally translated as adjectives, meaning "lawful" and "unlawful," as in *hoc fās est dictū* = this is lawful to say. In such phrases, the ablative of the supine occurs for only a few common verbs and does not take either an object or modifiers; it stands alone, as in the examples just given.

PARTICIPLES

The very name of the Latin participle indicates that it participates in the functions of both verb and adjective. As verb forms, participles have mood and tense and, if active from transitive verbs, may take objects. They may be modified by adverbs or by adverbial prepositional phrases. As adjectives, they modify nouns, pronouns, or other words used as nouns, and they agree with these in gender, number, and case. The active present and passive perfect participles are the two regularly employed to express the action of verbs adjectivally. The active future participle is rarely used as a pure adjective except in poetry and in later prose. However, when active future and passive perfect participles are combined in compound tenses with the appropriate forms of the verb *sum* = I am used as a copulative, they become predicate adjectives in agreement with the subject.

The word "copulative" comes from the passive perfect participle *cōpulātus* of *cōpulō* = I join. It means that *sum* merely unites or connects two words rather than signifying being or existence. The active future participle with *sum* constitutes what is called the "first" or "active periphrastic conjugation," to denote immediate futurity. "Periphrastic" comes from a Greek word meaning "a circumlocution," so that a periphrastic conjugation is a "round about way" of expressing an idea for which Latin had no simple verbal forms. For example, *mulierēs labōrātūrae sunt* means "the women are about to (go to) work," and the active future participle *labōrātūrae* is feminine nominative plural in agreement with *mulierēs*. The active future infinitive, which combines the accusative of the active future participle with *esse*, was probably taken over into the regular conjugations from the first periphrastic. A so-called second or passive periphrastic conjugation is formed by combining *sum* with a gerundive in agreement with the subject, as in *urbs capienda est* = the city must be taken. Though the passive perfect system is not usually called "periphrastic," it could be so denominated because it combines *sum* with the passive perfect participle in agreement with the subject to express an idea for which the simple Latin passive system had no forms, as in *urbs capta est* = the city was (or has been) taken.

The active present and passive perfect participles are also used in the construction called the "ablative absolute." In this construction the participle is basically adjectival, not verbal. The construction may also occur simply with two nouns or with a noun and an adjective. Though in these cases the nonexistence participle of *sum* may be supplied mentally, it was probably not conceived of as actually forming part of the construction; the second noun or the adjective stood on the same footing as would a participle.

Active present participles when used as nouns or in the ablative absolute regularly have the ablative ending short -*e*, but when used as adjectives have the ablative ending long -ī. Examples are *dictum ā sapiente quōdam est* = it was said by a certain wise man (or philosopher), and *Caesare praesente Cicerō rēgem Dēiotarum dēfendit* = with Caesar present Cicero defended king Deiotarus. "In the presence of (or before) Caesar (as presiding judge)" would probably be expressed with the preposition *cōram* and the ablative, *cōram Caesare*; the ablative absolute expresses simply an attendant circumstance, such as that Cicero was defending Deiotarus, perhaps before the senate, and Caesar happened to be there. Long -ī appears in the ablative when a present participle is used as an adjective, as in *a homine sapienti numquam peccātur* = by a wise man a sin is never committed (literally it is never sinned).

Latin frequently uses an active present or passive perfect participle in agreement with a noun where English would use a subordinate or coordinate clause, as in *damnātum poenam sequī oportēbat* = (if he was) condemned, it was proper (for) punishment to follow (him). This construction permits in Latin the actions to be put in chronological order in the sentence but the less important one to be subordinated to the more important. For example, to render the above example literally in English would reverse the order of the actions: "punishment ought to follow (him once he has been) condemned." Similarly, a noun and a passive perfect participle may express in Latin what in English would require an abstract noun and a genitive or a subordinate clause, as in *ante conditam urbem* = before the founding of the city, or before the city was (or had been) founded.

GERUNDIVE

Despite the close resemblance in form of the gerundive to the gerund, they differ in function. The gerundive is a passive adjective that connotes immediate futurity, duty, obligation, or necessity. Because of the connotation of futurity, it is sometimes called a "passive future participle." Occasional gerundives are active intransitive in meaning, as are *secundus* (*-a*, *-um*) = following, second, or favorable, and *moribundus* (*-a*, *-um*) = dying.

The gerundive may be used as an ordinary adjective, as in *uir laudandus* = a man to be praised, but this use as a simple epithet is not common and is mainly confined to verbs of emotion. The gerundive is more common predicatively in agreement with the object of various verbs, as in *Catulus tabulārium faciendum cūrāuit* = Catulus saw to (literally cared for) a state archive being built, or Catulus was responsible for building the state archive. The concept here of something to be done verges on that of purpose and thus suggests the even more frequent employment of the gerundive in a prepositional phrase governed by *ad* to denote purpose. This construction usually replaces a simple gerund with *ad* when otherwise the active gerund would have an object. The object becomes the noun governed by *ad* and is modified by the adjectival passive gerundive. In either case the whole prepositional phrase signifies the end of motion, as in *mīlitēs missī sunt ad urbem capiendam* = troops were sent to take the city (literally to the city to be taken).

Latin employs three different constructions to connote purpose: first *ad* with the gerund alone or a noun modified by the gerundive; second a relative clause of characteristic connoting purpose, as in *mīlitēs missī sunt quī urbem caperent* = troops were sent who should (or to) take the city; and third, an ordinary adverbial purpose (or final) clause in the subjunctive with *ut* = so that (negative *nē* = so that not, as in *mīlitēs missī sunt ut urbem caperent* = troops were sent that they should take the city, and *hostēs urbem mūnīuērunt nē caperētur* = the enemy fortified the city so that it should not be taken.

The second common use of the gerundive is in combination with forms of the verb *sum* = I am, to make what is called the "second (or passive) periphrastic conjugation," which expresses future necessity, as in *cōnsul creandus est* = a consul must be elected. In this construction the gerundive, like the passive perfect and the active future participles in similar compound forms, is in fact a predicate adjective in agreement with the subject. A dative of reference is customary with this construction to indicate the person involved, or on whom the necessity lies, instead of an ablative of agent with the preposition *ā* (*ab*); this dative is usually, though inaccurately, called a "dative of agent." Only when there is a second dative of a person (not a thing) as indirect object is the agent expressed by the ablative with *ā* (*ab*) in order to avoid ambiguity. Thus *grātia mihi referenda est* means "thanks are to be rendered by me (literally as far as I am concerned)," but if the thanks are to be rendered to me by a friend, the sentence runs *grātia ab amīcō mihi referenda est.*

The second periphrastic is frequently used impersonally, as may also be the passive mood in general. Thus *pūgnandum est* = fighting is to be, or is necessary. In this construction the neuter gerundive looks like an accusative gerund, but the context shows the difference. It is neuter because it modifies and agrees with the concept involved in itself, here "fighting." The impersonal passive periphrastic resembles a simple impersonal passive, such as the present *curritur* = there is a running, or people are running, or the perfect *cursum est* = there has been a running, or people ran, or even running is completed, or the race is finished.

In conclusion, the uses of the various moods and tenses of the verb are all related to their basic connotations. In the finite systems, the chief syntactical demarcation is between the uses of the indicative and those of the subjunctive, in both dependent and independent clauses. The indicative, stating fact, as it ordinarily does, is usually simple to account for in a main clause; in a subordinate clause it is occasionally hard to grasp the precise line between it and the subjunctive, as with temporal *cum* = when, with *dum* = while, or in relative clauses. The key to understanding the constructions of the subjunctive is that the speaker, in using it, disassociates himself from the factuality of the statement; that is, he feels uncertainty, whether this implies unreality, contingency, probability, volition, or wish. The syntax of the nonfinite forms is easy of comprehension except in the case of the variety of infinitival constructions and in the differentiation between the use of the infinitive and that of subordinate clauses introduced by *ut* = (so) that, or (with the result) that, *nē* = (so) that not, and *ut nōn* = (with the result) that not. The verbs that take one or the other of these constructions must be learned by observation.

XIII

VERSIFICATION

When early men began putting laws, religious prescriptions, and legends or myths into oral form and sought to communicate them not only to one another but to succeeding generations, they must have come to realize that memorization and transmission were easier and more accurate if their thoughts were expressed in phrases that had repetitive patterns of sound, whether rhyming or rhythmical. Certainly the earliest literary survivals, whether of poetry or of legal and religious ordinances, generally show such patterns. Composition in any kind of repeated pattern, whether of sound, of stress, or in some literatures of thought, is called "verse." This term comes from a noun of the fourth declension *uersus* literally = a turning, from the verb *uertō* = I turn. This word was applied to a furrow, because the plough either turned up the soil or turned back and forth in ploughing a field. Then the word was applied to a line of plants in a furrow and hence to any line, including a line of poetry as distinguished by its repetitive pattern of sound. By extension, verse has come to be used in English for composition in verses. It applies properly to the external form, whereas poetry, from a Greek verb meaning "I make," covers both form and content.

Both verse and poetry stand in contrast to speech, which normally has no regularly repeated pattern of sound. This latter is called "prose," from *prōsa*, a term that represents a corruption in pronunciation, which occurred as early as the first century A.D., of the nominative feminine singular of the Latin adjective *prōrsus* (-*a*, -*um*) = straightforward, or right on. This word in turn had already been reduced from the passive perfect participle *prōuersus* or *prōuorsus* of *prōuertō* = I turn forward. *Prōsa ōrātiō* was therefore "speech that goes straight on," ordinarily without any regular pattern. The adjective then came to be used without *ōrātiō* as itself a noun. In modern literature the clear distinction of form made by classical writers between prose and verse has become blurred. Free verse purports to have more of a sound pattern, though not a regular one, and a more poetic character than prose, and some prose claims to have poetic content and to merit the title "prose poem."

The repeated pattern of sound may take various forms in different literary traditions. In the Hebrew psalms the repetition is one of thought in two halves of a verse, each comprising approximately the same number of syllables, as in the English translation, "The Lord is my shepherd; I shall not want . . ." Anglo-Saxon poetry, particularly the epic *Beowulf*, divides the verse into two sections by a marked pause. Each section contains two strong or stressed syllables, which are generally alliterated, that is, they begin with the same letter. Apart from this repetitive pattern of stress and sound, the halves may differ considerably in the number of weak or unstressed syllables that they contain, though they tend to show in general an equivalence of speech time rather than of syllables. For example, *Beowulf* line 95 is scanned as follows: "lēóman tō lēóhtade//lándbūèndum." It shows two main stresses in the first half, before the caesura, and two main and one secondary in the second half. There is alliteration of *le*- . . . *le*- in the first half with *l*- in the second. This verse is the second of a couplet which states that "(God established) the brightness (of sun and moon) for a light to dwellers in the land." There is constant variation in Anglo-Saxon verse from this metrical norm; the oral delivery of the verse must have permitted considerable liberty as to meter.

In later English verse, the repetition that constituted meter came to be one of successions of accented and unaccented syllables, normally alternating. But since this becomes very monotonous, often two or even three unaccented syllables intervene between successive accents. When the unaccented syllable precedes the accented, the rhythm is called "iambic"; when the accented precedes the unaccented, it is called "trochaic." A pure iambic line from Shakespeare is: "What blóódy mán is thát? he cán by hís repórt." The line "To bé or nót to bé—thát is the quéstion" shows a shift of the fourth accent to follow directly, with a pause in delivery, on the third and then two unaccented syllables before the fifth accent and a final unaccented syllable thereafter. In English meter the rhythm is therefore given by the word accent. Often a further pattern is fixed by making the ends of verses rhyme, again in various repetitions of final sounds. It seems, from comparing the metrical conventions of many Indo-European languages, that the use of repeated patterns of word accents with unaccented syllables intervening may have been inherited from the original tongue or tongues.

QUANTITATIVE METER

The earliest surviving Latin verse was in a form that the later Roman writers on metrics called "Saturnian," from the name of the god supposed to have ruled over Italy in the Golden Age. The rhythm of Saturnian is thought by most scholars to have been set by word accent, but since the surviving lines show very irregular patterns of accent, and since the place of the word accent in early Latin was probably different from that in classical Latin, there is little agreement on the form of the repeated pattern. A strong minority of scholars even maintain that the repeated pattern was one of syllabic quantity and was borrowed from Greek metrics. Of what appear to have been the only two major literary works in Saturnian, namely a translation of Homer's *Odyssey* by the poet Livius Andronicus (c. 284–c. 204 B.C.) and an account of Rome's first war against Carthage, the *Bellum Punicum* by Naevius (c. 270–c. 201 B.C.), relatively few lines survive, and other fragments of Saturnian are equally scanty. The total does not afford sufficient grounds for a conclusive judgment about the basis of the rhythm.

Since Andronicus came from Tarentum and Naevius from Campania, both thoroughly Hellenized areas, and since each also wrote dramatic works in Greek quantitative meters, it is entirely possible that the rhythm of their narrative poetry was at least influenced by Greek metrical practice. The debate on the nature of the Saturnian rhythm is significant principally insofar as it bears on the difficult question of the relation of word accent to verse stress in classical Latin poetry.

Greek poetry from the beginning, namely from Homer, who composed perhaps as early as the eighth century B.C., used repeated patterns of sound based on syllabic quantity rather than on word accent, that is, on the alternation in various patterns of long and short syllables. Since classical Latin verse was quantitative in imitation of Greek verse, the only other Indo-European language independently to show quantitative meters is Sanskrit, the language of the Indo-European occupiers of India. The use of accentual meters in other languages derived from Indo-European suggests that the parent language used word accent to establish its rhythms. This, however, does not prove that Indo-European did not also recognize quantitative meter, evidenced in both Sanskrit and Greek. In view of the probable use of such meter in Sanskrit, it does not seem likely that the pre-Homeric Greeks arrived at quantitative meter on their own or that they derived it through the Mycenaean proto-Greeks from the non-Hellenic Minoans, whose culture flourished in Crete from the mid third to the mid second millennia B.C.

Greek poetry was initially closely allied to music, and its rhythms were conceived of in musical terms. Thus syllabic quantity represents the musical time allowed for the pronunciation of a syllable. The assumption of only two quantities, long and short, was a simplification of what must have been in speech a much greater variation in time of pronunciation. Indeed, in some verse patterns a long syllable may stand in positions normally assigned to a short syllable, which indicates that, in speech, syllabic quantity could be adjusted to musical needs.

The musical basis of Greek rhythms creates problems of pronunciation that are impossible to solve because of the lack of any clear evidence as to the overall sound of ancient spoken Greek. In the first place, the musical accompaniment to verse presumably had a repeated stress, which is called in Latin an *ictus* = beat. This usually, though not necessarily, fell on a long syllable, and it might fall on a syllable other than that bearing the normal spoken word accent. Second, in spoken Greek there was a tone of voice on a given syllable in each word, which was not necessarily that which bore the word accent. The voice might be raised or lowered on the given syllable, or possibly it might rise and fall. In the Alexandrian period (323–30 B.C.) Greek scholars used marks to help foreigners put the right tone on syllables. An acute mark or accent (´) indicated a rising tone, a grave accent (`) a falling tone, and a circumflex accent (ˆ) a rise and fall of tone. Since a rise and fall of tone on one syllable appears difficult to utter, possibly syllables marked with a circumflex accent had a steady, sustained tone. Some modern languages, such as Chinese, still have a tone change. In them, to give a syllable the wrong tone may completely alter the meaning of a word. If the tone change and the word accent fell on different syllables, then Greek verse had to take account of three types of sound emphasis: word accent, tone change, and musical ictus. The ictus might or might not fall on the same syllable as either of the other two.

Latin poets very early borrowed the Greek system of quantitative meter as part of their general imitation of Greek literary forms and techniques. However, tone change seems never to have had the importance in spoken Latin that the introduction of written tone accents shows that it had in spoken Greek. On the other hand, Latin word accent appears to have been even more marked than was the Greek. Whatever the position of the word accent in early Latin, it became fixed in classical Latin to one of two syllables, either the syllable before the last, called the "penult," if this was long, or the third syllable from the end, the "antepenult," if the following penult was short. Thus the position of the word accent in Latin came to depend solely on the quantity of the penult.

Even the two earliest named Latin poets, Livius and Naevius, who used the possibly accentual Saturnian rhythm for their epics, also wrote dramatic poetry in Greek meters based on syllabic quantity. The most outstanding early Latin poet, Ennius (239–169 B.C.), employed the meter of Greek epic, the dactylic hexameter, for his versified account of early Roman history, the renowned *Annales*. He set the pattern for such later didactic and epic poets as Lucretius and Vergil.

When Greek quantitative meters were applied to Latin, the musical stress or ictus might fall on any syllable dictated by the particular quantitative pattern used by the poet. But in spoken verse, the stressing of syllables other than those bearing normal word accents would make the recognition of words difficult. Statistical studies have shown that in fact Latin verse has a considerable coincidence of word accent and verse ictus, often as high as fifty percent. Particularly in the verses of Vergil the two coincide in the first and in the last two of the six metrical units called "feet." If, for example, in a typical verse, Vergil, *Aeneid* II 2, the ictus is indicated by ′ above the metrically stressed syllable and the word accent by a ‚ below the syllable bearing it, correspondence and diversity appear as follows:

índe toró pater Aénēās sīc ōrsus ab álto

Apart from this effort to make the spoken words recognizable by coincidence of musical ictus and word accent at key points in the verse, it must be assumed that either the ictus or the word accent, or both, were not so strongly emphasized as to obscure the other. Thus the modern tendency to lay heavy stress on syllables bearing the musical ictus is probably exaggerated, if not wrong. However, it is not easy for a modern reader to preserve the values of both musical ictus and word accent in reading Latin verse aloud.

A further difficulty in the adaptation of Greek quantitative rhythms to the Latin language was that in Latin words the relative frequency and sequence of long and short syllables differed from those in Greek. Hence the achievement of the Latin poets in adjusting Latin words to the Greek rhythmical patterns without so distorting their order and syntactical relations as to obscure the meaning is remarkable. In the *Odes* of Horace (65–8 B.C.) the word order is rendered unusually complicated by the metrical requirements, and in consequence much attention is necessary to recognize the syntactical groupings. Nevertheless Horace achieved an extraordinary success in fitting the Latin language into complex Greek lyric rhythms, which have almost invariable metrical patterns. To a lesser degree,

Vergil faced the same problem. However, since the rhythmical pattern of dactylic hexameter verse was repetitive and allowed the flexibility of substituting a long syllable for two shorts, Vergil could preserve a more normal word order than could Horace. Also some of Vergil's departures from prose order are for poetic, rather than metrical, reasons.

Because grammatical relations have in Latin a larger role in giving meaning than does mere word order, the rearrangement of the normal prose order of words to fit fixed metrical patterns did less to obscure sense than it would in a language which, like English, depends heavily on word order for meaning. Whether the Romans of the late Republic and early Empire still expected their poetry actually to be accompanied by music, they in any case remained strongly conscious of the musical basis of their rhythmical patterns and may well have actually either chanted or sung their verse rather than simply reading it, as moderns tend to do.

The Romans applied to the whole subject of versification the term *prosōdia* = prosody. This comes from a Greek noun which basically means "to (or accompanying) a song," and which connoted primarily word accent or verse stress. It came to cover also the other elements of verse making: quantity, meter, and scansion.

SYLLABIC QUANTITY

Quantity has heretofore been considered as that of vowels only, which are by nature long or short. The rhythm or meter of Latin verse depends, however, not on the length of vowels alone but on the length of syllables comprising both vowels and consonants. There are as many syllables in a Latin word as there are separately pronounced vowels or diphthongs. Syllables end where possible with a vowel, so that single consonants are pronounced with a following vowel or diphthong rather than with a preceding one. When two consonants come together, however, they must ordinarily be pronounced separately for clarity. In such cases, the first is pronounced with the preceding vowel and the second with the following one. This is true whether the two consonants come within a word or at the end of one and the beginning of the next.

Because of the necessity in speech to distinguish the sounds of two successive consonants, either within a word or between two successive words, the syllable ending in a consonant takes longer to pronounce than does a syllable ending in a vowel. Theoretically a succession of a consonant followed by a short vowel followed by a consonant should take about the same time to pronounce as would a consonant followed by a long vowel, while the pronunciation of a syllable comprising a consonant, a long vowel, and a consonant should take longer. However, both the Greeks and Romans, in discussing verse quantity, neglected this additional time and treated all syllables that end in a consonant as equal in length, whatever the quantities of their vowels.

Thus in Latin meter a syllable whose vowel is followed by two or more consonants, that is, which itself ends in a consonant, is generally long even if its vowel is short. The two or more consonants may be within a word or one at the end of a word and one or more at the beginning of the following word. But when a syllable ending in a consonant is last in a word and not followed by another word beginning with a consonant, as frequently occurs at the end of a verse of poetry, the final syllable is not lengthened unless its vowel is by nature long. When a syllable containing a short vowel is lengthened by a final consonant, the consonant is said to "make position" and the syllable to be long "by position."

The only exception to the lengthening of a syllable containing a short vowel when this is followed by two consonants is when the two consonants are a mute followed by a liquid. In this case the syllable may be short or long, because the mute and the liquid may either be pronounced closely together with the vowel of the following syllable or be separated so that the mute goes with the preceding vowel at the end of the first of two syllables and the liquid with the following vowel at the beginning of the second. If the mute and the liquid are pronouced together and the preceding vowel is short, then the first of the two syllables is short; if they are pronounced separately, then the first syllable is long whether its vowel is long or short. The mutes are all the plosive consonants: voiceless p, t, $c(k)$, and qu; voiced b, d, and g; and the aspirated voiceless ph, th, and ch. The liquids are l and r.

The double consonants x $(c[k]s)$ and z (dz), in which the

single written sign represents two consonant sounds closely combined, count as double consonants and make position, even though
they would not have been separated as much in speech as would two
less combined successive consonants. Likewise consonantal *i* and *u*
make position when they follow another consonant; they never
precede one. The only exceptions are *qu* and occasionally *gu*, which
represent single consonant sounds though written as two letters.
The consonant *h* does not make position after another consonant,
whether it stands alone or in combination with a consonant, as in *th*.
Clearly aspiration was not sufficiently strong in Latin to be recognized as a distict consonant sound.

In sum, the quantity of a Latin syllable which ends in a vowel is
that of the vowel, and its quantity is said to be "by nature," that is,
short by nature if the vowel is short, and long by nature if the vowel
is long. Syllables within a word in which the vowel is followed by a
consonant in the same syllable, or at the end of the word when the
words ends with a consonant and the following word begins with
one, are always treated as long whether the vowel in them is long or
short. If the vowel in such a syllable is short by nature, the syllable
is said to be long "by position."

Heretofore a long mark (¯) over a vowel has indicated its natural
length. In illustrating meter, however, the long mark is used to indicate a long syllable; short syllables do not bear a short mark (˘)
unless one is needed to emphasize their shortness. This double
significance of the long mark arises because in marking syllabic
quantity in verse, it is customary to indicate the quantity of the
syllable only over its vowel or diphthong, not over the whole
syllable.

Following are some examples to illustrate syllabic quantity:
First syllable short because it ends in a short vowel: *pa-ter* =
father.
First syllable long because it ends in a long vowel: *māter* =
mother.
First syllable long long because it ends in a diphthong: *moē-nia*
= walls.
First syllable long because it contains a short vowel followed by a
consonant in the same syllable: *tēr-ra* = earth.
First syllable long because it contains a short vowel followed by

a double consonant which is, so to speak, shared between the first and second syllables, though probably actually pronounced mainly with the second: *sā-x-um* = rock. This is sounded as *sāc-sum*.

First syllable long because it contains a long vowel followed by a consonant in the same syllable: *cōn-sul* = consul. In such a word, the quantity of the *-o-* cannot be determined by the length of the syllable in verse, since it is in any case long by position. Such a vowel, in a syllable that would in any case be long because the vowel is followed by a consonant, is therefore said to have "hidden quantity," which must be determined by some other means, for example, in *cōnsul* by the principle that vowels followed by *-ns-* were always pronounced long.

First syllable with a short vowel pronounced short or long, depending on how a following mute and a liquid are divided: *pa-tris* = of a father (first syllable short) or *pāt-ris* (first syllable long). With this may be contrasted *mātris* = of a mother, in which the *-ā-* of the first syllable is long, so that the syllable itself is long by nature regardless of whether the word is divided *mā-tris* or *māt-ris*.

In verse, the whole line is treated as if it were a continuous spoken unit. In consequence when a word within the line ends with a syllable containing a short vowel followed by a final consonant, and when the following word begins with a consonant or consonants, the final syllable of the first word is long by position, just as it would be within a word. This holds true even when the final consonant is a mute and the initial one a liquid, since in this situation the separation in speech between the words prevented the possibility of pronouncing the mute and the liquid together. If a verse ends in a syllable whose vowel is followed by a consonant, the quantity of the syllable ordinarily remains that of its vowel, since the verse was considered as having ended and any consonant or consonants at the opening of a following verse rarely served to "make position."

When a word ending in a final short vowel is followed by a word beginning with two consonants, the situation is more complicated. If the two initial consonants are a mute and a liquid, a preceding final short vowel usually remains short, as in *tālia, flāmmātō* = such things, burnt (the words are not syntactically connected); *claūstra fremūnt* = the door bars roar (that is, on being opened); *dērige grēssum* = direct (your) step; and *īmōque trahēns* = and drawing from the depth. The Romans avoided placing a final short vowel before words beginning with other combinations of consonants, which normally can be pronounced together at the opening of a word but which would ordinarily be separated within a word, as before initial *sc-*, *st-*, and similar combinations that do not comprise a mute followed by a liquid. On the rare occasions when a final short vowel precedes an initial combination of such consonants, the vowel is usually lengthened as if within a word, as in *nūllā spēs* = no hope, where *nūlla* is feminine nominative singular in agreement with *spēs*; or *Brōntēsquē Steropēsque*, two proper names.

METRICAL FEET AND VERSES

Short and long syllables are combined in various sequences to form metrical units called "feet." A foot is the smallest unit used to measure a verse, and it may simply be repeated a given number of times or combined with other types of feet to form a sequence which itself may be repeated. Such a sequence is known by the Greek name *cōlon* (or *kōlon*) = a limb or member; its plural is *cōla*. A verse, or a longer metrical unit than a colon, may contain a determined number of similar feet or a regular pattern of different feet or a succession of cola. The verses or lines of the poetry that is usually first met in the study of Latin each contain a fixed number of basically similar feet, for instance, six dactyls in the hexameter verse of epic or six iambs in the senarius of comedy. Monotony is avoided by not having each verse consist wholly of six dactyls or five iambs but of substituting other metrically equivalent feet within the verse, without departing from the prescribed total of feet.

Verses may be combined into larger groups, which in English are called "stanzas," from an Italian noun meaning "a room," or "a stopping place," which in turn derives from the active present participle *stāns* of the Latin verb *stō* = I stand, or I stop. Latin has no term corresponding to "stanza"; the closest one in ancient metrics is the Greek *strophē* literally = a turning, which was applied to the three stanzas of a Greek tragic chorus, in which the first, the *strophē* proper, was followed by a metrically symmetrical *antistrophē*, and the concluding stanza was a nonsymmetrical *epōdē* = aftersong.

In Latin poetry successive lines occasionally end in similar sounds, as in *ferēbat/uolēbat* = he was bearing/he was willing, or *mouentem/petentem* = moving/seeking. These are frequent enough in Vergil to suggest to some scholars that they represent a survival of rhyme from early Latin verse. However, Latin is so replete with similar endings that it may be questioned how far such repetitions of sound really constitute rhyme, which is used so much in English verse to emphasize the line divisions of stanzas. Christian poetry in the late Empire did elevate to literary status both word accent as a basis of rhythm and rhyme, probably because these features had continued to characterize the popular Latin verse of the Roman proletariat during the classical period while literary verse of the upper classes passed more completely under the domination of Greek practices.

Two other types of echoing sound, called "alliteration" and "assonance," are not uncommon in Latin poetry, and assonance is particularly frequent between the ends of lines. Alliteration, a mediaeval term from *ad* = to and *lit(t)era* = letter, means the repetition of the same letter or sound, usually at the beginning of successive words or of words close enough to each other that the repetition is noticeable. Alliteration may also occur within words, especially in syllables on which the musical ictus falls. Examples are *mūrmura māgna minārum* = the great murmurs of threats, and *flāmmāntia mōēnia mūndī* = the flaming ramparts of the universe. An extreme example of alliteration that runs over into a second verse is Vergil, *Aeneid* IV 460–461, *nōcēs ēt uērba uocāntis/uīsa uirī* = the voices and apparent words of (her) husband calling (her).

Assonance, from the rare verb *assonō* = I respond (in sound) to, is the repetition in successive or closely placed syllables of vowel sounds but not necessarily of the accompanying consonants. Examples are *mūrmura*, in which the two first syllables are in complete assonance, and Vergil, *Aeneid* III 277 and VI 901, which are identical, *āncora dē prōrā iacitūr, stānt lītore pūppēs* = the anchor is tossed from the prow, the sterns rest on the beach. In this verse there is assonance of *-ora* twice, with a following *-ore* and a close approximation in *-ur*. The resemblance in sound of successive line endings may also be regarded as assonance. In general, alliteration is usually a repetition of initial consonant sounds and assonance is a repetition of internal vowel sounds, though even the few examples given suggest that this is only a rough approximation.

The general term for the patterns of short and long syllables that distinguish verse from prose is "meter," derived from the Greek noun *metron* = measure. Thus in English, meter or measure refers specifically to the component feet of verse or generally to the different types of feet. The different meters of Greek and Roman verse ordinarily take their names from the type of foot used in each and the number of feet. Occasionally the feet are reckoned in dipodies, from a Greek word meaning "two feet," since in Greek metrics pairs of like feet were often considered as a single metrical unit. Hence a line of six iambic feet may be called in Greek an "iambic trimeter," because only three dipodies are counted, or in Latin an "iambic senarius," when the six feet are considered individually.

The meters that most closely approach the rhythm of ordinary speech are called "iambic" and "trochaic." The iambus, or iamb, from a Greek word of uncertain origin, contains a short syllable followed by a long one bearing the ictus, namely ˘ ´. The trochee, from a Greek noun meaning "running" because of its tripping rhythm, has a long syllable bearing the ictus followed by a short one, namely ´ ˘.

Since the study of Latin poetry usually begins with Vergil, the metrical form of his verses, called "dactylic hexameter," is the one that is first met. In the dactylic hexameter, the basic foot contains a long syllable which bears the ictus followed by two short syllables, giving the pattern ´ ˘ ˘. This foot takes its name "dactyl" from the Greek noun *daktylos* = finger, because the quantities of its syllables, a long and two shorts, resemble the lengths of the joints of a finger. The Greek term "hexameter" $=$ six measures, or feet, indicates that in this line the Greeks counted the individual feet, not the dipodies. The reverse of the dactyl, two short syllables followed by a long one bearing the ictus (ˇˇ ´), is called an "anapaest," from a Greek verbal adjective meaning "struck back," because in it the dactyl is, so to speak, knocked into reverse. More complicated feet in Greek and Latin verse may be found in any systematic Latin grammar.

In all metrical verses, in order to avoid the monotonous repetition of the same syllabic patterns, substitution is possible. Normally there is substituted for the basic foot some other foot, whose syllables yield the same musical time as do the syllables of the basic foot. In iambic and trochaic meters, this requirement of equivalency would limit substitution to a foot of three short syllables, called in Greek a "tribrach." If a tribrach is used in an iambic verse, the ictus falls on the middle syllable, the first of the two shorts substituted for the long, thus ˇˊˇ If a tribrach is used in a trochaic verse, the ictus falls on the first syllable, again the first of the two shorts substituted for the long, thus ˊˇˇ. In order to increase the possibility of substitution in iambic and trochaic rhythms, both dactyls and anapaests were regarded as needing only the time of three, instead of four, short syllables and could thus be substituted in those rhythms. The same was done with a foot comprising two longs (¯¯) called a "spondee," from a Greek noun meaning "libation," or a "ceremony of pouring a libation." The slow, measured spondaic rhythm was appropriate to such solemn religious functions as libations. Feet in which syllables are substituted which by nature are longer than those that they replace are called "irrational." The position of the ictus in an irrational foot depends on its position in the basic foot.

The place of the ictus in any foot reflects not merely the pattern of the meter but also the musical rhythm. A verse whose feet have the ictuses on the first syllables is said to be in a "descending" rhythm, passing from stressed to unstressed syllables, while a verse having the ictuses on the last syllables of feet is in an "ascending" rhythm. Because of the musical difference of these rhythms, basic feet of an ascending or descending rhythm cannot normally be substituted for basic feet in the opposite rhythm, for example, an iambus in a trochaic rhythm and vice versa, or an anapaest in a dactylic rhythm and vice versa. When this does occur, as occasionally happens, it usually brings two ictuses together and interrupts the musical alternation of stressed and unstressed syllables.

In the dactylic hexameter, a spondee may be substituted in any of the first four feet. An anapaest cannot be substituted, since its rhythm is ascending, while that of the dactyl is descending. Nor can a rare foot of four short syllables, although in metrical time equivalent to the dactyl, be substituted in dactylic hexameters. It does occur occasionally, reduced in delivery to three times, in iambic and trochaic rhythms, especially in comedy, where the quick succession of short syllables reproduces rapidity of speech. Such rapidity would hardly suit the dignity of dactylic verse, especially if a foot of four short syllables followed on the two shorts of a dactyl, to yield a total of six.

The fifth foot of the dactylic hexameter is regularly a dactyl. When a spondee occurs in the fifth foot, as it does frequently in early verse and occasionally in Vergil, the verse is called "spondaic" and acquires a tone of solemnity. If all of the first four feet are spondees but the fifth is a dactyl, the verse is still slow and solemn but is not called "spondaic."

The last foot of the dactylic hexameter is always of two syllables, thus metrically a spondee. However, in Greek and Latin metrics, the final foot of a verse may be short even when the meter requires it to be long. This possibility of a *syllaba anceps* = two-way syllable arises from the natural pause at the end of the verse, which fills out the missing short time. Thus the final foot is represented as $\stackrel{\smile}{}$, where the mark $\smile$ stands for either short or long. The two characteristics of the ends of verses, namely that position is not made and that a final syllable may in fact be long or short (*syllaba anceps*) when the meter prescribes a long, show that the Greeks and the Romans did regard the total verse as a metrical unit, or colon, independent of the preceding or following verse. Within the verse, there is a metrical continuity of syllables which disregards divisions between words.

STANZAS

Verses containing only one type of foot, with substitutions, most
frequently occur in a continuous series with the same number of
feet in each verse, as in the iambic or trochaic dialogue of Roman
comedy or in the epic *Aeneid* of Vergil, where dactylic hexameter
succeeds hexameter except for the occasional break of half-verses,
whether these were left incomplete at Vergil's death or were
deliberate variations. However verses differing in length and often
containing a variety of feet may be composed in stanzas. The
simplest form of stanza has only two verses in the same meter but
of different lengths. Such a stanza of two verses only is called a
"distich," from a Greek noun meaning "two lines."

The most common distich in Latin verse is one named "elegiac,"
from the Greek term "elegy" (of uncertain derivation) for this
type of verse and for poetry composed in it. The elegiac distich or
couplet has as its first verse a regular dactylic hexameter, with substitutions, though verses with a spondee in the fifth foot, called
"spondaic verses," never occur. The second verse of the couplet
comprises two incomplete half-hexameters; that is, each half consists of two dactyls followed by a single syllable bearing the ictus.
At the central break the single syllable must be long, but at the end
it may be a syllaba anceps, namely either long or short. The
metrical effect in the center is to bring together one ictus on the
single long syllable of the third foot and a second on the opening
long syllable of the fourth foot, so as to create a necessary pause or
syncopation at this point. Similarly the verse ends with an ictus on
the single syllaba anceps constituting the sixth or final foot, with a
similar metrical sense of syncopation at the end of the line. The
second verse is often called an "elegiac pentameter" because two
and a half plus two and a half dactyls add up to five. But in fact
it comprises six feet, of which two are incomplete. The substitution
of spondees occurs freely in the two complete feet of the first half;
in the second half such substitution almost never occurs.

Because of its alternation of smoothly flowing dactylic hexameters with syncopated pentameters, the elegiac couplet came to be
used frequently for poetry of reflection or emotion, particularly by

the Augustan poets Tibullus, Propertius, and Ovid to express the emotion of love. Because of the eminence of these poets, Roman elegy is thought of as love poetry, but the elegiac couplet was never limited only to this mood. For instance, at the end of the first century A.D. Martial used it for the bulk of his satirical epigrams. Moreover love poetry was written in other, more lyric meters, as by Catullus and Horace.

Roman dramatic and lyric poets, like the Greek, commonly used verses in which different feet were combined according to a given pattern; such meters were probably intimately connected with music. There may be a succession of verses of the same pattern. More frequently, verses of different metrical patterns are joined in stanzas, usually of four verses in length, as in many of the *Odes* of Horace. Such verses may take their names from the main type and number of feet in them, but more often are called after Greek poets who first or prominently employed them. For example, the Alcaic and Sapphic verses and stanzas preferred by Horace take their names from two Greek lyric poets who composed on the island of Lesbos about 600 B.C.

SPEECH PHENOMENA IN VERSE

Roman verse was composed primarily to be recited or sung. It therefore displays a number of phenomena of speech, particularly in its older or more popular forms. Vergil's verse shows not only assonance and alliteration but other characteristics of speech which had become accepted in the literary language of his day.

In reciting longer verses, such as the dactylic hexameter, it is convenient to pause slightly for breath. Such a pause usually occurs about the middle of a verse. If it falls within a foot, the pause is called a "caesura," that is, a "cutting," from the Latin verb *caedō* = I cut. A caesura after the initial long syllable of a dactyl or spondee is called "masculine," and one after the first short syllable of a dactyl, thus between the two shorts, is called "feminine." If the pause comes between two feet, it is called a "diaeresis" from a Greek noun meaning "a tearing apart." A diaeresis after the fourth foot is not uncommon in Vergil's bucolic (from Greek *boukolos,* an adjective or noun meaning "tending cattle") or pastoral (from Latin *pastor* = one who feeds, especially sheep) poetry and is called a "bucolic diaeresis." But in the *Aeneid* the commonest pauses are either a caesura in the third foot or a diaeresis between the third and fourth. However, this pause must have varied in intensity and in place. In reading aloud, it should be made at a natural break in the sense or syntax, rather than by adhering to any fixed rule. Some verses are so composed as to suggest two slight pauses; others seem so closely knit as to suggest none. In the elegiac pentameter, the second line of the elegiac distich, the syncopation produces a marked diaeresis in the middle. Caesuras or diaereses presumably occurred also in longer iambic, trochaic, or lyric verses, but again their intensity and place must have been flexible.

The other common speech phenomenon in Latin verse is called "elision," meaning "a squeezing out," from the verb *ēlīdō* = I squeeze out. Modern Italian, particularly in the south, still slurs or eliminates final vowels, and this was presumably true in classical Latin. In verse this tendency was recognized metrically by eliminating two types of final vowel sounds before an initial syllable beginning with a vowel, a diphthong, or an *h*-; namely a final vowel or diphthong, or a vowel followed by a final -*m*. Aspiration was apparently slight in Latin, so the slurring or running together of final vowels or diphthongs before *h*- as well as before initial vowels or diphthongs must have been easy. It is more curious that final -*m*, though it made position before an initial consonant, did not prevent elision before an initial vowel, diphthong, or *h*-.

Exactly what happened in pronouncing an elision is unknown. Weak vowels, such as a final short -*e*, may have been completely dropped; stronger vowels, such as a final long -*ā*, may have been merged with the following vowel almost like a diphthong; and final -*m* may have produced a nasalization of the following vowel with the loss of the preceding one. The metrical quantity of the single metrical syllable which results from elision is that only of the second syllable, the initial syllable of the second word. It is unaffected by the quantity of the first vowel, the one in the final elided syllable of the first of the two words. Since it is not known exactly how the Romans in speech merged the elided syllable into the following one to produce what became metrically a single syllable, a modern reader of Latin verse should simply omit the elided, or first, vowel, diphthong, or vowel followed by *-m*. For example, the opening of the third verse of the *Aeneid*, which runs *multum ille et* = and he much, should be read as *mūlt īll et* and written, to indicate the elisions, *mult(um) ill(e) et*. This phrase contains five syllables but counts metrically as only three, namely two long and one short.

In speech, the phenomena represented by elision at the ends of words in verse occurred also within words. It may result in the pronunciation of two vowels as one, or perhaps as a diphthong, by what is called "synizesis," from a Greek noun meaning "a binding together." For example, *mea* = my (feminine) may be slurred to something like *mya*, and *deinde* = then, originally *de-inde* = from thence, becomes only two syllables. Or there may be internal elision, as in *mī* for *mihi* = to me, *nīl* for *nihil* = nothing, or *antehāc* = before pronounced as *antyāc*.

In the verse of early Roman comedy, there is evidence that before *es* = you are and *est* = he is, elision may work in reverse, a phenomenon called "prodelision." For example, *crēditum est* = it is believed may be pronounced *crēditumst*, or *memoriā est optumā* = you are of an excellent memory as *memoriās optumā*. In the latter phrase, *memoriā optumā* is an ablative of description. Also, since final *-s* appears to have been lightly pronounced in early Latin, in such forms as *amātus es* = you have been loved and *amātus est* = he has been loved, it was easy to drop the initial *e-* and merge the two *s*'s, to produce *amātus* or *amātust*. In modern texts, to distinguish prodelided forms from corresponding simple forms of declension or conjugation, an apostrophe is inserted. For example, the preceding examples would be printed *crēditum'st*, *memoriā's*, *amātu's* (or *amātus'*), and *amātu'st* (or *amātus't*). Vergil apparently did not recognize prodelision, since when there is elision before *es* or *est* in his verse, the resultant syllable has the metrical length of the *es* or *est*, not that of the preceding syllable, as in any other case of elision. Also Vergil did not prodelide over final *-s*. By his day, the various phenomena of speech, recognized in early verse, were, by careful writers, being either eliminated or formalized into metrical rules.

That these phenomena continued to be regular features of daily speech is illustrated by a story told by Cicero in his treatise on divination, *Dē Dīuīnātiōne* 40.84, to the effect that when in 54 B.C. Crassus was leaving Italy from Brindisi for his disastrous expedition against the Parthians, a man selling figs that came from a district called Caunus was crying his wares simply as *Cauneās, Cauneās* = Caunians, with both the feminine accusative plural *fīcōs* = figs and some verb meaning "buy" understood. Cicero comments that Crassus should have recognized a divine warning not to go. This story shows that *cauē nē eās* = beware lest you go was pronounced *cau'n'-eās*, with a synizesis of *cauē*, attested also in the verse of comedy, and an elision of the *-ē* of *nē*.

When elision does not occur where it would be expected, the phenomenon is called "hiatus," a Latin noun meaning "a gaping," from the verb *hiō* = I gape, or I yawn. In the verse of comedy hiatus is common when there is a pause for emphasis or at a change of speaker within a line. In Vergil, hiatus is infrequent. He occasionally employs it to avoid the loss of a monosyllabic exclamation before a vowel, as the *Ō* must be pronounced in *Georgics* II 486, *Ō ubi campī* = O where fields. He also sometimes permits it before a caesura or a diaeresis, as the final *-ō* must be kept before the initial *ho-* in *Aeneid* III 606, *sī pereō // hominum* = if I perish of men. Here the initial *h-* would ordinarily not prevent elision, but the caesura, indicated by //, causes enough a pause to allow it.

Another phenomenon of daily speech that was recognized by poets down to the time of Cicero is that called "iambic shortening" or *breuis breuians* = a short making short. The permanent phonological effect of this phenomenon of spoken Latin was not extensive. It caused the shortening of the originally long final *-ā* in the feminine nominative singular of the first declension and of the final long *-ē* in a few common adverbs of the second declension where the preceding syllable was short, as in *bene* = well and *male* = badly, and possibly of the final *-o* of the nominative of the first person singular pronoun *ego* = I, as against Greek *egō*.

But iambic shortening is a common metrical feature of early Latin verse, by which both at the ends of words and within words a long syllable may be treated metrically as short if it is preceded by a short syllable and if the metrical ictus (rather than the word accent) falls either on the immediately preceding short syllable or on the following syllable, whether long or short. Iambic shortening may be represented by the formula: $\smile\!\!-\!\!\stackrel{\prime}{-}$ may yield $\stackrel{\prime}{\smile}\!\!\smile\!\!\stackrel{\prime}{-}$. This formula indicates that in any given case either the first or the third syllable bears the ictus and the third syllable may be either long or short. An example of an iambic shortening in iambic verse, from Plautus, *Miles Gloriosus* 28, is *ăt ĭndĭlĭgénter* = but carelessly, where the syllable *in-* should be long by position before the following *-d* but is shortened by the preceding short syllable *ăt* and the following ictus on *-dĭ-*. Thus the first foot becomes an anapaest. The second foot is a normal iambus.

Although Vergil does not admit iambic shortening into his dactylic hexameters, traces survive under the Empire, for example, in a tendency to regard as short the final long *-ō* of the first person singular active indicative. This phenomenon was apparently generalized from verbs in which the long *-ō* followed a short syllable and was itself followed by a word accent or a metrical ictus. Similarly Juvenal, in the early second century A.D., once treats as short the final long *-ō* of the nominative singular *dēclāmātĭō* = a declamation, a feminine noun of the third declension. The last two words of his *Satire* X 167, a dactylic hexameter line, are *dēclā|mātĭŏ|fĭās* = (that) you may become (the subject of) a declamation. The upright lines placed to divide the feet show that the fourth foot is a spondee, and it is followed by the customary dactyl in the fifth. To achieve this dactyl, the final long *-ō* of *dēclāmātĭō* is shortened by iambic shortening, since the preceding syllable, *-tĭ-*, is short and the following long syllable, *-fĭ-*, bears the metrical ictus. The last foot is, as regularly, a spondee.

Not only does final *-s* seem to have been so lightly pronounced in early Latin that it permitted prodelision, but it also did not necessarily make position when preceded by a short vowel and followed in the next word by a consonant, as in the concluding feet of a dactylic hexameter by Cicero's contemporary Lucretius, *Dē Rērum Nātūrā* III 1025, *Āncŭs rĕlĭquĭt* = Ancus left, in which the *-us* remains short before the following initial consonant to yield the usual dactyl. Vergil, however, consistently regards a final syllable ending in *-s* and followed by an initial consonant as long, whether its vowel is short or long; he also does not use prodelision of *es* or *est* after final *-s*. It must before be assumed that, whatever may have been true of popular speech in his day, final -*s* had come to be fully enunciated in the literary language.

Final -*m* permitted the elision of its syllable before an initial vowel, diphthong, or *h*-. Despite this indication of some sort of light pronunciation, it made position before a following consonant, whether initial or internal.

Latin poets occasionally admit to their verses other phenomena of daily speech than those discussed here, which may be found in any systematic Latin grammar. The common usages of daily speech that have been considered reinforce the evidence of other metrical practices that Latin poetry was composed for oral recitation more than for visual reading. Although Latin verse reflects speech phenomena, it has standardized them to fit into regular metrical patterns.

SCANSION

The modern reader perforce becomes familiar with Latin meters more from the printed page than from listening. Hence his first introduction to the subject is likely to be mechanical, through study of the types of feet and verses and their metrical patterns of long and short syllables. The process of indicating metrical quantity, dividing into feet, indicating pauses, and so forth, is called "scansion" or "scanning," from the Latin verb *scandō* literally = I climb, which was applied to the climbing or rising up of the voice in reading aloud metrically.

In writing out scansion, it is customary to place the indications of quantity and so on above the verse being scanned, though occasionally the marks are found below. In marking by hand, the long mark (ˉ) or the short mark (˘) should properly be placed over the whole syllable, but since in printing it is easier to place them only over the vowel or diphthong in the syllable, this placement has also become conventional in handwritten scansion. It should therefore be kept in mind in scanning that the marks of quantity pertain to the syllables, and not to the nature of the vowels only, as they have previously done in this book and as they do in a dictionary. When the final syllable of a line of verse is anceps, that is, when it is by nature short but the metrical pattern requires it to be long, the syllable is sometimes marked long. It is preferable in scanning, however, to mark the final syllable of a verse with its vowel quantity, long if its vowel is long and short if its vowel is short, even though the short vowel be followed by a consonant. This practice develops familiarity with the natural quantities of vowels in final syllables. But in marking the quantities of final syllables in verses with the natural quantities of their vowels, one should remember that in many types of verse, particularly in the dactylic hexameter and the second verse of the elegiac distich, a short final syllable counts as long where the meter so requires, that is, where it is a syllaba anceps.

The ictus is usually marked by an acute mark (′) placed over the mark of quantity. In verse this mark indicates the musical or metrical stress, not the word accent.

The division between feet is shown by a single upright line (|). In writing out scansion, this line should be carried down from the row of scansion marks into the text, to be sure that it properly divides the syllables. If, however, a short vowel followed by a consonant ends a word before an initial vowel in the following word, although technically in scansion the final consonant should be carried over in pronunciation to the following initial vowel, so as to leave the preceding short vowel ending a short syllable, it is customary not to separate off the final consonant of a word in marking the scansion but to carry the line down between it and an initial vowel in a following word. Thus the end of the first line of Vergil's *Aeneid* would be scanned and divided *quī|prīmŭs ăb|órīs|*, not *quī|prīmŭ să|bórīs|*, = who first from the shores. It may be questioned whether in reading verse the Romans actually ran the words together by carrying over such consonants to begin the following syllable. When a verse concludes with a complete foot, it is helpful to indicate this by placing an upright line similar to those used to divide the feet within the line at the end of the row of scansion marks. In the process, a final short syllaba anceps should be regarded as concluding a complete final foot. If a verse concludes with a metrically incomplete foot, this can be indicated by placing at the end of the row of scansion the mark ⌃ and omitting the final upright line. The mark ⌃ is called a "caret" = it lacks; this word is simply the active present indicative third person singular of the Latin verb *careō* = I lack. The technical term for a metrically incomplete verse is "catalectic," from a Greek adjective derived from a verb meaning "to break off abruptly." A metrically complete verse is therefore called "acatalectic," a term in which the Greek negative prefix *a-* yields the meaning of "not broken off."

Pauses within a verse, whether caesuras or diaereses, are indicated by a double line, upright or sloping ($\|$ or $//$), in the row of scansion marks. When the double line indicates a diaeresis, it may be carried down into the text in place of the single line marking the division between the feet, particularly at the strong diaeresis in the middle of an elegiac pentameter, or the second line of an elegiac distich. Usually, however, the sloping double line is placed only in the row of scansion; in the case of a diaeresis, it crosses the upright divider between feet that extends down into the line of text.

Omission of syllables from feet is sometimes called "syncopation," from a late Latin verb *syncopāre*, which derives from a Greek noun *sunkopē* = a cutting off. It is indicated by a caret (ˆ) in the row of scansion.

These are the common indications used in writing out scansion. Other marks, not discussed here, are used to indicate that a long syllable stands in place of a normal short one, or two shorts in the place of one short, or that a long syllable is prolonged to three or four musical times. A few examples should serve to illustrate scansion.

The first example is an iambic senarius or iambic trimeter, namely six iambic feet with substitutions, from Plautus, *Miles Gloriosus* 49:

ĕdĕpŏl|mĕmŏrĭ|ā's ŏp|tŭmă |″—ŏffăĕ|mŏnĕnt|

The translation is "By Pollux, you are of an excellent memory (ablative of description)—(a change of speaker) the morsels advise me (to be)." The first foot is an anapaest in which the third syllable is long by position. The second is a tribrach, with the ictus on the middle short syllable, the first of the two short syllables that are substituted for the concluding long of an iambus. The third foot is a spondee in which the first syllable is the long *-ā* of the ablative singular of the first declension and there is prodelision of the *e-* of *es*; the second syllable is long by position. The fourth foot is an iambus in which the second syllable is again a long -ā of the superlative adjective in the feminine ablative singular agreeing with *memoriā*. Between the final long -ā of this foot and the initial short *o-* of the next there is hiatus because of the pause, a diaeresis, at the change of speaker. The fifth foot is a spondee in which the first syllable is long by position and the second is a diphthong. The last foot is an iambus, as regularly in this meter, though the last syllable in this meter may sometimes be a syllaba anceps.

A trochaic septenarius or tetrameter catalectic, with seven and a half trochaic feet and substitutions, also comes from Plautus, *Miles Gloriosus* 158:

$m(i)$ ĕquĭdēm|ĭ(am) ârbĭ|trĭ vī|cĭnī|sânt ″mḗaè|quĭd fĭ|ât dŏ|mĭ ⌃

The translation is "indeed now the neighbors are spies on me as to what goes on in my house." At the opening there is elision between $m(i)$ ĕ- so that the first foot is an anapaest with the ictus on the first short syllable, and the third syllable is long by position since it is followed by the two consonants -*m* and consonantal *i-*. The second foot is a trochee, which opens with the elision of -*am* before *a-*, and the *a-* is long by position and bears the ictus. Since the second syllable of the foot, -*bi-*, is followed by a mute and a liquid, it may be either long or short; here it is taken as short. The following four feet are spondees; in the first two (the third and fourth feet) the *i*'s are all long by nature. In the fifth foot, *sunt* is long by position and *mḗaè* is pronounced as a single long syllable by synizesis. The first syllable of the sixth foot is long by position, and the second is long by nature because in forms of *fiō* = I become, or I happen, the -*i-* is long even though followed by a vowel except in the infinitive *fierī* and the imperfect subjunctive *fierem*. The seventh foot is, as regularly in this meter, a trochee, though a tribrach may be substituted for it. The first syllable of the trochee here is long by position. The final foot is catalectic, that is, it consists of a single long syllable bearing the ictus. The lack of a second syllable, which places the musical or metrical stress or ictus at the end of the line, affords a certain syncopation before the initial stress of the following line. A pause or masculine caesura has been indicated in the fifth foot, but perhaps the verse was delivered slowly, because of the spondees, and without any pause. The trochaic septenarius was always common in popular Latin verse and preserved strongly the recognition of word accent in its rhythm. When, during the late Empire, accent emerged as the basis of rhythm in Christian poetry, this meter was often employed in hymns.

The dactylic hexameter, which is likely to be the meter first met in studying Latin verse, contains six dactylic feet with the free substitution of spondees, except normally in the fifth foot, and with the last foot always of two syllables, either a spondee or, with a syllaba anceps, a trochee. Characteristic is the first verse of the second book of Vergil's *Aeneid*:

cónticŭ|ḗr(e) ōm|nḗśin|tḗntī|qu(e) ŏ̄rǎ tĕ|nḗbānt|

The translation is "all fell silent and, intent, held their faces (i.e., turned toward Aeneas)." The first and, as regularly, the fifth foot are dactyls, while all the other four are spondees. There are two elisions, of the -e before *om-* and of the -e before *ōra*. All the syllables ending in consonants, that is, those in which the vowel is followed by two consonants, are long by position; the remaining long syllables end in long vowels and thus are long by nature. A masculine caesura falls readily in the third foot, at the break between the two coordinate clauses.

A famous line in which all the feet are spondees except the fifth, so that it is not technically spondaic but nevertheless by its slow movement gives an impression of a lumbering giant, the Cyclops Polyphemus, is *Aeneid* III 658:

mónstr(um) hōr|rénd(um) īn|fórm(e) īn|gḗnścuī|
lúmĕn ăd|émptŭm|

The translation is "a monster terrifying, shapeless, huge, from whom light (or his eye) had been removed." Further weight is given to the line by the three elisions, the first two of syllables ending in -m. In three of the syllables that are long by position, namely *mōn-*, *-gēns*, and *-ēmp-*, the vowels are probably also long by nature. But these hidden quantities do not affect the scansion, since this depends on the quantities of syllables, not of vowels. Only two long syllables are such by nature, *cuī* and *lū-*. The final -um is short by nature but takes the place of a long syllable as a syllaba anceps. A natural position for a masculine caesura is in the fourth foot, before the relative clause, which is separated off by a comma in most printed texts.

Vergil seldom used a spondaic verse with a spondee in the fifth foot. Two such lines, *Aeneid* III 12 and VIII 679, imitate from Ennius the ending *ēt māgnīs dīs*. The first is scanned as follows:

cŭm sŏcĭ|ĭs nā|tŏquĕ˝pĕ|nātĭbŭs|ĕt māg|nĭs dīs|

The translation is "with his companions and his son, and the great household gods." Of the five syllables that are long by position, namely *cum, -īs, et, mag-,* and *-nīs,* two also contain vowels long by nature, the two ending in the long *-īs* of the ablative plural of the second declension. The *-u-* of *cum* is short by nature, as is the *e-* of *et.* The *-a-* of *magnīs* is also probably short, although some regard it as lengthened by nature, as well as by position, by the following *-gn-.* A feminine caesura comes readily after the *-que,* which connects the pair of nouns *sociīs* and *nātō.* The *et* is placed second in the phrase which it connects to *sociīs nātōque,* namely *penātibus māgnīs dīs.* This phrase is translated here as if *penātibus* is an adjective modifying *dīs,* as does *magnīs.* However, *penātibus* may be a noun with *magnīs dīs* in apposition, to mean "the household gods (who are) great divinities." When a conjunction like *et* is placed second in a phrase it is said to be "postpositive," from the passive perfect participle *postpositus* of *postpōnō* = I place after, or postpone. In this verse, the caesura heightens the emphasis given by the conjunctions, since the *et* connects two main elements, the human and the divine, of which the former is subdivided by the *-que.* Although this is a spondaic verse, because of the spondee in the fifth foot, three of its feet are dactyls. The second spondaic verse, *Aeneid* VIII 679, in which Vergil imitated from Ennius the close *et magnīs dīs,* has four dactyls before the two concluding spondees. It is scanned:

cŭm pătrĭ|bŭs pŏpŭl|ŏquĕ,˝pĕ|nātĭbŭs|ĕt māg|nĭs dīs|

The translation is "with the fathers and the people, and with the great household gods." Thus the tone of solemnity is here given solely by the spondaic conclusion, with its recall of Rome's famous early poet.

The opposite effect, that of quickly galloping horses, is given by a well-known verse, *Aeneid* VIII 596, in which all the feet except the last are dactyls:

quădrĭpĕ|dāntĕ pŭ|trēm sŏnĭ|tŭ quătĭt|ŭngŭlă|cămpŭm|

This verse, which describes a cavalry charge, means, "the hoof smites the crumbling (or dry and dusty) plain with four-footed sound." In it the quantities are normal, that is, by position in those syllables that end in consonants, since their vowels are all short by nature, and by nature in those syllables that end in short or long vowels. The final syllable is short but counts as long by syllaba anceps. This verse moves so rapidly that it is not easy to find a suitable pause; perhaps a slight one would occur as a masculine caesura in the fourth foot after -*tu*. If so, the two halves are closely tied together not only by the lively flow of the meter but also by the agreement of *putrem* in the first half with *campum* at the end.

Catullus, the lyric poet contemporary with Cicero, addressed to his mistress Lesbia a famous couplet, no. 85 of his poems, which illustrates the elegiac distich, in which a dactylic hexameter is followed by a falsely named pentameter. The second verse actually has six feet, but the third and sixth are incomplete, that is, they constitute only half feet, so two and a half feet plus two and a half feet were regarded as making only five. This couplet is scanned:

$$\acute{o}d(i)\ \breve{e}t\ \breve{a}|m\acute{o}\overset{\prime\prime}{q}u\bar{a}|r(e)\ \breve{i}d\ f\breve{a}c\breve{i}|\acute{a}m\overset{\prime\prime}{f}\bar{o}r|t\acute{a}ss\breve{e}\ r\breve{e}|qu\acute{i}r\breve{i}s|$$
$$n\breve{e}sc\breve{i}\breve{o}|s\breve{e}d\ f\breve{i}\breve{e}|r\breve{i}^{\frown}|\overset{\prime\prime}{s}\acute{e}nt\breve{i}(o)\ \breve{e}t|\acute{e}xcr\breve{u}c\breve{i}|\breve{o}r^{\frown}$$

The poet cries "I hate and love—why I do this perchance you ask; I know not, but I feel that it is so (literally becomes) and I am crucified." The dactylic hexameter is normal; it contains two elisions, of -*i* before *et* and of -*e* before *id*. Four syllables containing naturally short vowels are long by position, *id*, -*am*, *for*-, and -*tas*-. The quantity of the remaining syllables is the natural quantity of their final vowels. The concluding syllable is short. Probably in delivery this verse would have a major pause or masculine caesura in the second foot, a spondee, and perhaps another lesser one, but still a masculine caesura, in the fourth foot, also a spondee. Indeed, a printed text will probably have a colon after *amō* = I love and a comma after *faciam* = I should do.

Both halves of the pentameter consist of two dactyls followed by a single syllable, a long for the third foot, as regularly, and a short at the end, which counts as a long by syllaba anceps. In the first dactyl, the last syllable is an -*o* which is the ending of the first person singular active present indicative. This ending is properly long -*ō* but is here shortened by iambic shortening under the influence of the preceding short syllable and the following ictus on a long syllable. The verse of Latin comedy shows that *nĕscĭŏ* was frequently pronounced as a dactyl, especially in the phrase *nĕscĭŏ quid* = I do not know what, or something. The frequency with which the final long *-ō* of the first person singular of the active present indicative was shortened by iambic shortening when preceded by a short vowel and followed by an accent or ictus led in the early Empire to the general shortening of this *-o*, even when iambic shortening did not apply. In the second dactyl of the pentameter, the syllable *fi-* is short because the *-i-* of *fīō* = I become is short in the infinitive, as here, and imperfect subjunctive but is long elsewhere, even though preceding another vowel. In this verse also the syllables *nes-*, *sed*, *sen-*, and *ex-* are long by position though their vowels are by nature short. Only one syllable, *-ī*, is long by nature. In the second half there is elision of *-ō* before *et*. The lacking syllables (syncopation) in the third and sixth feet are indicated by the carets, and since the verse is incomplete, no final upright line is put at the end to mark a complete foot. The upright line in the middle might equally well be simply the double line above, indicating the diaeresis, carried down into the text.

These examples of scansion may suggest how to approach both scanning in writing and reading Latin verse metrically. The Roman schoolboy heard verses recited orally from childhood and had to memorize them at school. Thus he acquired a sense of the rhythms by ear and undoubtedly could read ordinary verse metrically without giving much thought to the lengths of the individual syllables. The swing of the meter and the quantities of familiar syllables carried his delivery along naturally.

Similarly, a Roman poet, such as Vergil, composed by ear, with an instinctive feel for the rhythm and music of his verse, and not by laboriously putting words together into metrical patterns of longs and shorts. Nevertheless the extraordinary metrical regularity of Vergil and even more so of Horace, whose complicated lyric meters show relatively few departures from the strict patterns of quantities, indicates that they composed their verses not only with an intuitive sense of musical quality but also with a fully self-conscious attention to the techniques of meter, such as quantity, caesura, coincidence of word accent and verse ictus in the last two feet of the dactylic hexameter, and other devices.

A modern person seldom hears Latin verse recited aloud—not enough to become imbued with a feeling for the various rhythms. He or she must therefore approach scansion analytically, in the fashion illustrated. He or she must recognize the lengths of syllables either by noting double consonants, reserving judgment if a mute is followed by a liquid, or by recognizing the quantities of endings of declensions and conjugations. Quantities of vowels ending syllables in the stems of words can sometimes be recognized by word accent, since the penult is long if accented and short if the antepenult is accented. Otherwise quantities must be learned by heart or looked up in a dictionary.

Actually, however, practice in scanning and reading the simple meters enables a person to discover such quantities through recognizing the other quantities given either by position or by familiar case and verb endings. He or she can then fill in the remaining quantities from the metrical pattern of the verse. It is sometimes suggested that the easiest way in which to begin to learn the scansion of dactylic hexameters is to mark the quantities of the syllables mechanically backward from the end, since the last two feet can normally be identified as a dactyl followed by either a spondee or a trochee with syllaba anceps. However, it affords better practice in scansion to take the verse from the beginning and scan it as it comes. By so doing, a person becomes steadily more familiar with the rhythm until he or she acquires the ability to read verses, especially dactylic hexameters, at sight without scanning them mechanically.

The modern recreation of the pronunciation of Latin, including quantity, ictus, and other metrical elements, undoubtedly fails to represent adequately what Latin poetry sounded like to a Roman. The poetic quality of Latin verse can nevertheless be fully recognized only if it is delivered orally with due attention to both the pronunciation of the sounds and the various metrical elements. For this reason every effort should be made to acquire as early as possible, by writing out the scansion of verses and reading them aloud, an ability to read metrically at sight.

XIV

POSTCLASSICAL LATIN AND
THE ROMANCE LANGUAGES

For centuries after the classical period of Ciceronian and Augustan Latinity, Latin was by no means a dead language. Although following the fall of the Western Roman Empire in the fifth century A.D. the speech of ordinary people in Europe became diversified into the various Romance languages, Latin remained an international language, both spoken and written, for learning, diplomacy, and the Church, at least into the seventeenth century, and in some parts of Europe much later. While the use of spoken Latin has today almost vanished, it is still occasionally used for written communication.

Ever since the Renaissance, however, there has been a canonization of classical (Ciceronian and Augustan) Latin and a neglect of later forms except as used in such fields as law, theology, or mediaeval studies. In consequence, the study of Latin has become an academic discipline, recommended for its own sake, or as opening up the riches of Latin literature and the experience of Rome, or as an introduction to grammar or word building. Latin is no longer a currently used language, except for study of the literatures of Rome and the Middle Ages, theology, linguistics, Romance languages, or the like, for which it is still necessary. This separation from contemporary applicability should not obscure the continuing vitality of Latin as a language both in itself, through its literature, and in its descendants, still today living tongues.

FORMS OF POSTCLASSICAL LATIN

During the Republic, the several Italic dialects and various early dialectal forms of Latin had failed to achieve the status of literary use because of the predominance of the Latin used by the upper classes at Rome, and particularly by Roman authors. Yet it is clear from statements in ancient grammatical and other writings and from the later linguistic changes in Latin itself that the spoken Latin of ordinary people, both in Rome and even more so elsewhere in Italy and the provinces, retained many so-called archaic features and also preserved or acquired regional peculiarities of pronunciation, form, and even syntax.

As the literary language became more elaborate and complex in the hands either of writers trained in rhetoric or of school teachers eager to inculcate their own stylistic virtuosity, it drew further and further away from the ordinary spoken Latin. In the mid second century B.C. the plays of Terence, written to please a cultivated circle of aristocrats, already showed a more polished style than those of the down-to-earth Plautus of a generation earlier. In the mid first century B.C. Cicero, acknowledged master of classical Latinity, nevertheless used in his intimate letters a much more colloquial style and vocabulary. Sentences are simple and direct, but often allusive, as might be conversation with a friend. The vocabulary is that of everyday life, and it is sprinkled with Greek words or quotations. In his essay on the ideal orator, *Ōrātor* 67, and elsewhere, Cicero calls such a style "everyday speech," *sermō cotīdiānus*, or *cottīdiānus*, or *quotīdiānus*; various spellings are given. In one of his letters, *Ad Familiārēs* IX 21.2, he speaks of *plēbēius sermō* = speech of the ordinary people, as well as of *cotīdiānīs uerbīs* = everyday words. Other terms are found in different writers, but the one that has become usual is *lingua uulgāta*, or *uulgāris* = language of the crowd (*uulgus*), or vulgar Latin.

Despite the dominance of the styles of Cicero in prose and

Vergil in epic verse, literature and inscriptions of the early Empire preserve evidence that vulgar Latin was commonly in use outside of the cultured classes. Probably under Nero, emperor from 54–68 A.D., an author of the court circle named Petronius composed a novel of adventures among people of the lower classes, portions of which have been preserved under the title *Satyricōn*. This title is generally held to be a Greek genitive plural, with *librī* understood, and to mean "(Books of) Satires." Whether the contents are really satirical, or caricature, or plain exaggeration each reader must judge. The *Satyricōn*, particularly in its conversations, contains popular words, confusions of gender and case, mistakes of construction and mood, omission of words and syllables easily supplied by the hearer, which is called "ellipsis" from a Greek noun meaning "leaving out," and similar characteristics of popular speech in almost any culture. The city of Pompeii, south of Naples, was destroyed by an eruption of Vesuvius in 79 A.D. Thus the scribblings on its walls, called in Italian "graffiti" = writings, preserve the ordinary Latin of the mid first century A.D. Lead tablets dating from throughout the two and a half centuries of the early Empire (30 B.C.–235 A.D.) contain curses invoked in vulgar Latin by uneducated people against their enemies. These tablets, which were buried in spots supposedly efficacious to effect their harmful work, are known as *dēfīxiōnēs* = formal declarations, especially curses. By the second century A.D., inscriptions commemorating persons of the less educated classes or from the provinces cease to be as carefully written as were earlier ones even of poorer persons. What seem to be errors in such evidences of the speech of the uncultured masses may at times be due to the individual composer or inscriber of the inscription. But they are more likely to represent philological, morphological, or stylistic changes that were occurring in popular speech but which failed to find admission to the by then fixed and jealously guarded classical literary language.

Stylistically, vulgar Latin prefers short sentences strung together coordinately in a loose style to the long sentences with elaborate subordination which are found in Cicero's periodic style. The omission of connectives (asyndeton) and the coordination (parataxis) rather than subordination (hypotaxis) of clauses, both of which had been features of early Latin, are preserved in popular style. The vocabulary is picturesque, with many diminutives, hybrids, borrowings from Greek, and slang terms. Pronunciation was varied and affected by local dialect or foreign speech. In short, the spoken Latin of the Empire continued to develop, as would any living language, while the literary language tended to remain faithful to the classical norms, though even in it, poetic words were adopted into prose, prepositional constructions began to take the place of cases, and popular touches appeared. By the end of the third century A.D. the gap between the two forms of Latin may have been as great as is that between the English of Shakespeare's plays and contemporary speech—mutually intelligible but still quite different.

In the late third century A.D. an anonymous schoolmaster prepared a list of words frequently misspelled, as well as presumably mispronounced. This *Appendix Probī*, so designated because it is preserved at the end of a grammar written by an otherwise unknown Probus, shows how far popular Latin had departed from classical norms. The *Appendix* gives the proper classical forms of words that at the time it was written had already changed their spelling and presumably their pronunciation, followed by their contemporary, popular forms, as in line 53, *calida, non calda* (hot); line 60 (repeated in line 184), *caelebs, non celeps* (bachelor); line 139, *aper, non aprus* (boar); and line 221, *uōbīscum, non uōscum* (with you). Similarly, soon after 400 A.D. an apparently well-connected western nun wrote a description of her pilgrimage to the Holy Land in the vulgar Latin of the period as employed by Christians. In her account, called *Peregrīnātiō Aetheriae* = the travel of Aetheria, she describes her approach to Mt. Sinai as follows in section 39.4: *Quī montēs cum īnfīnītō labōre ascenduntur, quoniam non eōs subīs lentē et lentē per gīrum, ut dīcimus in cochleās, sed tōtum ad dīrectum subīs ac sī per parietem, et ad dīrectum dēscendī necesse est singulōs ipsōs montēs dōnec perueniās ad rādicem propriam illīus mediānī, quī est speciālis Syna* = these mountains are ascended with infinite labor, since you do not go up them slowly and slowly in a circuit, as we say by spirals, but you go wholly straight up as if up a wall, and it is necessary to descend straight down each mountain, until you come to the proper base of that middle one, which is specially Sinai. This account is understandable but hardly classical in style.

Christians had initially been recruited primarily among speakers of Greek in the eastern Mediterranean. Only slowly did the Church and Christian writings begin to use Latin. Just as the earliest Christian missionaries and the writers of the New Testament had adopted the current Greek of the Hellenistic world, known as "common" (*koinē*) Greek, so the early Roman Christians employed the Latin of the ordinary people and avoided the literary style as identified with upper-class paganism. The African writer Tertullian, in the early third century A.D., was one of the most vigorous users of this popular Christian Latin. But its greatest monuments were composed by two Christian scholars of the late fourth and early fifth centuries A.D., at a time when the Church had come to terms with pagan literature and when these scholars themselves often wrote in a fully Ciceronian style.

The first of the two monuments is the *Confessions* (*Confessiōnēs*) of St. Augustine, in which shortly before 400 A.D. he recorded the stages of his conversion to Christianity in a tone of intimate address and confession to God. Even more important in the formation of the Latin of the later Western Church was the translation of the Bible (*Biblia*) into Latin prepared by St. Jerome over the years from about 380–404 A.D. In this he partly used earlier Latin versions of the Bible, as for the Psalms, partly adapted the earlier Latin versions, and partly made his own new translations either from the Greek or, for much of the Old Testament, directly from the Hebrew. The earlier Latin versions had followed the Greek translations of both the Old and the New Testaments quite literally, and St. Jerome, though he corrected errors, did not wish to alter too drastically the familiar texts. Thus his version reproduces in Latin many Greek words, expressions, and constructions. Similarly, in translating from the Hebrew he tried to conform his Latin style and expression to those of the Hebrew. Thus the Latin of his Vulgate Bible, while basically the popular Latin of his day, also introduces Greek and Hebrew elements, which passed into the Latin of the Church, that is, into later ecclesiastical Latin.

Any language develops particular vocabularies and styles for professional uses. Latin technical writings on such topics as agriculture and medicine show both specialized vocabularies and styles, and many traces of popular speech. But the professional writing that the Romans particularly bequeathed to the Middle Ages and later times was jurisprudence. The great scholars of the Roman law, whose works were extracted by order of Justinian for the *Digest* (*Dīgesta*) during the early sixth century A.D., mostly had flourished at the end of the second and the beginning of the third centuries A.D. Their Latin is still classical in grammar, though specialized in vocabulary and in idiom of expression. But Justinian's compilers also preserved the still valid laws in the *Code* (*Cōdex*). This work comprises edicts, also called "constitutions," mainly of the emperors from Constantine at the opening of the fourth century A.D. to Justinian; relatively few edicts of emperors earlier than 300 A.D. were regarded as worth including, and none from before Hadrian in the early second century A.D. These edicts of the late Empire, that is, those which date from after 300 A.D., are composed in an elaborate and wordy style that had become typical of the documents, whether legal or state, which emanated from the imperial chancery, in which the edicts were drafted.

This style was inherited by the papal and royal chanceries of the Middle Ages. By then, however, the chanceries issued chiefly public documents. Law had become the speciality of judges and lawyers, who were often churchmen. They went back to the more classical Latin of the *Digest*, rather than using the fulsome style of the *Code*. Mediaeval legal Latin is therefore simpler than mediaeval chancery Latin, although it remained technical and full of specialized formulas. Characteristic of late imperial and mediaeval chancery Latin is the use of elaborate titles and of verbs in the third person instead of in the second. This style is preserved in the Italian use of the third (instead of the second) person singular and plural except in the most intimate address for the singular and the most formal for the plural. Italian also preserves such forms of address as "His (not Your) Highness" or "His Excellency."

As early as the second century B.C., Romans had begun to settle overseas, often in advance of actual Roman conquest. Traders, perhaps largely from South Italy where Greek was as commonly spoken as was Latin, moved into the Aegean. Since they found there the vigorous Hellenistic civilization, they adopted Greek rather than imposing Latin. When Rome conquered first Greece and Macedon, then Asia Minor, and finally Syria and Egypt, her governors and commanders used Latin officially. But since by the first century B.C. educated Romans spoke Greek fluently and admired Greek culture, they made no efforts to establish Latin as the general language in the eastern Mediterranean. Even soldiers and other ordinary Romans must have found it easier to learn Greek than to try to do business in their own tongue. In consequence, the Roman world east of the Adriatic remained largely Greek speaking. Outside of Greece and western Asia Minor, older native languages had survived alongside Greek and continued in use, such as Aramaic in Judea and Egyptian in Egypt, even though Greek was so much a second language in Egypt that papyri from the Hellenistic and Roman periods are universally in Greek, rarely in Latin, and hardly at all, except for religious purposes, in native Egyptian.

In the west, the situation was very different. In Gaul and Spain, and eventually in Germany, Britain, and along the Danube, the Romans met inferior civilizations. Therefore Latin, as the language of both conquest and culture, prevailed over the local languages. Even in Africa, where the Carthaginians had diffused their Semitic language, Punic, this had not penetrated deeply enough or produced a sufficiently strong culture to resist Latin. While the dispersion of Romans into the western provinces was not widespread until the Empire, some veterans and other Romans had settled in Spain by 200 B.C., in southern Gaul by 118 B.C., and in Africa by 100 B.C. In the later Republic, commanders like Pompey in Spain and Caesar in Gaul granted Roman citizenship generously to natives, who either already spoke Latin or had to learn it. Under the early Empire, the quartering of legions in the western provinces meant not only increased recruitment of native-born soldiers but also the stimulation of trade, conducted in Latin, and the settlement of veterans and of other Romans drawn thither by the army or by economic opportunities. Already during the first century A.D., provincials appeared in the Senate and administration; some were easterners but the bulk were westerners. Westerners became particularly important in Latin literature. Thus, whereas under Roman rule the eastern part of the Empire retained its Greek language and Hellenistic civilization, the west was thoroughly Romanized and Latin became the language of government, the army, and culture.

Just as in the east native languages continued alongside Greek, so in the west both native languages and elements of native culture, particularly of religion, survived alongside Latin and Roman ways. In culture this combination resulted in a measure of absorption of local features by the Roman overlay. In language it showed up as the survival of native words and even constructions in local Latin. It has been suggested that the Latin of each province tended to preserve characteristics of the spoken Latin of the period of initial settlement, just as French Canadian preserves elements of the spoken French of the early eighteenth century, or as the more isolated older parts of the original American colonies retain features of seventeenth century English. This contention cannot be proved, however, for want of evidence about the early spoken Latin of the provinces. The study of the Romance languages indicates that the three principal factors which differentiated their initial development were absorption from the underlying native languages, contact with different Germanic dialects, and isolation during their formative period, the Dark Ages, from about 500 to 800 A.D.

In short, during the late Empire the difference always present in Latin between the literary and the spoken languages widened as the literary remained conservatively classical and the spoken continued to develop. The literary did show professional specialization, notably in chancery and legal Latin. Vulgar Latin also began to be differentiated, first into ecclesiastical Latin, influenced by Greek and Hebrew through the translation of the Bible, notably in Jerome's Vulgate text. Second, vulgar Latin began to develop regional peculiarities resulting from the absorption of elements from the native tongues. These linguistic regions were usually even smaller than the Roman provinces, or than the modern nations that have succeeded them, and are represented by the dialects of the various Romance languages.

During the Middle Ages these varieties of Latin continued in active use. Classical Latin was always the literary standard, particularly in periods of revival of interest in the great Roman writers, as under Charlemagne around 800 A.D. and in the more famous Italian Renaissance, which began about 1300 A.D. Chancery Latin survived in the chanceries of kings and particularly of the Catholic Church, where it is still used in the Vatican. Legal Latin was used both for the canon law of the Church and for civil law, particularly after the rediscovery of Justinian's collections, the *Corpus Iūris Ciuīlis* = the body of civil law, about 1100 A.D. Direct study of the *Corpus*, particularly of that section known as the *Digest*, replaced the use of its mediaeval adaptations and made Roman law the dominant element in the formation of the laws of the various nations of modern Europe. Even in England it strongly influenced the development of the common law, which derives from Anglo-Saxon and Norman-French antecedents. A less polished form of legal Latin, much mixed with vernacular words and constructions, continued to be used in mediaeval charters, deeds, and similar documents.

Vulgar Latin also remained in common use throughout the Middle Ages. Its ecclesiastical form was the common language of the Church, used for the study of theology, for teaching, for the service, and for hymns and other religious poetry. Only recently did decisions of the Second Vatican Council, which concluded in 1965, permit the use of vernacular tongues in services of the Catholic Church. On the one hand, this makes the service more intelligible to ordinary people, whose knowledge of Latin is slight or nonexistent; on the other, it breaks the continuity and destroys the universality of a habitually familiar, if unintelligible, form of service.

During the Middle Ages and even down into the eighteenth century all educated people spoke and wrote Latin. Because mediaeval teaching was primarily in the hands of churchmen, the Latin of students and scholars tended to be ecclesiastical in character, and was therefore another continuation of the vulgar Latin of the later Empire. In addition to ordinary documents, such as letters and treatises, there are preserved from the Middle Ages plays and poems, particularly the student songs known as "goliardic," from a term used for court jesters and buffoons. The best known of these songs, which begins *Gaudeāmus igitur, iuuenēs dum sumus* = Let us therefore rejoice while we are youths, is in fact not attested before the eighteenth century, but is nonetheless typical of the genre.

A feature of both church hymns and goliardic verse is the use of word accent as the basis of rhythm, probably as a continuing tradition from the use of word accent to determine rhythm in early Latin verse and in popular poetry throughout the whole Roman period. The founder of Christian Latin hymnology was St. Ambrose, bishop of Milan in the mid fourth century A.D. His hymns, written for congregational use, have accentual rhythms. Though educated Roman Christian poets, such as Prudentius around 400 A.D., composed hymns and epics in the classical quantitative meters, and though throughout the Middle Ages quantitative meters were still used by learned poets, accentual meters prevailed in popular song, in which rhyme also became common.

In sum, the various specialized forms that Latin assumed during its postclassical history were not at all mutually unintelligible. Any language develops such popular or specialized variants, and in some cases these become distinct languages, as in the survival of Sanskrit for the religious language of Hinduism as against the spoken dialects of Hindi, or of Old Church Slavonic in Russia as against modern Russian, or even of Latin in the Catholic Church as against the contemporary tongues spoken by its multilingual membership. But a modern reader of classical Latin ordinarily finds no difficulty in understanding any form of later Latin. Mediaeval deeds and charters may present to such a reader words of non-Latin origin, unfamiliar terms invented for new forms of land tenure and the like, or constructions that have departed a long way from the norms of classical Latin. Legal and ecclesiastical Latin may show specialized vocabularies and formulas. But the modern reader should find no problem with hymns, student songs, or the writings of well-educated scholars and authors, especially of those as familiar with classical Latin as were, for instance, Dante (1265–1321), Eramus (c. 1466–1536), and Milton (1608–1674). The varieties of later Latin are not mutually exclusive. They shade one into another, to the extent that speakers or writers were well or poorly educated. At no time would the users of Latin have been unable to understand any variant that they encountered, except insofar as regional differences of pronunciation arose under the influence of the various vernacular tongues and the interruption of spoken communication between different regions.

THE ROMANCE LANGUAGES

When the western Roman Empire was broken up, during the fifth century A.D., into various kingdoms established by invading Germanic tribes, only in outlying areas, such as the Rhine frontier or Britain, was Latin wholly replaced by the Germanic language of the invaders. In the more central provinces, the barbarians, impressed by the higher culture and administration of the Romans, attempted to live alongside them, to use their law and forms of government at least for the Roman inhabitants, and to adopt their culture. Moreover, on the frontiers Christianity was generally swept away along with Roman culture by the invaders, as it was in England by the Anglo-Saxons. But in the more central areas the barbarians, if not already Christianized, soon were converted, as were the Franks in Gaul. In consequence, Latin continued in use in the services and life of the Church. In short, Latin remained the language of law, administration, education, and the Church.

Since the ordinary people, particularly the farmers, had German settlers quartered in their houses and placed upon their land, the two peoples gradually coalesced, with a consequent interaction of speech. During the Dark Ages (c. 500–800 A.D.) Latin remained predominant, but its various regional dialects were further differentiated according as each was affected by the language of the local occupying Germans. The breakdown of centralized control, not only at the imperial but even at the provincial or kingdom level, interrupted trade and intercommunication, so that each region followed its independent linguistic course. When Charlemagne about 800 A.D. sought to reimpose both cultural and political union at least on western Europe except for Spain, the local speeches had already developed into distinct languages. In North Africa the development of a local Latinate speech was cut short when the highly Romanized Vandal kingdom was conquered first by the forces of the Byzantine emperor Justinian in the first half of the sixth century A.D. and then by the Muslim Arabs in the late seventh century. The Arabs pushed on into southern Spain, where they imposed their culture, rule, and language, until the region was finally reconquered by the Spaniards in the late fifteenth century.

The languages that developed in western Europe south of the Rhine, except for Britain and south Spain, and also in Rumania, are called "Romance" from the late Latin adverb *rōmānicē* = in Roman fashion, which was used with such late verbs as *fābulāre* or *parabolāre* = to speak. These verbs produced respectively the Spanish *hablar* = to speak and the French *parler*, with the same meaning. The verb *parabolāre* is derived from the Latin transliteration of the Greek noun *parabolē* = a comparison, hence a parable. In the Vulgate, *parabola* is used generally for "word" or "speech," and the verb was made from it. Since to speak in Roman fashion was contrasted with the barbarian languages, the adverb *rōmānicē* came to be used both as a noun and as an adjective to denote the forms of Latin spoken during the Dark Ages. In much the same way the Byzantine Greeks, though they had abandoned Latin as a language, continued until the fall of Constantinople in 1453 to speak of themselves as *Rōmaioi* = Romans, in contrast to their barbarian neighbors, such as the Slavs and Turks. Variations on this term continued to be used in popular modern Greek until this century, and may still occasionally be heard.

Today the major Romance languages of western Europe are Portuguese, Spanish, French, and Italian. One more Romance language flourishes in the eastern Balkans, Rumanian. Though the Rumanians claim to be descended from Trajan's Roman settlers of Dacia, the province north of the Danube between the Carpathians and the Black Sea, it seems more probable that their ancestors were refugees from various Balkan areas, forced north across the Danube into the security of the mountains and isolated there by invading Slavic peoples.

Although the main Romance languages are these five, all through the Middle Ages and down into modern times many more local dialectal forms have existed. Besides Portuguese and Spanish,

Catalan is still spoken in northeastern Spain. Modern French was originally the dialect of a limited area around Paris known as the Ile de France, where the kingdom was first established. Like Latin earlier, it came to overshadow the language of southern France, Provençal, and such dialects as Walloon, which is still spoken in northern France and Belgium. Similarly, in Italy dialects differ so much that a man from Venice can hardly communicate with a Sicilian except through the common medium of literary Italian. This last is basically the dialect of Florence, which became standard because of the excellence of its writers during the Renaissance. The various Romance dialects have preserved more of Latin the more isolated they have been. For instance, in Sardinian a table is still called by the Latin *mēnsa*, not, as in Italian, *tavola* (from Latin *tabula* = tablet). In Alpine valleys dialects called "Ladin" (Latin) and "Romansch" (Roman) are only dying out in the mid twentieth century. And of the major Romance languages, Rumanian remains by far the closest to its Latin parentage.

Romance philology is the study of the development of the Romance languages and of their phonological, morphological, and syntactical similarities and differences. It supplements the evidence of later Latin literature and inscriptions in providing evidence for vulgar Latin. Just as comparison between forms and sounds in the Indo-European languages makes possible a reconstruction of Indo-European, so a comparison of the Romance languages makes possible a reconstruction of vulgar Latin. Whatever their various borrowings either from earlier native languages or more particularly from the languages of the invading German tribes, the Romance languages are for the most part Latin in vocabulary and grammar.

Only in the later Middle Ages (1100–1300 A.D.) did the Romance languages begin to develop vernacular literatures, a term derived from the Latin noun *uerna* = a home-born slave. In Italy writers like Dante (1265–1321) and Petrarch (1304–1374), in England Chaucer (c. 1340–1400), and in other countries similar authors raised vernacular literature to the highest levels. In consequence, Latin lost the cultural primacy that it had until then enjoyed. Yet Dante debated whether to compose his *Divina Commedia* in Latin or in Florentine Italian, and Milton (1608–1674), author of the great English epic *Paradise Lost*, was also an excellent Latinist in prose and verse, who served as Latin secretary to the government of Oliver Cromwell.

DECLINE OF LATIN

The Renaissance is a period not easy either to date or to define, but if Dante is taken as its earliest harbinger in Italy and Milton as its last fruit in England, the period of some three hundred and fifty years between them dealt three severe blows to the primacy of Latin as the language of international diplomacy, culture, religion, and learning. First, the vernacular literatures established themselves as in their own right superior to anything, practically speaking, that had been produced in Latin since the days of Cicero and Vergil. No longer did scholars and authors feel that only through Latin could literature reach its highest achievement. Second, the Protestant Reformation, one of the results of the Renaissance, held that the scriptures and in general the Christian message should again be put into language intelligible to ordinary men, just as it had been by the writers of the Greek Old and New Testaments and by St. Jerome in his Vulgate Bible. Thus Latin was no longer the universal language of religion, though it continued to be so of the Catholic Church until the Second Vatican Council in 1965. Finally, Renaissance writers and scholars, attracted to the great literature of the Ciceronian and Augustan ages, condemned as inelegant, not to say illiterate, the various forms of post-classical Latin and thus divorced the study of Latin from the actualities of contemporary life.

Yet Latin gave way slowly. Only after Milton's time did it cease to be an international language for European diplomacy and learning. Not until the second half of the nineteenth century did it begin to lose its place as the foundation of a liberal education. And only in the second half of the twentieth century has the Catholic Church abandoned it as the universal tongue of religious services.

Down to the end of the nineteenth century, each nation continued to speak classical Latin according to its pronunciation of its own language. Thus there were French, Italian, Spanish, German, English, and other ways of enunciating Latin. In the latter half of the nineteenth century studies were undertaken in Germany and elsewhere to recover so far as feasible the classical pronunciation. During the twentieth century this reformed pronunciation has been generally adopted in Germany and the United States, and by mid century it was fairly well established in England as against the older English pronunciation, which was also used in the United States down to around 1900. The reformed pronunciation has not been so widely accepted in France, Italy, or Spain; and the Catholic Church still follows the Italian pronunciation, which those trained in Catholic schools often adopt. English and American lawyers pronounce such Latin tags as are common in the law with a pronunciation slightly different from that formerly used in England and the United States.

The recreation of a uniform pronunciation of Latin has undoubtedly been beneficial in helping scholars of different nations to understand one another. It has also heightened appreciation of the literary quality of classical writings, since the Greeks and Romans conceived of literature in oral terms, so that reading it aloud properly is an important approach to a full enjoyment of it. Nevertheless this change in pronunciation, which came at a time when Latin was losing its educational primacy, created a break between the older generation, accustomed to the traditional pronunciations, and the younger, who read Latin with the reformed sounds.

Although because of these trends the study of Latin can no longer claim to be essential to a liberal education or for many professional careers, it still should occupy a significant position in education. Many of the arguments often used to justify Latin are, however, ancillary. It does indeed help with an appreciation of grammar, whether of the Romance languages or of English. It aids in understanding much of the vocabulary of these languages. It provides a rigorous intellectual discipline because of the relative orderliness of its grammar and the precision of its expression. But these educational aims may be achieved by the study of other more contemporary languages or by a course in general linguistics. More important, Latin is an essential tool for advanced study in many fields, as in English, German, or Romance literatures, in most areas of mediaeval studies, and to some extent in theology, law, and even science. But the study of Latin makes its most significant contribution to a liberal education by opening up a new dimension of the past. It affords an introduction to the achievements in literature and other fields of a culture that is still the foundation of the civilization of western Europe and the Americas.

LATIN AND ENGLISH

Caesar, on his two demonstrations in force into Britain in 55 and 54 B.C., found the island occupied by various tribes who spoke dialects of Celtic. A century later, in 43 A.D., the emperor Claudius initiated the Roman conquest of Britain. When the emperor Domitian recalled his successful commander Agricola in 84 A.D., Roman arms had penetrated into north Wales and well up into Scotland. Early in the second century A.D. the emperor Hadrian had a great defensive wall built across northern Britain from Newcastle on the Tyne to Carlisle on the Solway, and except for occasional pushing of the defenses further up to the Edinburgh-Glasgow line, this remained the northern limit of the Roman province until the late fourth and early fifth centuries A.D., when successive emperors, and finally Honorius in 410 A.D., withdrew the regular legions for the protection of the continental provinces against invading Germans.

The inscriptions that survive from the nearly four centuries of Roman occupation are uniformly in Latin, with no trace of Celtic. Nevertheless it is safe to assume that, as in other provinces, the native language continued to be spoken by ordinary people. The Celtic languages that survived among peoples on the fringes of the former Roman province show certain borrowings of vocabulary from Latin. However, the development of a Romance language parallel to those that were formed on the continent during the Dark Ages, a language in which Latin would have been transformed by contact first with the local Celtic and then with German, was prevented by the ruthlessness of the Germanic occupation of Britain.

During the fifth and early sixth centuries A.D. at least three Germanic tribes, namely the Jutes (c. 449), the Saxons (c. 497), and the Angles (c. 547), moved across the North Sea into Britain. By 500 A.D. they had overrun practically all of the former Roman province. These tribes, known collectively as the Anglo-Saxons, in their homelands in northern Germany along the coasts of the North Sea had probably become somewhat familiar with Latin either through the penetration of Roman traders or because their members had served as auxiliaries in the Roman army, and perhaps they had borrowed some Latin words. In Britain, they seem to have made an almost clear sweep of the Romanized Celts, who were either slaughtered or forced into the peripheral areas of Scotland, Wales, Cornwall, and across the English Channel into Britanny. In these areas Celtic languages have lasted down into modern times, except that Cornish ceased to be spoken by about 1800. Also the native Celtic of Ireland, Erse, is still used, albeit with the considerable support of nationalistic feeling. The legends of King Arthur and his knights may preserve in a much romanticized form tales of the resistance offered by the Romanized Celts to the Germanic occupation, particularly along the borders of Wales.

In Britain, therefore, there was no merger of Germanic invaders with Romanized natives, such as occurred on the continent, and thus no development of a Romance language. Anglo-Saxon, as spoken in various dialects after the occupation, and its derivative English remain in basic structure and vocabulary Germanic. Nevertheless there began at once and has continued an ever increasing borrowing of vocabulary from Latin into English. Some Latin words the Anglo-Saxons may have brought with them from Germany; others they may have picked up from the local inhabitants for things with which they had not previously been familiar. For instance, Latin *castra* = camp survives as the name of the city Chester or in compound city names like Winchester. From Latin *mīlia* (*passuum*) = a thousand (of paces) derived English "mile," from (*uia*) *strāta* = a paved road came "street," *uīnum* yielded "wine." There were a limited number of these early loan words.

Christianity had apparently not penetrated deeply into Roman Britain, and whatever may have existed there must have been wiped out by the pagan Anglo-Saxons. During the fifth century A.D. Christianity was introduced into Ireland, whence Irish missionaries carried it into northern England during the early seventh century. But the most significant missionary was a certain Augustine, sent by Pope Gregory the Great in 597 A.D. He began the conversion of southern England to the Roman form of Christianity. The Church introduced many Greek words, already adopted into Latin, or Latin words connected with its services or life. For instance, the Greek *monastērion*, in Latin *monastērium* = monastery became in English "minster," used for a monastery church; Latin *altāre* gave English "altar"; and the closing phrase of the Latin liturgy, *īte; missā est* meaning "go; it is (you are) dismissed," provided a name for the ceremony, "mass." Some nonliturgical words seem also to have been introduced by the Church. For example, late Latin *cappa* = hood, or cape, yielded "cap," and *culīna* = kitchen gave "kiln."

The Church also substituted the Latin alphabet for the Anglo-Saxon runes, letter forms which centuries earlier the Germans had probably derived across the Alps from a northern form of the Etruscan or Latin alphabet. The Anglo-Saxons at first kept a few letters from the runic writing. For *th* they used two runic signs with almost equivalent sound value, the thorn (þ) and the eth or crossed *d* (ð), and they kept a third sign, the wyn (ƿ), for a sound approximating consonantal *u*. The thorn and eth were finally dropped in favor of *th*, and the wyn was replaced by a double *u*, or *w*. Much later, English applied the *i longa*, written as *j*, to the sound that it now represents, since *y* had come to serve for consonantal *i*. Similarly, since *w* roughly replaced consonantal *u*, written as *v*, the letter *v* came to represent its present sound. The addition of these three letters, namely *j*, *v*, and *w*, brought the English alphabet to twenty-six instead of the Latin twenty-three.

The great intake of Latin vocabulary into English began with the conquest of Anglo-Saxon England by William the Conqueror and his Norman French followers in 1066. A century and a half earlier, around 900, Scandinavian freebooters called Northmen, Norsemen, or Normans, had occupied northwestern France along the Channel and up the Seine Valley. There the local population had already developed a Romance language, a dialect of Old French, in which Latin had both changed into a vernacular and absorbed Germanic elements from the speech of the Franks who had settled in northern France in the mid sixth century A.D. The Normans, relatively few in number, added a few Scandinavian words to the vocabulary but on the whole adopted the local dialect as their tongue.

In England, Norman French remained for some two centuries the language of the court, of administration, of higher ecclesiastics, and of the law. The mass of the population continued to speak their native tongue, which developed during these centuries from Anglo-Saxon (Old English) into what is called Middle English. In consequence, the interactions of the two vocabularies were varied. Some Norman-French words of Latin origin wholly displaced the Germanic. For example, "agriculture" from Latin *agricultūra* supplanted Anglo-Saxon "earthtilth," and "noble" from Latin *nōbilis* replaced Anglo-Saxon "aethel," which survived as the personal name Ethel. In court circles, curiously, "prince" and "duke" were adopted from the French derivatives from Latin *princeps* and *dux*, but English "king" and "queen" resisted French "roi" and "reine" from Latin *rēx* and *rēgīna*. In many cases both types of words continued in use, as Sir Walter Scott describes in *Ivanhoe* by an amusing talk between two Anglo-Saxon serfs. One serf points out to the other that the animals that they tend are called "swine," "ox," or "calf," but when these animals are served up to the Norman overlord, they become "pork" from Latin *porcus*, "beef" from Latin *bōs, bouis*, or "veal" from Latin *uitellus*.

Although the influence of Norman-French was primarily on the vocabulary of government, the church, law, and culture, it also reached into daily life. For example, Latin *caldārium* = a hot bath produced French "cauldron" and English "caldron," and Latin *pōēna* = penalty yielded French "peine" and English "pain." By the middle of the fourteenth century English had begun to establish itself as the language even of the upper classes. At the same time, the kings of England were asserting their claim to large sections of France outside of Normandy and therefore came into closer contact with the French court and French culture, and with the dialect used in Paris and the surrounding Ile de France, that is, with the linguistic predecessor of modern French.

These multiple contacts with Latin, either direct or indirect, have made the vocabulary of English rich in synonyms. In some cases the Anglo-Saxon and Latin derivatives survive alongside one another, such as "virgin" from Latin *uirgō* alongside English "maiden." Derivatives of the same Latin word were adopted at different periods. For example, *monastērium* contributed not only "minster" but the more learned "monastery," and the Greek *presbuteros*, a comparative adjective meaning "older," was used in ecclesiastical Latin as the noun *presbyter*, which became in early English "priest" but was also revived by Scotch Calvinism in its antique form "presbyter," from which comes the term "Presbyterian." Sometimes two forms of a Latin derivative were taken over from French. For example, the Latin diminutive *capitellum*, from *caput* = head, was used for the block on the top of a column and yielded English "capital," but it was also applied metaphorically to the heading of a column or page of writing and then to the division marked off by the heading, whence derived French "chapitre" and English "chapter."

About 1500 the Tudor monarchy presided over, and helped to stimulate, the beginning of the Renaissance in England and of the slow standardization of its language into Modern English. The revival of secular learning encouraged direct familiarity with Latin literature. Latin had remained the language of the Church and, along with Norman French, of law. In the latter field, many legal tags became part of the English vocabulary. For instance, a writ requiring somebody to produce the body, that is, the person, of a prisoner in court, and thus to prevent abuse of power by long imprisonment without trial, is still known as a writ of *habeās corpus* = may you have (produce) the body. A corpse resulting from murder is a *corpus dēlictī* = body of a crime. In trading, *caueat ēmptor* = let the buyer beware.

After 1500, Latin words often became Anglicized directly, such as "ire" from Latin *īra* alongside English "anger," or "conflagration" from Latin *conflagrātiō* alongside English "fire," or alongside English "loving" the adjective "amatory" from the Latin *amātō-*

rius, -a, -um = loving, formed on the perfect passive participle *amātus, -a, -um* of the verb *amō* = I love. In many cases, Latin provided the adjective for an English noun. For example, "lunar" from Latin *lūna* = moon is the adjective correlated with the English noun "moon." Often the Latin word appears unchanged in English, as do *senātōr, cōnsul, maximum, data, exit, animal,* and *āctor*; so much so that it is often hard to know whether to regard such words as English or to italicize them on the ground that they are still Latin. Such continuous borrowing extending through centuries has frequently left not two but three synonyms in English, one of Germanic and two of differing Latin derivation, such as English "kingly" alongside "royal" and "regal" from Latin *rēgālis.*

As England's overseas contacts extended, Latin derivatives were adopted not only from French but also from other Romance languages. The vulgar Latin term for "horse" was *caballus,* as against the more elegant *equus.* This became French "cheval" and yielded English "chivalry." The Italian derivative "cavallo" contributes the English "cavalry." English "alligator" represents Spanish "el lagarto," whose definite article *el* is Latin *ille* = that, and whose noun comes from Latin *lacertus* = lizard.

The foregoing examples suggest how deeply indebted the vocabulary of English has been to Latin since the earliest Germanic invasion into the Roman province of Britain. They also show how much Latin has enriched English not only with terms for new objects or concepts but especially by building up that variety of synonyms which makes English so expressive a tongue.

Latin words have been deliberately introduced into English as scientific or technical terms. This learned borrowing stands apart from the natural and almost unconscious adoption of Latin into English through familiar daily use. For instance, a botanic term like *gladiolus* = little sword, for a flower with long pointed leaves, has become its accepted name. Some technical terms are rather artificial, like the American "elevator," built on the Latin verb *ēlevāre* = to raise up, for something that the English more simply call a "lift." Many are modern composites from Greek, such as "telephone" and "telegraph," whose Greek components mean respectively "far sound" and "far writing." Occasionally this practice has resulted in bastard compounds, such as "automobile," in which *auto-* comes from a Greek demonstrative which may mean "self," and "mobile" is from the Latin adjective *mōbilis* = mobile. The word should either be purely Greek, *autokīnēton*, as indeed it is in modern Greek, or wholly Latin, *ipsimobile*.

Sometimes the Latin derivative has by usage departed far from its original meaning. For example, "radio" was adopted as a combining form from Latin *radius* = a rod, which also came to mean "a line," such as the radius of a circle, or a ray of light or electricity. When "radio" was combined with the Greek derivative "telegraph," the result was the word "radiotelegraph," which means "far writing by a ray (of electricity)," for which an alternative expression is "(to communicate) without a wire," shortened to "wireless." "Radiotelegraph" was abbreviated to "radio." This word came to be used not only for the method of communication but also for the actual apparatus employed to send and receive a message, for the message itself, and as a verb for the process of transmission. Thus it would be possible, if inelegant, to say "by radio he radioed a radio to announce his arrival."

Despite the wealth of Latin derivatives in the English vocabulary, Latin grammar and syntax have had little effect on the Germanic structure of English. Like Latin, English descends from Indo-European and inherited a basically similar pattern of declensions, genders, numbers, and cases for nouns, and of conjugations, voices, moods, tenses, persons, verbal nouns (infinitives), and verbal adjectives (participles) for verbs. As the language has been modified and developed, these have largely been sloughed off. For instance, while nouns still show singular and plural number, except in a few words, such as one deer and two deer, and while differences in plural endings, such as horse-*s* as against ox-*en*, are survivals of differences in declension, case survives only in the personal pronouns, as in "I," "my," "me," and gender survives only in that of the third person singular, "he," "she," "it." What seems like a case ending for the genitive of possession, namely '*s*, is in fact a contraction of "his"; that is, "the man his coat" became "the man's coat."

Similarly in the verb, the subjunctive has almost vanished. Only a very precise speaker would express a present contrary-to-fact condition with an imperfect subjunctive: "if I were able, I would come." Changes of stem or ending to indicate tense are common, as in "sing" and "sang," or "love" and "loved." But both tense and mood have come to be represented mainly by compounding with forms of the auxiliary verbs "to have" and "to be." Verbal endings for person and number exist only in the present third person singular: "he, she, or it moves," as against the general form "move." In consequence of this simplification, it would be difficult for speakers of English to reproduce the grammatical and syntactical aspects of the highly inflected Latin. This difficulty has been obscured by the application to English of the formulations of Greek and Latin grammarians. Though this works as well as it does because of the common Indo-European characteristics, it often results in misrepresentation of the English grammar and syntax. Fundamentally, English must depend chiefly on word order, rather than on grammatical form, to show the relationship between words, phrases, and clauses.

From the beginning of English literature until at least the middle of the nineteenth century, writers of both prose and poetry usually had a thorough grounding in the classics, particularly in Latin. Many in consequence sought to copy the more elaborate Latin periodic sentence. For instance, Milton's *Paradise Lost* opens with a prepositional phrase, "Of man's first disobedience," and there follow various subordinate phrases and clauses until the main verb "sing" is reached at the opening of the sixth verse. The subject is then expressed by the vocative, "O heav'nly Muse," and this in turn is modified by various subordinate clauses, until the sentence finally concludes with the sixteenth verse. This may sound very Latinate, but anyone who attempts to render into Latin the complex prose of Milton or of such authors as Samuel Johnson and Edward Gibbon soon finds that their long sentences must be broken down into simple component parts before being reconstructed in Latin periodic sentences. It is in fact easier to build into Ciceronian periods the straightforward style and short sentences of a contemporary newspaper article. The resemblance of more elaborate English style to Latin is therefore a matter of similarity of effect, within the limitations of the lack in English of elaborate stem changes and endings, rather than of any real correspondence of grammar or syntax.

Broader aspects of the influence of Latin culture on that of England and the United States include such practical matters as the survival of the calendar established by Julius Caesar. Protestant England and her American colonies only in 1752 adopted the slight reform that in 1582 Pope Gregory had introduced into Caesar's calendar. Also the months still keep in English their Latin names, in curious contrast to the days of the week which, except for Saturday, are Germanic.

More profoundly, the Romans, either in their own achievements or by adapting and transmitting what they took over from the Greeks, laid the foundations of the culture of western Europe, and hence of the Americas, in practically all fields, except perhaps natural science, namely in government, law, art, philosophy, and literature. Natural science, although its modern development was stimulated by a study of ancient science, has not only progressed so far but has also altered scientific concepts so fundamentally that it may claim to represent a modern creation. Music has probably to a less degree rejected its classical precedents, but it also has in modern times come a long way from its classical, Byzantine, and mediaeval background.

In general, not only does knowledge of Latin contribute to an enlargement and understanding of English vocabulary and suggest fascinating leads into the history of words. Far more significantly, even a rudimentary acquaintance with Latin opens the way to an appreciation of the Roman inheritance in contemporary western culture as well as of the Roman achievement itself, an achievement that has perennially attracted and inspired later generations.

XVI

HISTORICAL AND ORAL
APPROACHES

The linguistic history of Latin extends from the dispersion of speakers of Indo-European from somewhere in east central Europe during the third millennium B.C. to the Second Vatican Council in the middle of the twentieth century A.D., and is not yet closed. Latin was probably the speech of the first Indo-European people to move into Italy during the second millennium B.C. Its speakers were crowded by later comers into a small pocket in the lower Tiber Basin. Certainly an intelligent observer visiting Italy around 700 B.C. would have regarded Latin as the least likely of the languages of Italy to become the general language of western Europe. Even if he had discounted Etruscan as not giving promise of a literary future and as alien to the general Indo-European pattern of languages that was spreading over western Europe, and even if he had felt that the Osco-Umbrian dialects were too fragmented and too limited to be widely diffused, he would almost certainly have prophesied that Greek, though spoken in scattered settlements along the coasts of southern Italy and Sicily, would, because of its connection with the civilization and culture of Greece, dominate over the more backward languages and cultures of Italy. Although Latin was influenced by these neighbors, though not to any extent by the later linguistic arrivals in Italy, Punic and Celtic, it retained until very late remarkably archaic morphology and syntax. It probably began to be written as early as the sixth century B.C., in an alphabet derived from the western Greek colonies through the mediation of Etruria. But an extensive literature is attested only from the mid third century B.C., and it developed under the strong influence of Greek style, literary genres, and quantitative meters.

During the three centuries from about 300 B.C. to the beginning of the Christian era, Roman conquest made Latin the dominant language first of Italy and then of the western Mediterranean. In the east, it did not replace Greek, which had been imposed throughout the area by the conquests of Alexander and the kingdoms created by his Hellenistic successors. Greek represented for the Romans the language of a culture which, initially more advanced than theirs, always remained a model to imitate and against which to match their own cultural achievements. Even in the west, local tongues survived as the speech of ordinary people well down into the Roman Empire, and in some provinces, such as Gaul, Britain, and probably Spain, until its end. During the three centuries of conquest, Roman writers achieved a fusion between borrowed Greek intellectual forms and concepts and the Roman spirit, ideals, and point of view. This fusion culminated in the literary achievement of the classical period, notably in the works of Cicero and Vergil. Even so, the written text always remained secondary to the spoken word.

The creation of a distinguished native literature at once imposed the overlay of a standard language of culture on the variety of spoken forms of Latin and, by creating an exalted norm of attainment, led later writers to imitate it rather than to create new modes of expression. In consequence, while literary Latin remained relatively static, spoken or vulgar Latin continued to develop and to diversify through technical use, through regional variation resulting from contact with native tongues, and through independence of development.

When in the fifth century A.D. different Germanic peoples, each with its own Germanic dialect, occupied the western Roman provinces and eventually Italy itself, regional variation was accentuated by absorption of vocabulary and perhaps of features of speech from the occupying Germans. At the same time the collapse of the central Roman government and the rivalry of the new Germanic kingdoms prevented intercommunication between regions. Thus by 800 A.D. what had begun as dialects of Latin in western Europe had developed into distinct Romance languages, except in those areas where the conquerors had made a clean sweep of the Romanized population and established either Arabic or a German tongue, namely in North Africa, southern Spain, the German frontier, and England..

Although the peoples of the western regions thus came to speak mutually unintelligible languages, Latin continued to be the universal spoken and written language of culture, government, law, and the Church. The specialized forms that developed for each subject never became so distinct as not to be generally intelligible. Only around 1300 A.D. did the Romance languages begin to be employed for vernacular literatures of as high a quality as had been created in classical Latin. And only in the seventeenth century did the rivalry of the vernacular tongues prevail over the dominance of Latin in these fields and begin to reduce Latin from a currently spoken language to an artificially nurtured perpetuation of a classical tongue. Today, the study of classical Latin still affords an unequaled discipline in language, style, and thought; an insight into linguistics, grammar, and the formation of vocabulary; and most significantly, an introduction to the common cultural ancestry of western Europe and of the Americas.

Fully to appreciate Latin as a language and to comprehend its literature requires a more subtle understanding of its morphology and syntax than results from the traditional and formal presentation of classical Latin which is found in analytic textbooks and systematic grammars. Such an understanding is derived in part from a historical approach to the development of the language. The often seemingly arbitrary idiosyncrasies which appear among the classical forms and constructions resulted from a long history. In the maturing of classical language there operated not only regular patterns of change but also divergencies and cross influences. The latter reflected local variations that developed in daily speech. To the extent that consistent patterns of change can be traced either within the surviving evidence for the growth of Latin or by comparison with similar patterns in other languages, the historical approach to Latin can claim to be scientific; insofar as various features must be accepted as unexplained deviations, Latin grammar remains a purely descriptive account of what is actually found. Thus the pronunciation, morphology, syntax, and versification of classical Latin should not be regarded merely as diverse phenomena of the language at one period of its long history but as the end results of the history. An appreciation of the history shows that the characteristics of classical Latin are more integrated and correlated than they appear to be at first sight. It also affords an insight into the problems and methods of general linguistics.

An understanding of classical Latin is also helped by another approach, one much stressed in contemporary teaching of the language. This approach is called the "oral" or "direct" method. The oral or direct method should supplement, not replace, study in the traditional manner of the grammar of classical Latin. It presents Latin as it was presented to young Romans, through the voice and ear rather than through the printed page and eye. It emphasizes immediate grasp of the meaning of a whole phrase or sentence instead of the attainment of this meaning by the painstaking translation and putting together of the individual words.

Meaning in any language depends on more subtle elements than merely the dictionary definition of words, the grammatical use of forms, or the syntactical construction of phrases, clauses, and sentences. The context in which a word or phrase occurs colors its connotation. In speech—and written Latin was always meant to be read or spoken aloud—voice, gesture, or musical accompaniment contributed to the effect. Despite the progress that has been made in the last century toward a better understanding of the pronunciation and metrical rhythms of Latin, a modern person still labors under the handicap of being unable to hear Latin as Cicero or Vergil might have delivered it. Moreover, a beginner lacks the feeling for overtones of meaning in words that comes only from wide reading. Finally, it is almost impossible today to live with Latin in the sense of hearing it as a normal daily speech and thus to absorb it mainly by the ear rather than by visual reading, analysis, and memorization.

Nevertheless good progress can be made toward a fuller comprehension of Latin by combining with the systematic study of forms and constructions both a historical realization of how classical Latin grammar came to be as it is, and also an effort to cultivate comprehension through the ear rather than through the eye only. Whereas in English meaning depends largely on a determined word order, the elaboration of forms and suffixes in Latin permits a much more flexible word order without serious impairment of meaning. Hence a Latin sentence, particularly in the more complex periodic style of Cicero or the intricate adaptation of word order to meter in the *Odes* of Horace, requires comprehending a phrase, clause, or sentence in its entirety. The oral or direct approach encourages progress from word-by-word reading and translation to immediate grasp of the meaning of larger units of expression. It also leads on from the conscious consideration of form and construction to an instinctive response to the significance of forms and constructions in the contexts where they appear. The comprehension of whole thoughts instead of single words leads to an appreciation of differences in style and of the various ways in which a given thought may be expressed. It also brings the realization that grammatical rules did not restrict a Cicero or a Vergil to rigid patterns of expression. The so-called rules are merely generalizations and systematizations of the practices of writers, and what seem to be exceptions are more often subtle attempts to make meaning clearer by deviating from normal usage.

Latin was, and still is, not a fixed and somewhat arbitrary system of forms and constructions into which thought is straight-jacketed. It was, and might still be, a fluid, developing, living language. It was also, and should still be, primarily a spoken, not a written, tongue. Ease and fluency in reading, writing, and speaking Latin are best attained by combining the three approaches, the systematic, the historical, and the oral or direct. The principal reward for acquiring a command of Latin is to become acquainted directly with a great literature which deeply conditioned the later literary forms of western Europe and the Americas and which gives expression to the spirit, concepts, and ideals of the Roman government, law, philosophy, and religion; in short, with a civilization and culture without which the patterns of European and American culture would be very different from what they are because of their Latin inheritance.

BIBLIOGRAPHY BY CHAPTERS
INDEX TO BIBLIOGRAPHY
GENERAL INDEX

BIBLIOGRAPHY BY CHAPTERS

The books listed here are primarily ones available for purchase. Books published in the United States were checked in *Books in Print, 1974,* and the few books published in England, and one or two in France and Germany, were checked against the corresponding lists of books in print in those countries for 1973 or 1974. Some important older books are listed even though out of print in the hope that they may be available secondhand or in schools or public libraries. Many useful older books are not listed because they no longer appear to be readily available except in large university or public libraries.

Attention is invited to the lists of textbooks in Greek and Latin published from time to time in *The Classical World* and *The American Classical Review*. Lists in the latter journal tend to be fuller, but as of spring 1975 the most recent issue was *ACR* 2.3 (June 1972): 105–145. In this bibliography, therefore, citation is from *The Classical World* 68.4 (Dec. 1974–Jan. 1975): 129–165, referred to hereafter as *CW List* 1975. In that list, a single heading: "V. Language Books," pp. 251–252, includes books on pronunciation, the history of Latin, morphology and syntax, and versification. Because of its mixed contents, this heading is not cited in the separate listings on these topics.

Attention is also invited to articles by authoritative scholars on such topics as "Alphabet," "English Language," "Indo-European Languages," "Latin Language," "Linguistics," "Romance Languages," and "Writing" in recent editions of the *Encyclopaedia Britannica,* 11/13th ed. (1910–1920), 14th ed. (1929), and 15th ed. (1974). There is no article on "Linguistics" in the 11/13th ed. The 15th ed. is divided into two sections, *Micropaedia* or *Ready Reference* (10 vols.) and *Macropaedia* or *Knowledge in Depth* (19 vols.); the articles in the latter are fuller and more informative. "Latin Language" has a brief article in the *Micropaedia,* but is discussed only under "Romance Languages" in the *Macropaedia,* XV, 1033–1035. Similar articles may be found in other longer modern encyclopedias.

The books in this Bibliography are arranged to correspond to the chapters in this book, though many have relevance to chapters other than those under which they are listed. Each book is briefly described. For reprints, the publisher and date of the original is also given. For books published in the United States and England, the United States publisher is given first, even if the English edition is the original. Initials of authors' first and middle names are expanded where possible, to aid in finding them in library catalogues. Books available in paperback editions are marked "pb." Books out of print are indicated "o.p." Books for which no date of publication is given are marked "n.d."

1. LANGUAGE AND LINGUISTICS

Most books on linguistics are too full and technical for use in connection with the study of elementary Latin. Only three are therefore given:

Arlotto, Anthony Thomas, *Introduction to Historical Linguistics;* Boston, Houghton Mifflin, 1972. This recent and useful book presents linguistics simply and with illustrations drawn largely from the Indo-European languages, which are discussed in ch. 8. Special alphabetic signs used in linguistics are set forth in Appendix 1.

Leroy, Maurice, *Main Trends in Modern Linguistics* (trans. and rev. Glanville Price from the French *Les grands courants de la linguistique moderne;* Paris and Brussels, Presses Universitaires, 1963); Univ. of California Press, and Oxford, Blackwell, 1967. This book affords a good initiation to modern linguistics. The Introduction and Part One trace the history of linguistic studies from antiquity to the second half of the nineteenth century in a straightforward manner. Part Two deals with the work of the Swiss linguist Saussure, whom Leroy considers the most important figure in modern linguistics. Part Three describes the various schools and theories of linguistics current in the twentieth century. While emphasis is laid on French scholarship, the contributions of other countries are fully set forth and the bibliographical notes mention relevant literature down to 1967.

Palmer, Leonard Robert, *Descriptive and Comparative Linguistics: A Critical Introduction* (in Studies in General Linguistics); New York, Crane, Russak, and London, Faber and Faber, 1972. This is a full revision of the author's much earlier *An Introduction to Modern Linguistics* (1936). It offers an introduction to linguistics which is too advanced for beginning students of Latin. The author uses much technical terminology, many quasi algebraic formulas, and a system of abbreviations which must be learned to follow the argument. The text is illustrated with charts and figures. The two parts deal respectively with descriptive (synchronic) linguistics and historical and comparative (diachronic) linguistics. The second part has interesting chapters on writing, etymology and change of meaning, and language and culture. Two appendices discuss the Indo-European languages. There is a good bibl., a table of phonetic symbols, a list of abbreviations used in the text, addenda, and indices of authors and subjects.

BIBLIOGRAPHY TO CHAPTERS 2-3

For an application of structural linguistics to Latin, see: O'Brien, Richard J., *A Descriptive Grammar of Ecclesiastical Latin Based on Modern Structural Analysis,* described in bibl. 14.1.

2-3. INDO-EUROPEAN

Watkins, Calvert, in *The American Heritage Dictionary of the English Language;* Boston, American Heritage and Houghton Mifflin, 1969; New York, McGraw-Hill, and pb. Dell, 1970. Pp. xix–xx discuss Indo-European and the Indo-European languages. Pp. 1496–1502 present more fully the presumed form of the Indo-European language and what may be learned from its vocabulary about society and thought. Pp. 1505–1550 give a list of common Indo-European roots. On the back end papers are a table of the Indo-European sound correspondences and a chart of the Indo-European family of languages, both of which show more clearly than does the first table in this book the derivation of later languages from earlier protolanguages.

Lockwood, William Burley, *Indo-European Philology: Historical and Comparative* (in Hutchinson's University Library: Modern Languages); Atlantic Heights, N.J., Hillary House (Humanities Press), from London, Hutchinson's, 1969; also pb. This is a brief and readable introduction. It opens with a history of research into Indo-European and a classification of the various Indo-European languages. Ch. 7 presents the evidence from Greek, Latin, and Sanskrit for Indo-European. Ch. 12 discusses the contribution of the comparative method to a fuller understanding of language and society. Intervening chs. deal with the Germanic and Celtic languages.

Crossland, Roland Arthur, "Immigrants from the North," ch. 27 of *The Cambridge Ancient History,* 2d ed., I, part 1, pp. 824–876 (with bibl. pp. 989–993); Cambridge Univ. Press, 1971 (originally publ. as fasc. 60, 1967). This chapter, probably too scholarly for beginning students, presents the linguistic and archaeological evidence for the dispersion of the speakers of Indo-European and for their original homeland, with discussion of various views and of the difficulties with each. Crossland on the whole accepts the usual view that the dispersion took place gradually during the 3rd and early 2nd millenniums B.C. and that the differentiation into the separate Indo-European languages took place during the dispersion rather than after speakers had settled in given areas. For Indo-European speakers in Italy, see pp. 854–855.

Crossland, Ronald Arthur, and Birchall, Ann, eds., *Bronze Age Migrations in the Aegean: Archaeological and Linguistic Problems in Greek Prehistory;* Park Ridge, N.J., Noyes Press, 1974, and London, Duckworth, 1973. This is a collection of papers delivered at a Colloquium on Aegean prehistory held at Sheffield Univ. in 1970. The papers are on the whole too specialized for beginning students of Latin. Several of the papers suggest that the correlation between cultural change as attested by archaeological investigation and linguistic change is not demonstrable and in particular that the Bronze Age in Greece did not produce such extreme changes from the Neolithic Age as to necessitate the assumption of massive invasions which might have brought primitive Greek into the Hellenic peninsula. One paper argues that the most likely period of change for the dispersion of the speakers of Indo-European may have been the "neolithic revolution." However, the spread of the cultivation of cereals and the domestication of animals from the northern Middle East into Anatolia, the Balkans, the Danube Valley, and western Europe would not appear to have been coincident with the dispersion of the speakers of Indo-European from some area north of the Black Sea.

4. LANGUAGES OF ANCIENT ITALY

Pulgram, Ernst, *The Tongues of Italy: Prehistory and History;* Westwood, Conn., Greenwood Press, n.d.; from Harvard Univ. Press, 1958. This gives a lively account of the archaeological and linguistic history of Italy from prehistoric to modern times. Books II and III cover the languages of Italy before the Roman conquest and the spread of Latin in consequence thereof. The emphasis is on archaeological and ethnographic rather than on purely linguistic aspects of the tongues discussed.

Whatmough, Joshua, *The Foundations of Roman Italy* (World History Series 48); New York, Haskell House, 1971; from London, Methuen, 1937 (in Methuen's Handbooks of Archaeology). Although now old, this presents more fully than does Pulgram the archaeological and linguistic evidence for the various peoples of Italy before the Roman conquest.

Two of the non-Italic peoples of Italy, the Etruscans and the Greeks, strongly influenced the development of early Rome and to some extent early Latin. For the Etruscans, see:

Pallottino, Massimo, *The Etruscans* (trans. J. Cremona from the Italian *Etruscologia,* 6th ed., 1973; ed. with additional notes David Ridgway); Indiana Univ. Press and London, Allen Lane, 1975. This thorough revision of a well-known book by a distinguished Italian Etruscologist discusses in ch. 1, pp. 37–63, the complex question of the peoples and tongues of "Italy at the Dawn of History." The author concludes that various peoples and tongues met in Italy during the 2nd and early 1st millennia B.C. and that today it is impossible to distinguish their various contributions to the pattern of peoples and tongues of c. 800 B.C. In ch. 2, pp. 64–81, the author argues that the disputed and probably insoluble questions of Etruscan origins and of their language are less important than the formation of Etruscan civilization on the basis of the earlier

Villanovan culture and under a variety of external influences. For the influence of the Etruscan language on Latin, see pp. 202–203. At the end Ridgway provides a good section of "Notes on Further Reading," which lists the many earlier books in English on the Etruscans. Translations of previous editions of Pallottino's book were published by Penguin/Pelican and are now o.p.

For the Greeks two fairly recent books are:

Woodhead, Arthur Geoffrey, *The Greeks in the West* (Ancient Peoples and Places 28); New York, Praeger, and London, Thames and Hudson, 1962. This well-illustrated book deals with the Greek colonization and settlement in the west and the history of the various resulting city-states. It does not discuss in detail Greek influence on early Rome or early Latin. The bibliography is useful.

Boardman, John, *The Greeks Overseas;* Penguin/Pelican A 581, 1964. Ch. 1, pp. 175–231, discusses "Italy, Sicily, and the West." For Italy the emphasis is on contact and conflict with the Etruscans and Phoenicians rather than on any contact with early Rome. The chapter has a brief bibliography.

Since the Celts and the Carthaginians were peripheral to early Rome and had little influence on early Latin, discussions of these two peoples are not listed here.

5. THE ALPHABET

Diringer, David, *Writing* (Ancient Peoples and Places 25); New York, Praeger, and London, Thomas and Hudson, 1962; Eng. ed. is listed as in print in 1973; U.S. ed. is not listed in 1974. This provides a short and general treatment of the development of writing throughout history in all parts of the world. The Phoenician, Greek, and Latin alphabets are discussed on pp. 112–177. This book summarizes the author's much fuller:

Diringer, David, *The Alphabet: A Key to the History of Mankind,* 3d ed., with the assistance of Reinhold Regensburger (from Eng. 1st ed., 1948, which derived from an Italian original, *Il Alfabeto,* 1937); New York, Funk and Wagnalls, 2 vols. (text and plates), 1968.

Gelb, Ignace Jay, *A Study of Writing;* Univ. of Chicago Press, rev. ed. 1963 (and reprints, from 3d ed., 1952); also pb. This general study of the origin, development, and classes of writing uses primarily the forms developed in Egypt, the ancient Near and Middle East, and Anatolia (Hittite) but also draws on forms developed elsewhere in the world. Too theoretical for beginning students, it also essentially concludes with the creation of a fully alphabetic writing by the Greeks and does not show how the Latins derived their alphabet from the Greeks via the Etruscans. Gelb finds four stages in the development of writing: (1) the sign is a direct picture; (2) the sign represents a word, generally of one syllable; (3) the sign represents a syllable, which is generally that of the word for which it stood extended to the occurrence of the same sound in words of different meaning; (4) the sign stands for a single consonant or vowel, that is, the writing is fully alphabetic.

For the Etruscan alphabet, see:

Pallottino, Massimo, *The Etruscans* (described in bibl. 4) pp. 209–213, with table on p. 211. On p. 100 is a brief discussion of the adoption of the Etruscan alphabet by the Romans.

For the Latin alphabet, see:

Gordon, Arthur Ernest, "On the Origins of the Latin Alphabet," *California Studies in Classical Antiquity* 2 (1969): 157–170. This article surveys the history of scholarly opinion as to whether the Romans borrowed their alphabet directly from the Greeks, probably at Cumae, or from the Etruscans. Gordon concludes in favor of borrowing from the Etruscans.

Gordon, Arthur Ernest, *The Letter Names of the Latin Alphabet* (Univ. of California Publications: Classical Studies 9); Univ. of California Press, 1973. This booklet collects first the ancient evidence for the Latin pronunciation of the letter names and then the modern views on this subject. A conclusion, pp. 59–65, presents the view expressed in the text, that during the Republic the letter names were phonetic, that is, for vowels their long sound and for consonants the consonants followed by long *ē* except for *hā, kā,* and *qū.* But perhaps beginning with Varro (1st cent. B.C.) and certainly by the late Empire the names of the semivowels were spelled with a short *e* followed by the consonant.

Gordon, Arthur Ernest, *The Manios Fibula* (Univ. of California Publications: Classical Studies 16); Univ. of California Press, 1975. The title of this still (summer 1975) unpubl. pamphlet may not be exact. Gordon writes that he has reexamined the fibula and various discussions of its falsity or genuineness and concludes that the weight of scholarly opinion favors accepting it as genuine. For the text of the inscription, see E. H. Warmington, *Archaic Inscriptions* (described in bibl. 7–12.1), pp. 196–197.

Gordon, Arthur Ernest, "The Duenos-Vase Inscription," *California Studies in Classical Antiquity* 8 (1975). The title of this still unpubl. article may not be exact and no pagination is as yet available. This vase, now in Berlin, is probably of the 4th cent. B.C.; see E. H. Warmington, *Archaic Inscriptions* (described in bibl. 7–12.1), pp. 54–57.

For Roman numerals and the Roman calendar, see:

Anderson, William French, "Arithmetical Computations in Roman Numerals," *Classical Philology* 51.3 (July 1956): 145–150. This brief article, if available, might show interested students that mathematical operations can be performed with Roman numerals. Anderson admits, however, that the Romans have left no specific statements that they used such a method rather than the abacus, to which references are rare and late.

Michels, Agnes Kirsopp, *The Calendar of the Roman Republic;* Princeton

Univ. Press, 1967. This scholarly study presents the construction of the republican calendar, its various special days, and its development. Though difficult, the book might interest students wishing to investigate Roman Life. At the back is a schematic Roman calendar and a reconstruction of a painted one.

6. PRONUNCIATION

Allen, William Sidney, *Vox Latina: A Guide to the Pronunciation of Classical Latin;* Cambridge Univ. Press, 1965. This gives a detailed and at times technical, but recent, discussion of Latin pronunciation. At the end Allen collects relevant passages from Latin grammarians and other ancient authors and provides a summary of his recommended pronunciation of letters and diphthongs referred to the standard pronunciation of southern British English. On pp. 84–85 he argues that the Latin word accent was one of stress. He also published a companion volume, *Vox Graeca,* ed. 2, 1974.

Sturtevant, Edgar Howard, *The Pronunciation of Greek and Latin* (in William Dwight Whitney Linguistic Series); Gröningen, Bouma (U.S. agent Chicago, Argonaut), 1968; from 2d ed., Philadelphia, Linguistic Society of America and Univ. of Pennsylvania, 1940 (enlarged from 1st ed., Univ. of Chicago Press, 1920); o.p. Though even the reprint seems to be o.p., this book, if obtainable, is a standard and full discussion, using the ancient evidence.

Kent, Roland Grubb, has two books which, though too detailed for the elementary student, afford for the teacher more detailed discussion of Latin phonology and morphology, but not of syntax, than does this handbook. Both were originally publ. in Baltimore by the Linguistic Society of America; the first is still in print in a reprint, the second unfortunately o.p. They are:

The Sounds of Latin: A Descriptive and Historical Phonology; Millwood, N.Y., Kraus Reprint, n.d.; from 3d ed., 1945 (from 1st ed., 1932); pb.; and

The Forms of Latin: A Descriptive and Historical Morphology; 1946; o.p.

7-12. MORPHOLOGY AND SYNTAX

1. *General*

Palmer, Leonard Robert, *The Latin Language* (in The Great Languages); Atlantic Heights, N.J., Humanities Press, 1961; from New York, Barnes and Noble, and London, Faber and Faber, 1954 (and reprints). This offers a fuller and more technical treatment than does this handbook of the history of the Latin language and its comparative and historical grammar.

Bennett, Charles Edwin, *The Latin Language: A Historical Outline of Its Sounds, Inflections, and Syntax* (in Bennett's Latin Series); Boston, Allyn and Bacon, 1907; o.p. This book though old and hard to obtain, affords a clear and systematic introduction to the various topics treated in this handbook. It was meant to supplement Bennett's *New Latin Grammar* (also o.p.), described in bibl. 7-12.2.

Warmington, Eric Herbert, *Archaic Inscriptions*, vol. IV of his *Remains of Old Latin* (4 vols., 1935-1940; in Loeb Classical Library); Harvard Univ. Press, and London, Heinemann, 1940. From this are quoted the early Latin inscriptions in chs. 5 and 7; a fragment of Ennius in the latter ch. comes from Warmington's vol. I: *Ennius and Caecilius* (1935, rev. 1956).

2. *Grammars*

During the late 19th and early 20th cents. several useful systematic Latin grammars were published in English, all presented along much the same lines, according to traditional patterns of morphology and syntax. These have not been replaced as sources in which students may find fuller discussions and paradigms of the material covered in this handbook, where they are often referred to as "systematic Latin grammars." For a listing of books in print on Latin grammar, see *CW List 1975*, p. 251. This does not, however, include the grammar by Lane (below), or Beare (see bibl. 13); both are listed in *Books in Print 1974* as still available in reprints. This handbook has drawn chiefly on:

Allen, Joseph Henry, and Greenough, James Bradstreet, *New Latin Grammar for Schools and Colleges* (rev. George Lyman Kittredge and others); New Rochelle, N.Y., Caratzas Bros., 1975; from 2d ed., Boston, Ginn, 1903 (and reprints; from 1st ed., 1892, and reprints).

Also in print are:

Hale, William Gardner, and Buck, Carl Darling, *Latin Grammar* (Alabama Linguistic and Philological Series 8); Univ. of Alabama Press, 1966; from Boston, Ginn, 1903.

Gildersleeve, Basil Lannau, and Lodge, Gonzales, *Gildersleeve's Latin Grammar;* New York, St. Martin's, 1971; from 3d ed., Boston, Heath, 1894 (rev. from 1st ed., 1867).

Lane, George Martin, *A Latin Grammar for Schools and Colleges;* three reprints are listed in *Books in Print 1974,* namely New York, AMS Press, 1970; Westport, Conn., Greenwood Press, n.d.; and St. Clair, Mich., Scholarly Press, 1970; all are from a posthumous edition by Morris Hickey Morgan, New York and London, Harper, 1898 (and reprints). This grammar is considerably fuller than the preceding three.

Buck, Carl Darling, *Comparative Grammar of Greek and Latin;* Univ. of Chicago Press, 1933 (and reprints). This is still a standard reference book for students of both languages. Its introduction discusses well the Indo-European family of languages and the separate developments of Greek and Latin. On pp. 165–167 Buck holds that the Latin word accent involved both stress and change in tone (pitch).
    The following two books are useful, if obtainable:
Bennett, Charles Edwin, *New Latin Grammar* (in Bennett's Latin Series); Boston, Allyn and Bacon, 3d ed., 1918 (and reprints; from 1st ed., 1895); o.p. This is shorter than the three first grammars listed above. It was supplemented by Bennett's *The Latin Language* (see bibl. 7–12.1).
Lindsay, William Martin, *The Latin Language: An Historical Account of Latin Sounds, Stems, and Inflections;* New York, Hafner, 1963; from Oxford, Clarendon Press, 1894; o.p. This, although even the reprint appears to be o.p., is a magisterial historical Latin grammar. A shorter version, also o.p., is:
    A Short Historical Latin Grammar; Oxford, Clarendon Press, 2d ed., 1915 (from 1st ed., 1895); reprint 1937; o.p.
    Two useful books specifically on syntax are:
Woodcock, Eric Charles, *A New Latin Syntax;* Harvard Univ. Press, and London, Methuen, 1959; U.S. ed. apparently o.p.; Eng. ed. in print as of 1973. This work serves to expand the statements on syntax in this handbook.
Handford, Stanley Alexander, *The Latin Subjunctive: Its Usage and Development from Plautus to Tacitus;* London, Methuen, 1947; o.p. This, if obtainable, gives a good and full account of the subjunctive.

3. Dictionaries

The *CW List* 1975, pp. 254–255, gives a number of Latin dictionaries and word lists. This handbook has depended chiefly for quantities and spellings on:
Lewis, Charlton Thomas, *An Elementary Latin Dictionary;* Oxford Univ. Press, 1915 (rev. from 1st ed., New York, Harper, 1890); a U.S. ed., New York, American Book, 1915, is o.p.
    Much fuller is:
Lewis, Charlton Thomas, and Short, Charles, *A Latin Dictionary,* Oxford Univ. Press (Clarendon Press), 1879. The U.S. version, *Harper's Latin Dictionary* (later publ. New York, American Book), is apparently o.p.
    A new and much fuller Latin-English dictionary is in course of publication:
Oxford Latin Dictionary; Oxford, Clarendon Press. Begun in 1968, this had in 1973 completed fasc. IV (ending with *liberō*). Completion of the estimated 8 fascs. is envisaged about 1980.

The most thorough Latin dictionary, with definitions and citations in Latin, is:

Thesaurus Linguae Latinae; Leipzig, Teubner. This is sponsored by five German learned academies. Publication in fascs. was begun in 1900 and by 1974 had reached into the letter *O,* although until then nothing had appeared on *N.* This claims to give every occurrence of all words except the most common in classical and early Christian Latin literature. It is a work of reference for scholars and major libraries.

The most convenient etymological dictionary of Latin is in French:

Ernout, Alfred, and Meillet, Antoine, *Dictionnaire étymologique de la langue latine;* Paris, Klingsieck, 4th ed. rev., 2 vols., 1967; from 4th ed., 1959–60 (from 1st ed., 1 vol., 1932). This, in print in France in 1974, is a useful work of reference for anyone desiring to trace the origins of a Latin word, its history and meaning, and parallels in other Indo-European languages. It is clearer and easier to use than a similar dictionary in German:

Walde, Alois, *Lateinisches Etymologisches Wörterbuch* (in Indogermanische Lehr- und Handbücher, 2 Reihe: Wörterbücher), 3d ed. by Johann Baptist Hofmann; Heidelberg, Winter, 2 vols. publ. in 21 fascs., 1938–1954; from 1st ed., 1908; with an index vol. in 4th ed., 1965; o.p.

13. VERSIFICATION

Rosenmeyer, Thomas Gustav, Ostwald, Martin, and Halporn, James Werner (in the Eng. ed. the names appear in the order Halporn, Ostwald, and Rosenmeyer), *The Meters of Greek and Latin Poetry;* New York, Bobbs-Merrill (also pb. Library of the Liberal Arts 126), and London, Methuen, 1963. This is perhaps the best introduction to Greek and Latin versification for students.

Raven, David Sebastian, *Latin Metre: An Introduction;* Atlantic Heights, N.J., Humanities Press, and London, Faber and Faber, 1965. This is more technical and complicated than Rosenmeyer et al. The author published a companion volume, *Greek Metre: An Introduction,* 1962.

Cooper, Charles Gordon, *An Introduction to the Latin Hexameter;* New York, St. Martins, and Melbourne, Austl., 1952. This offers a brief (70 pp.) but clear analysis of all aspects of hexameter verse, especially Vergil's.

Platnauer, Maurice, *Latin Elegiac Verse: A Study of the Metrical Usages of Tibullus, Propertius and Ovid;* Hamden, Conn., Shoe String Press, 1971; pb. reprint of Cambridge Univ. Press, 1951, o.p. This small book gives a statistical survey and discussion of the metrical usages of the three poets with respect to verse pauses (caesura, diaeresis, etc.), proportions of dactyls and spondees, vowel quantity (including hiatus, elision, and other metrical practices), and word order and idiom. While too technical for a beginning student, it serves to illustrate with elegiac examples many of the more generalized statements in this handbook concerning versification. For the meters of Roman comedy, with which beginning students are not ordinarily concerned (although examples are cited in the text of ch. 13), reference may be made to:

Hammond, Mason, Mack, Arthur Mordecai, and Moskalew, Walter, eds., *T. Macci Plauti Miles Gloriosus;* Harvard Univ. Press, 2d ed., 1970 (rev. from 1st ed., 1963). The sections in the introduction on meters, prosody, and so forth (pp. 29–57) give a survey of the meters and forms used by Plautus, with a bibl. on pp. 64–65.

A general treatment is:

Beare, William, *Latin Verse and European Song: A Study in Accent and Rhythm;* Atlantic Heights, N.J., Hillary House (Humanities Press), and London, Methuen, 1957. This affords a full and lively discussion of classical Latin metrics in relation to other metrical systems. It continues down into mediaeval and later Latin metrics. On pp. 53–54, Beare holds that the Latin word accent was one of change of tone (pitch), not of stress.

14. POSTCLASSICAL LATIN AND THE ROMANCE LANGUAGES

1. *Postclassical Latin*

Marx, Walter Herman, *Claimed by Vesuvius;* Wellesley Hills, Mass., The Independent School Press, 1975. This textbook is an introduction to the ordinary Latin of the mid 1st cent. A.D. as attested in the many inscriptions, graffiti, and tablets from Pompeii and Herculaneum, destroyed by the eruption of Vesuvius in 79 A.D. The book also includes a few selections from the account in Petronius' *Satyricōn* of the dinner given by a rich freedman called Trimalchio, the *Cēna Trimalchiōnis*. For three available editions of the *Cēna*, see *CW List* 1975, p. 243.

To them may be added:

Smith, Martin S., *Petronius, Cena Trimalchionis;* Oxford, Clarendon Press, 1975. This edition has appendices on the question of the date and on the colloquial Latin.

The *CW List* 1975, p. 255, offers a brief selection of readers, dictionaries, and grammatical works for Later Latin. Helpful older books on vulgar, ecclesiastical, and mediaeval Latin, chiefly publ. in Eng., are mostly o.p. Probably the most useful book both publ. in the U.S. and still in print is the now old:

Grandgent, Charles Hall, *An Introduction to Vulgar Latin;* New York, Hafner, 1962; from Boston, Heath, 1907 (and reprints; in Heath's

Modern Language Series). This covers in four main sections vocabulary, syntax (including inflections), phonology, and morphology.

To this may be added, as also publ. in U.S. and still in print:

Harrington, Karl Pomeroy, *Medieval Latin;* Univ. of Chicago Press, 1962; pb. reprint from Boston, Allyn and Bacon, 1925 (in College Latin Series). This is primarily an extensive anthology of selections. Its preface of 9 pp. summarizes the changes from classical to mediaeval Latin.

Also deserving mention are:

Strecker, Karl, *Introduction to Medieval Latin* (trans. and rev. Robert B. Palmer from the German of 1932); Berlin, Weidman, 1957, and reprints. This short book is devoted primarily to bibls. on various aspects of mediaeval Latin, which the translator updated from 1932 to 1957. The introductions to the various sections afford a valuable survey of various aspects of mediaeval Latin.

O'Brien, Richard James, *A Descriptive Grammar of Ecclesiastical Latin Based on Modern Structural Analysis;* Chicago, Loyola Univ. Press, 1965; pb. This book would not be useful to a beginning student desiring to learn contemporary ecclesiastical Latin. Despite the promise of its title, almost all of its materials and examples are drawn from classical Latin. Its analysis is of classical grammar and syntax. Its presentation and terminology are those of advanced structural analysis of language, not those familiar from more traditional grammars. A student unfamiliar with advanced linguistics would find it hard both to understand and to follow.

2. *The Romance Languages*

Posner, Rebecca Reynolds, *The Romance Languages: A Linguistic Introduction;* Gloucester, Mass., Peter Smith, n.d.; from Garden City, N.Y., Anchor Books, pb. 1966. This short and clear book discusses the character of the Romance languages, their common Latin background and how this became differentiated, the linguistic differences among the modern Romance languages, and the differences within each between literary and nonliterary forms.

Elcock, William Dennis, *The Romance Languages* (in The Greek Languages); Atlantic Heights, N.J., Humanities Press, n.d.; from New York, Macmillan, and London, Faber and Faber, 1960 (and reprints). This excellent book is much fuller than Posner, probably too full for elementary students. It discusses vulgar Latin, influences from other languages (particularly German), mediaeval Latin, the formation of the Romance vernaculars, and the development therefrom of the modern Romance languages.

15. LATIN AND ENGLISH

Kent, Roland Grubb, *Language and Philology* (in Our Debt to Greece and Rome); New York, Cooper Square, 1963; from Boston, Marshall Jones, 1923 (and reprints; later reprints New York, Longmans Green). Despite its title, this short book deals chiefly with the Latin element in English. Introductory chs. discuss language in general and Greek and Latin in particular. Despite its age, it affords a good introduction for elementary students.

Most histories of the English language discuss the Indo-European and Germanic origins and the contributions of other languages, including Latin, at various periods in the history of English. Scholars differ as to whether Latin elements in Anglo-Saxon were wholly brought by the Anglo-Saxon invaders from their contact with Latin on the continent or were in some instances adopted from Latin elements in the Celtic spoken in England. The difficulty is to determine whether the Anglo-Saxons wholly wiped out or swept out the Romanized Celts or whether a substratum remained, chiefly on the land, to intermingle with the invaders. Here may be mentioned only one of several books on English:

Weekley, Ernest, *The English Language;* New York, Academic Press (formerly Seminar Press), and London, Deutsch (distributed N.Y. by British Book Center); 2d ed., 1952; from 1st ed., New York, McBride, and London, Benn, 1928. On pp. 76–87 Weekley regards the Latin element in Anglo-Saxon as brought from the continent, not borrowed from British Celtic.

There are several books on the Latin element in English, which usually afford an introduction on the periods at which various Latin elements came into English. Of these, perhaps the best and fullest is unfortunately o.p.:

Johnson, Edwin Lee, *Latin Words of Common English;* Boston, Heath, 1931; o.p. This opens with a description of the various periods in which Latin borrowing into English occurred, with examples for each period. It provides a lengthy discussion, with full examples, of the forms and meanings of Latin words borrowed into English in various ways. There is a full index of the words cited as examples.

Still in print are, among others:

Grummel, William Charles, *English Word Building from Latin and Greek;* Palo Alto, Pacific Books, pb. 1961; from Washington Univ. Press, 1958. The 1961 reprint was not seen. The 1958 original is inconveniently printed by photo-offset in such a way that the book, opening from the bottom, must be reversed on turning each page. This is a textbook for classroom use. A good introduction, pp. 1–10, covers the formation of English, the Indo-European languages, and Latin elements in English. The lessons provide exercises on derivations from Latin (pp. 11–66) and from Greek (pp. 67–90).

Burriss, Eli Edward, and Casson, Lionel, *Latin and Greek in Current Use;*

Englewood, N.J., Prentice-Hall, 2d ed., 1949; from 1st ed., 1939. This is also a textbook for classroom use with lessons and exercises.

Nybakken, Oscar Edward, *Greek and Latin in Scientific Terminology;* Iowa State Univ. Press, 1959 (and reprints). This concentrates on Latin and Greek terms in biology and medicine, and is aimed toward premedical students.

INDEX TO BIBLIOGRAPHY

The numbers refer to the section, and where relevant the subsection, of the Bibliography where the book is discussed.

GENERAL INDEX

INDEX

The quantities of Latin vowels are not marked. Latin words and proper names are not indexed when they serve simply to illustrate forms or constructions. The cases of nouns are indexed individually. The tenses of verbs are indexed under the moods, that is, under indicative, subjunctive, imperative, infinitive, participle, supine, gerund, and gerundive.

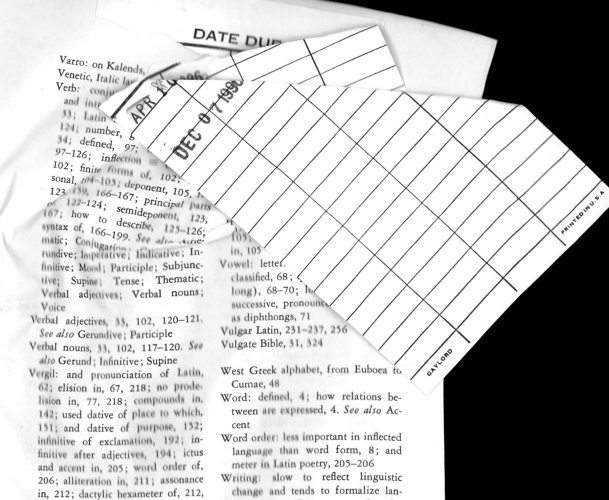

292